John — You [illegible]
to "pray" for [illegible] !
Best personal regards
Gordon Long

Livin PO In Sandbed Hell

by

Dr. Gordon Long

Southern Charm Press

Southern Charm Press, 150 Caldwell Drive, Hampton, GA 30228
Visit our Web site at www.southerncharmpress.com

The publisher offers discounts on this book when purchased in quantities. For more information, contact: toll free: 1-888-281-9393, fax: 770-946-5220, e-mail: info@southerncharmpress.com

Printed in the United States of America
First Printing: April 2001

Library of Congress Control Number
LCCN 2001087678

Long, Gordon Dr.
Livin PO in Sandbed Hell / Dr. Gordon Long

ISBN 0-9702190-7-5

Cover design by Ginuwine Graphics

Dedication

Estelle Mariah Hillis Long and Thomas R Long, two tough survivors who parented seven kids in the sandbeds of Georgia. Their successes were above average, considering what they didn't have to work with since being PO was a constant thing. Mushy love, never, we never did a lot of hugging and yet we never doubted the affection we had for each other as a family.

TABLE OF CONTENTS

LIVIN PO IN SANDBED HELL

INTRODUCTION

It is a strange world that we are born into, and the only way to know just how strange, is to live long enough to recognize who we really were, and maybe who we are now. I suspect the only way to get to that information is to sort out some of the strange things that happened to us, that we participated in, and maybe some of the things we actually caused. Naturally, everybody knows all those things are going to be noble, kind, considerate, and generally uplifting for human kind, especially the ones that directly seem to involve things we could have altered the course of, had not some evil devils kept us from the natural "good" only you or I just plainly recognize as the real "us" of this whole story.

What I am now, or became after what I consider a logical stopping point is just plainly not important right now. In fact, I would sorta like for you to have to ponder on just what the hell this person could be like as an adult. Maybe there will be a question as to whether or not attainment of adulthood could or should even be a possibility. To tell the truth, I have some real questions about just when this thing called adulthood happens.

Too often, you and I both know people who are from forty to sixty years old who have never stopped being children and then on the other hand, it seems some kids are born nearly thirty years old. These are the ones who drive the average "adult" nuts. Adults who are on the low side of average have this threatened feeling, and want to call that kid a smartass. That same SA might be pretty accurate, if he called his accuser a dumbass, however, if the kid really were an SA, he would keep that to himself. Otherwise, where I was brought up, all hell would break loose and that was particularly true if the DA was in some position of authority, as little as it may have been - for instance - breathing.

Since I have lived for so damned long, it is going to be necessary that I consider, at least at this point three separate divisions in this epoch to end all epochs. Just for your information, either wisdom, or the lack of material, may cause considerable shoving together of "stuff", so there is a chance it may really become just one epoch. Under some conditions, after writing all this "stuff" down, it just may turn out to be an interesting catharsis, which after sanitizing will leave nothing except a bunch of ifs, ands, and buts, and perhaps mostly butts. Now get this straight, if this is just going to make me feel good, one silly grin on my face is flat not good enough. Do you get the impression that I have this penchant for digressing [a.k.a. wandering around]? With minimal tailwind, I will get worse, most likely.

I think a good ending point for this epoch will be when I became six thousand three hundred and seventy two days old. If you just casually look at that number, you may jump to the conclusion that I think I'm at least in some third order reincarnation. Don't head for the calculator, I was about six months shy of being eighteen years old, and was getting aboard the *Nancy Hanks* for my first train ride ever, from Millen, to Atlanta, Georgia, [a place I had never been before], ready for induction into the United States Air Force. To give you an idea of what you might expect, Millen is a really little town about twenty miles from Girard where I was born, raised, jerked up, or reared - your choice. Neither Millen nor Girard had any census bureau designation as a Metropolitan Statistical Area. Girard had about three hundred people, and I think that was wishful thinking, 'cause its doubtful if counting people, chickens, and dogs the tally would have been that high. About eight hundred people lived in Millen and to get there and the train station for the *Nancy Hanks*, you had to go through Sardis, which I suspect in 1950 actually had three hundred people living there.

Girard was a farming community, to the best of my knowledge there was never any industry of any sort that would have supported a mangy dog, aside from two cotton gins and one hell of a lot of moonshiners. I think maybe there were three or four people who were financially, but not necessarily socially, middle class, everybody else qualified as being poor, or worse PO [pronounced as in Edgar Allen POE]. Let's get something straight right now; if you don't know the difference between poor and PO, you just never have really been PO. Don't get me wrong, what I am about to try to tell you about is not the usual story about having to walk ten miles to school everyday, rain, shine, hot as hell, snow, ice, and uphill in both directions. I was a depression baby, born in 1933, so some people ask, "How can you talk about the depression since it was over before you were six years old?" I have a perfectly honest answer - we had our very own private depression until 1950. If I have a message, it is to just examine what life was then and there, and what it was not. Maybe this entire effort is really about *motivation*, and if you stay with the story to the bitter end, you will understand how motivation really can move mountains, and more importantly even in some instances, move young kids to do and be things they really might think would be out of their reach. Some of these things along the way were belly laughs at the time, some pretty sad, some just things, and things that may not mean much of any thing. Those funny things are a hell of a lot more so after escape from the situation and looking back!

There will be one hellacious attempt to change every name possible. I'm nowhere nearly as concerned about lawsuits as I am about twelve gauge shotguns. In many cases, if I take a little license with the truth, it won't be too much variation from what really happened. Sometimes there were some really good guys who were straight arrows, and if they, or their families will let me, I'm going to name them correctly. After they read all the trashy stories that surround their act of kindness or humanity, it could easily be understood if they choose to be an unnamed and unwilling contributor.

CHAPTER I

BIRTHING, YOUNGENS AND LIVIN PO

Birthing in my family wasn't such a big deal, or so I thought, until last week when I got a phone call from one of my two living brothers on the eve of my birthday. He has been rather regular about calling each year. Since I am old, it should be obvious that he is about the same age as God. He explained to me, after all these years, why he doesn't forget my birthday. Pretty simple, he was allowed to stay home from school the day I was born which would have made him about eight. Even at his age he still recalled that respite from the third grade saved him from some type of torture, either real or imagined. Needless to say, formal education was not something he was heavily into.

Big families were not at all unusual in my world - My oldest sister is well into her 80's, I think she was married when I was about two years old, excuse me if my recollection of the wedding is a bit less than vivid. A justice of the peace in Allendale, South Carolina most often performed weddings around Girard. In fact, my wedding was the only one my Mama got to see, even though a whole carload of us went to Greenwood, South

Carolina with plans to attend one brother's wedding, but we misjudged how long it would take, and it was over by the time we arrived.

All seven of us were conceived and birthed in the same old iron beds. I think a real live medical doctor was in attendance, but I'm not positive. One good thing about being the youngest of seven was, from what I was told, I didn't have to worry about learning to walk at an early age. My feet didn't touch the floor until I was three, since I was passed from one sister or brother to another. Naturally, even to this day, irrespective of how often I correct them - telling them I am the youngest doesn't mean squat to them - I am still and will forever remain, the baby!

There are millions of us rural Youngens who were brought up in similar circumstances, and in the same kind of houses. Notice I said houses, irrespective of what I may write about any, and everything, there was one huge amount of "home" and family in our old house. 'Member when I said we were PO, the way we got to live where we did was that my granddaddy lived 'across the field' from us. He gave my father eighty acres of his land, and Daddy built his house there, about five hundred yards away and much closer to a public road. Public, yeah, but not public enough to be paved until about 1960. When I mentioned large families were common, granddaddy, who died before I was born, had a small army. I had more uncles and aunts than anybody I ever knew down there. There was Aunt Ida, Rena, Lessie, Bessie and Cora. Then there was Uncle Jim, John, Garnett and another one who died as a baby. The strange thing about it was that granddaddy John Perry Long must have been land PO as well as money PO because he gave every child a farm of about the same size.

Daddy built that old house with the help of friends and family I am sure, and they moved into it sometime before the First World War. I can tell you now; Daddy was not about to ever be called a 'finish' carpenter. Irrespective of his lack of skill as a carpenter, that old house withstood the onslaught of Mama and him, seven kids, and my mother's Mama. Grandmamma was the only grandparent I ever knew. She was there, and known to many as Miz Susie, from about 1926 or 28 until she died in 1943. Since she had a room to herself from the time I could remember, that cut down the space left for the rest of us. Altogether there were three bedrooms, a dining room, a sleeping porch, a hall, and a front porch. Double beds were everywhere, and it was uncommon for there not to be at least two in each bed. We didn't sleep on the front porch, but that old house was kept at "overflowing."

The entire house was yellow pine, including the floors, walls, ceilings and the weatherboards on the outside. One thing about those old boards though was that there was never any piecing, every board ran the entire length of the room, whether ceiling or floor, and the outside weatherboards were twenty feet long. At first the roof was made of cypress shingles, which were later covered with tin. That happened after the second fire because of a spark from one of the chimneys. I got a first hand look at a bucket brigade from working at the well on the second fire. Thank God for an old bell put up on a huge post about fifteen feet in the air and a strong pull rope to make it work. Everybody had one, and everybody knew that when a bell went off anywhere, except at 12:00 Noon, you started lining up your eyes on the direction of the ringing. It didn't matter who it was, who you were, or what color either, you used the fastest means available to get there and help. There must have been thirty or forty people there from everywhere in less than fifteen minutes. That old well got the workout of a lifetime, nearly running out of water, pulling about two gallons per bucket up faster than you could imagine possible. The water was poured into the waiting buckets, which went back down the brigade line to the ladder and to the line of men up on the roof. Saving a house meant saving the structure, and while there wasn't much thought about mental distress from the fear, but it took me many years to overcome the mental terror caused by the knowledge of how everything we had, and it wasn't much, could have gone up in fire and smoke so rapidly.

Scrubbing and cleaning, PO style meant something special to me. We didn't have much of anything, but we did have more washtubs than I think was safe for people with our lack of station in life. The reason I knew we were "over tubbed" was that we would work in the fields Monday through Friday, and sometimes through Saturday morning. Saturday afternoon was set aside for going to Girard, however, it didn't matter what time we finished with the field work, before we could go to town, we had to scrub the floors. I along with the brother nearest to me in age got to know every board in that entire house. It is doubtful if you have ever heard of a corn shuck scrubbing board, however that was the weapon of destruction to dirt and crud. These were hand made from corn shuck [husks], selected for long length, dipped in boiling water, twisted as nearly into a rope as possible and with every bit of strength we had, we pulled the shucks through two rows of one inch holes on a board about a foot long and mounted on a hoe handle at about a forty degree angle. Then you were ready to attack some wood floors!

Gotta have water, so get two number three sized washtubs and fill them by pulling the water up from the well bucket-by-bucket full. One tub was for renching [rinsing] and the other was the scrub tub, into which was put about three cups of homemade soap chips and about one half can of pure Red Devil Lye. By itself that Lye stuff will almost make the water boil. We moved every stick of furniture out of the room, and started scrubbing. Believe me, there is a major difference between moping and scrubbing. All this was under the watchful eye of Mama, who was the world's champion at 'jerking a knot' in a youngen. By the time those pine boards were bleached as white as sheets, it was time to rinse, that was also know as 'renching' the floor. Up to this time, I just sort of casually mentioned that Daddy wasn't a 'finish' carpenter, maybe he was really a long way from that, cause the floor in every room was way out of level, except every room was catawonkus in a different direction. Anyway, the water would run toward whichever way was the low side. Sometimes a pretty good bit of water and suds would start to congregate in a small pool so we had to do some real Georgia "Sand bed engineering" to solve the problem.

Those were six-inch yellow pine boards in the floor, but they weren't tongue in grooved, so we would take our pocketknife [every male from six years old owned at least one knife] and push out the crud that had crusted up and which worked as packing between the boards, to let the water out. One person would be left to finish draining off the water and to use the drying cloths before putting the furniture back in. While that was happening, the next room was getting the action. That kept on going until every room had been done. Now that was absolute evidence of just too damned many washtubs around one house. But going to Girard on Saturday afternoon was worth it all. Maybe you can't figure that out, but seeing just about anybody other than brothers, mules and hogs and ...was bound to be some help to all concerned. Before you start thinking we were going to Girard to buy something, try to understand, "PO don't jingle" in a pocket no matter how you try to fake it or shake it!

* * *

It is amazing what you stir up in the recesses of your mind when you think about all the odd things that happened in and around that old house. I bet very few of you have ever seriously thought of, or maybe even will admit to knowing about bedbugs. To be perfectly honest, I have never seen, or been bitten by one, and there is an overwhelming reason for that. Beyond all the floor scrubbing, there was a twice a year ritual in the Spring and Fall that made sure we never had those vermin, or what ever the hell they were. Yes!!!. There were such things as wooden bedsteads back then, however, it you wanted to incur a tirade, all that was necessary was to tell Mama that we should have wooden bedsteads and get rid of those old cast iron things we had. Wooden bed frames could not have withstood the punishment meted out to those old iron beds and the slats under the springs. On the first few warm weeks of spring, the pronouncement was made, "its time to do the beds", and by 'jingoes' we did just that. All it took was to strip the beds, wash the sheets, beat the old cotton mattresses and put them in the sun. Then we would take the wire springs outside, along with the slats. Next, we disassembled the frames and took all of the parts out to the big tubs of hot water, which had been filled from a cast iron wash pot. It takes a while to boil a huge pot of water, and the second one had to be started immediately, because it took about three full pots to do the job on all those bed parts. The process was to dip as much of the entire bed parts as possible, and pour hot water over the parts that wouldn't fit into the tubs. Next, the bed slats were done the same way, first one end was dipped into a hot tub, then the other, and then came the pouring of scalding hot water from a small bucket for the small section that wouldn't fit into the tub.

I always pictured those little suckers running from one end of the bed slat to the other, and heaving a sigh of relief that their speed had saved them from the boiling cauldron. Only to have to run back toward that hot end they had just left, and stopping on the dry spot in the middle of the bed slat to give each other high fives to celebrate their success, and at that instant have some damned vicious youngen scald their asses. Like I said, I have never seen a bedbug, I guess that operation was somewhat like the statement I stole and adapted from somewhere about the value of having an old 45-70 caliber Springfield rifle which I called my 'elephant gun'. I always tell people that after I got that gun, I neither saw an elephant, nor had to actually shoot one, so it must be mighty good protection.

* * *

Energy conservation was something we had never heard about, however, we did know something about fireplaces. The old house had four fireplaces, just don't get the idea that they looked like or were as big as the Cartwright's on the Ponderosa, or some ski lodge. They were functional, and small by most standards, able to hold about one big arm load of oak wood, and deep enough to accommodate a set of eighteen-inch firedogs. Firedogs are the same, to the best of my knowledge, as what I later heard called fire irons and andirons. They are the things the wood rests on so a draft will let the wood burn faster, which means hotter. Let me tell you, wood burning faster means hotter and that was much better in an old corncrib of a house, especially since no one had ever even heard of, or thought of insulation. If you were either the woodcutter, or wood toter who had to bring wood in for the fireplace, you would have been an evangelist for insulation. What we had for the construction of the house was a bunch of rough cut two by four studs with an outside covering of square cut one by six pine boards, put on with a three quarter inch lap as weather boarding. On the inside, tongue and groove one by six boards, put on horizontally, covered the studs. The floors and ceilings were just square cut boards of the same size; both were 'air dried' and put together as tightly as possible. The only difference was the ceilings were stripped with two inch slats at the joints to keep dirt, and crud from coming through as the cracks opened when the boards had shrunk to their absolute smallest in the dry time of the year. The build up of 'whatever' in the floorboards worked pretty well to keep major airflow from freezing your feet, but there was nothing to make them warm. It was years before I understood that a house could be underpinned to keep the cold wind from whipping under the house at forty miles per hour.

It was pretty easy to be certain that most of the house building down there was done in warm to hot weather because too frequently knots would be left in the boards, and they would fall out either in the floors, ceilings, or side walls. That was where I first learned a good bit about air velocity and nozzles, especially when the temperature was below freezing, both inside and outside the house. It doesn't take a knothole to let wind in, however, if you want to know just how much air can zip between two tongue and grooved boards in an old house like that, you need to go through the Ides of March when the fields have been turned for planting. The wind sucks the moisture from the porous soil and everything is dry, and they become sand bed fields where the wind can pick up the grains of sand and drive it through every crevice in the house. The grit gets everywhere. I swear I thought it came through the glass in the windows, too.

Getting back to the fireplaces, those things had voracious appetites and if anybody stayed at the house the fire had to be fed in that room all day. Since we didn't know anything about fire screens, the fire had to be down to 'cool coals' before we went to bed. The hearths weren't sufficiently large to be sure one hot coal wouldn't pop and get out on those incendiary pine boards. The girls from farm families almost always wore dresses, and it was easy to know who had a house as wide open to cold weather as we did. That old story about burning up the side of your body facing the fireplace while the other was freezing was true. When you nearly roasted one side facing the fireplace, exposed legs hanging from the dress would turn a pink and white mottled color, and it would stay that way for at least two days.

You knew it was cold on the mornings when there was ice in the water bucket at the washstand on the sleeping porch and in the dining room. I had never seen and basically didn't know what a hot water bottle was until I left home, but I did know how to make effective use of bricks and flat irons. The thing to do was to scrub a few old oversized bricks clean, keep the ones from last year, or if there were enough flat irons to go around, use them. Put them in front of what was going to be the last fire of the evening, about two hours before you planned to go to bed, then wrap them up, either bricks or irons, in several layers of old bed sheeting and put them under the covers down at the foot of the bed. You could really have a good feeling for about three hours. Bed covers meant a top sheet, a bottom sheet, and up to 4 homemade quilts, and it was important that you get in a good sleeping position while still alert because the weight of the bedding didn't allow much moving around later.

I can't help but believe it was a total miracle that we didn't burn the old house down, and ourselves along with it, during all the years we lived like that. Later, when I was about sixteen, we went to what was called trash-burning stoves, made of tin, and we even got so "up town" that we paid nearly thirty dollars for one that actually had a thermostatically controlled draft. Man, that was something!! More heat, better control, and much less woodcutting.

* * *

Sleeping two in a double bed, particularly in really cold weather is not all bad. Even with quilts and hot bricks in the bed, the extra body heat seems to make it much better. I laugh when I read the knowledgeable kooks [on all matters] relating to kids growing up who say, that after a certain age, kids just must have separate beds. We didn't know there were such things as gays, homosexuals, or whatever. Furthermore, I don't believe there are any more documented cases in incestuous relationships in the south than in any other parts of the country. We did know an extra body sure as hell did help with warming up that frigid old bed. Thirty degrees outside meant thirty degrees inside.

Since my brother, Dean was so much older than I was; he was seeing a gal in Girard on a regular basis. However, there was no way he could get the pickup to go to town, so he would walk, or run the mile to see her. He would have been put on death row if he had been later than midnight coming home. I would be in bed asleep when he came in, usually after running the entire distance, and put his freezing body in the bed. The next morning, he would tell me how much he appreciated my rolling over and giving him my warm place. At first I thought he was lying to me. Then I decided he wasn't, and the fact that he just kept teasing me about my rolling over and letting him have my warm place, made me madder and madder. After getting really steamed about it, I made myself stay awake the next time he went to see the gal, and on his return, I pretended to be asleep. Sure enough, he started telling me in a loud whisper, "Roll over so I can get in the bed." I just grunted and half way moved, angling myself just right. He had his clothes off, and was pushing me to move out of my warm spot and just about the time his butt hit the bed, I let go with both feet, kicking him about three feet from the bed. He landed flat on his ass and made a hell of a racket. I just grunted a little bit more, obviously still asleep. He was swearing and muttering, but not too loud because he wouldn't have needed a warm bed if Mama and Daddy had heard what he was saying. He got the cold side of the bed and I damned nearly got a hernia from stifling the laugh.

Mama and Daddy knew he had been razzing me about stealing my warm place. I waited the next morning at breakfast until we were all seated at the table and eating, then I asked Dean, with a very straight face “Did you take my warm place last night?” He mumbled something or another, not about to let it out. In my ever-helpful manner, I said “I had a dream last night that you had come in and tried to get me to roll out of my place and I kicked you out of bed.” He damned nearly swallowed a biscuit whole. Mama and Daddy understood exactly what had happened. Whether or not he got me to roll over and give up my warm spot again, I don’t know for sure, but he never bragged about it again.

* * *

CHAPTER II

WOOD CUTTING, A FROZEN ASS, LUCIUS, AND THE MONKEY SAW

Cutting wood for heating and cooking was, for me, just a few paces ahead of the Stone Age. My earliest recall of cutting firewood was freezing my ass off. Long after the weather had gotten cold, we rode in a two-mule wagon, over to the old 'Andrews' place to cut oak wood. It wasn't that it would have been impossible to dress warmly, but somehow or another some sort of snide remarks were always made about 'long johns' or long underwear. They were also called 'union suits', though it never made any sense to me. One bad thing about them was the trap door on the back, another was that the wool itched, and nobody should ever itch. It wasn't just my family that felt that way, I don't think sales of long johns ever amounted to anything in that part of the country. I would sometimes wear two pairs of pants, but never, never long johns. Peer pressure, for sure, however if you had accused me of not wearing long underwear because of that, I probably would have hit you because I didn't know what peer pressure meant, but I would have most likely thought it wasn't good. I never had even heard of hypothermia, though I can remember my nearest brother and me being nearly blue, with our teeth chattering uncontrollably on that damned old two mule wagon. The Andrews place was about a mile from the house, so about half way there we would be so cold, the only thing to do was to 'lay some line' on the mules to put them into a full gallop to get there faster. We knew we were about as cold as we could possibly get, but we also knew that once we got there we could start a little fire, warm up some, and once we started swinging those axes, we would get warm. Looking back, I don't know how we survived; I still remember being so cold that I had no feeling in my hands and fingers, and the same for feet and toes. We never wore but one pair of cotton socks in our old brogan shoes, and usually wore only one pair of "infernal" overalls. Even work gloves, though they must have existed, might just as well have been from another planet. I am sure I was all of nine or ten years old, and Dean was nearly 15, when we were popping axes that were as sharp as we could make them with a mill bastard file.

We most often used round wood for heating, meaning that it was nothing larger than we could burn in the fireplace without splitting. We didn't want to cut a tree bigger than about six inches in diameter because we would have had to load the entire tree on the wagon bed, and most likely would have had to cut it into two pieces to get it loaded. Also, a larger tree that size meant we either had to cut a chip out, or carry a crosscut saw with us, both of which would have taken more time. The smaller ones we could cut to burning length at home with one swing of the ax, or two at the most. That is until we got the table saws. We would keep cutting down oak trees, and "climbing up" and loading them until we were convinced the old mules couldn't pull anymore through the sand bed roads. If you don't know about sand beds, have you ever heard of the Fall Line? Anyway, it is where the old shoreline was a "jillion" years ago, and buddy, that was one hell of a beach. I guess I could say that we had a house on the beach. Only problem was, the walk to the ocean was damned substantial, like eighty miles to Savannah Beach, Georgia.

Before you get too quick and wonder why we didn't cut our firewood before it got cold, let me tell you why. First, we were working so hard pulling fodder, picking green peas, picking cotton, shaking peanuts, picking dry peas, stripping and grinding cane, that there wasn't any time left. Second, we knew with "fat liddard" we could quickly get a bed of coals so hot that even green oak would burn. In case you don't know, fat liddard is the heart, rosin filled, center of long dead pine trees. Another thing was that undried oak had its own burn regulator because of the moisture, it lasted longer. It took me years to accept that dry wood was better than green wood for my fancy stoves, bought much later in my life.

There was another reason why we waited so late to cut oak wood for the fireplace that was more important than any other. Stove wood, cut from long leaf pine trees, took first place insofar as which wood had to be cut, split and stacked since we used it for the cook stove. Syrup wood for the syrup boiler, also cut from long leaf pines, was next on the list of importance. It was pretty logical when you think for just a second. There wasn't much you could do without food, most particularly, you just flat-out got to have cornbread, flour bread, hoecake and biscuits. Fact was, even with biscuits, if you can't have sausage, ham and fatback, along with syrup, nothing is going to go right.

I never heard much about stewardship of the land when I was growing up, though we understood the limited number of trees we had available. In retrospect, I wish I had all those beautiful long leaf yellow pines I helped cut up, pulling one end of a crosscut saw. We would get up in the morning, just after sun up, to start cutting stove wood. We knew the drill, hitch up the mules to the wagon, and make sure the axes were sharp. Daddy sharpened the crosscut saw and checked the 'set' of the teeth. Dean and I would load everything in the wagon with anywhere from one to two gallons of water in glass jugs and maybe four to six ham, sausage or barrel cheese biscuits for each of us. Sometimes we would use our little finger to poke a hole in a biscuit and fill it with cane syrup until it couldn't absorb any more. We wrapped the good eats in brown paper and then we were ready to go play push me, pull you with the crosscut saw. Daddy, like all overseers, would go around by the county road nearly five miles in the pickup to get to the woods at the edge of the "Big Field", while Dean and I had to take the mules and wagon across the branches, which are also known as little streams.

After getting there, we'd hitch the mules to a tree, make a choice of which tree we wanted to cut, and decide where we wanted to "throw it" [a.k.a. fell it]. Maybe you know all about making a tree fall where you want it to by using notches, and in some few instances, a wedge. However, to this day my wife and kids all believe it is some sort of sorcery that makes it go where I say it will. One sure way to cause a youngen to study the fine art of putting a tree down where you want it was to understand the penalties of not dropping it exactly where it should go. If the wagon was not far enough away, it could smash the wagon and the mules. To this day I don't even want to think of what would have happened to Dean and me if a tree had taken out the mules and wagon. However, if I had been assured of any reason to think the replacement would have been better and would even have looked remotely like a small tractor, it probably would have been a direct hit!

A more specific reason though was that when you dropped at least a sixteen inch diameter, seventy foot tall Long Leaf Pine and you knew each block of stove wood must be cut every twelve inches, some realization set in that you didn't want to pinch that damned crosscut saw. That meant the tree locked up on the saw in the cut and it couldn't be moved until the tree was pried, or jacked up. The way to avoid that was to have a sixty inch piece of syrup wood, or a big limb put about twelve feet from the stump, lined up across the path with where you planned to throw the tree, and it had better fall on it. Once the tree was down, and after cutting twelve to fourteen inch blocks off the tree trunk, up to the place where the piece of syrup wood or limb was, it was time to reset the log for another few cuts. Usually that was done by using a pry pole about ten feet long, and putting one of the last cut blocks under the tree as far up the trunk as you could get it, depending on how high it could be pried up.

Have you ever pulled one end of a six-foot crosscut saw? Even if the answer is 'Yeah', did you do it for a whole day, and then come back for several more? I think you can store up enough life experiences on that saw in about a week for an entire lifetime. Only problem is, I will have to be reincarnated several times to use up all my experiences.

After the tree was down, unless there was some interest in starting a major war, at least two bottles of kerosene had better have been loaded on that wagon. Pine trees have massive amounts of pine tar or rosin in them, and it will stick to anybody, anything, or any metal. Get it on a cross cut saw and it will stick after about six pulls. Kerosene is the magic potion. A glass bottle, with a properly sized corncob, which has either one or two grooves down the side and forced into the neck of the kerosene bottle will dispense just the right amount on both sides of the saw. Attack that tree and start cutting the first block off. You are only about sixty or more cuts away from finishing that one up. Can you begin to understand why I would dream about how to be somewhere else, anywhere else, except in the sand bed hell of Girard, and the sooner the better! I knew there had to be a better way to live!

Dean and I would make about the first six or eight cuts, and one or the other, or both, of the 'sawyers' would be getting a bit winded and the first one to "lose it" started getting yelled at because he was "riding" the saw and not pulling at the right time. Believe me, it went steadily downhill from there. Finally, when yelling at each other wouldn't work, and no more could be cut because those muscles just wouldn't work anymore, Daddy would usually hand the axe to Dean to start splitting the blocks. That used different muscles, so he would "shingle" the block, usually taking one "round house" swing for each approximately two-inch shingle. One reason I didn't get the axe for splitting back then was that I didn't have the weight for the axe swing, another was that no matter how hard I set my eye on that damned block, focused exactly where I wanted the axe to go, it just didn't go there. Fortunately for me, I discovered the affliction of poor aim was probably a good rather than a bad thing, thus I kept that problem for many years.

I could 'bolt' the shingles. That was done on the first block cut because it was the largest, turned on end, and used like a butcher block. It was the height needed to rest the shingles on to split them into two by two inch pieces of stove wood. "Shingling" came from when wooden shingles were about all anybody had to put on roofs. I was, and am, totally clueless about the origin of the term 'bolting' except that when Mama wanted more wood put in the stove, I was instructed to put a few more "bolts of wood" in the firebox. Since the bolter was using an axe held in one hand, while holding the shingle with the other hand, good aim was more than just a casual affair. However, it was different from splitting the big blocks since it never took more than one short swing of the axe. Being short a finger or three was a distinct possibility, but I still have all mine. This game of cutting wood, while not being totally mindless, went on until you thought you would lose your mind, because one tree after another was murdered and 'rendered' until you had hauled enough wagon loads of stove wood to last until next winter. In our case that was five or six cords, neatly stacked about thirty yards from the wood box in the kitchen by the cook stove. In case you want to know, a cord of wood is sixty-four cubic feet. For our stove wood, that meant a stack four feet high, and sixteen feet long.

* * *

Lucius was one hell of a stump digger, and was more than a big man. He was huge, 6' 6" at least, and not fat, but the biggest pair of overalls I have ever seen always seemed too tight on him. He was so black he looked almost purple and even more so when he was sweating. He was a tenant on Mr. Bonnie's place, but when he had some spare time, he would work for Daddy, digging fat liddard stumps. He got one dollar per stump, no matter how big it was, and Daddy wouldn't let him dig any small ones. Lucius was a piece of work. He would start on a two feet in diameter stump that looked like it had been there for twenty five years and by the time he got the hole about four feet deep, it was nearly eight feet in diameter which meant he had a rather wide and flat area in the stump hole to walk around in.

He would stop to take a pull on his water jug about every half hour and go back to digging. The first time I ever watched he seemed to be getting more strength the longer he worked. I thought he was just getting his second wind. As many times as I watched him, and he dug fifteen or twenty stumps for Daddy, he always seemed to get pretty happy at about the same place on every stump. He was sure to break into a song and belt it out at the top of his lungs. Most of the things he sang were Gospel songs, the best I could tell. Many of them seemed to be in "Tongues", anyway they sure were in some language I couldn't understand. He was digging all the time he was singing and that seemed to build up a thirst. After another drink of water, he would start talking to God, and a bunch of people I had never heard of. He would run around that stump down in that hole, and come flying out, just hollering and jumping around like he was on stage somewhere. Finally, after having dug down about six feet, he would cut the taproot off with an axe. We usually took a mule and pulled the stump from the hole, though I must say Lucius seemed to roll the stump from the hole just about as fast as the mule could pull it out. If it was humanly possible, I made it a point to try and be somewhere around so I could watch Lucius dig. He was more than a show, but I was careful not to be so close that I could be considered on the first row! That would have been too close, I couldn't be sure but what he might sling his shovel or axe from the hole during his conversations with whomsoever. What I didn't know at first was that his "water" was really white lightning, and he was drunk as a skunk by the time he got to about the same place on every stump.

Poor Lucius, he was a happy fellow, but he apparently got too happy for his own good. One story I heard was that he had a problem keeping his pants buttoned. Back then neither he nor any of us could afford zippers. It seemed he had major problems with his buttons away from home, and his wife, who already had six or seven youngens by him, was tired of his bruising her up when he was full of white lightning. Running around with other women as well as his bruising her up were both pretty serious to her, but together they were more than she was willing to take. His last drunk netted him about nine or ten shots from a semi automatic 22 rifle and ended his stump digging days forever. His wife was never charged in the shooting because the sheriff said it was justifiable. His wife was a good person, and Lucius was too, when he wasn't chasing women and sucking white lightning.

* * *

Now don't go nasty on me, but we got beyond "digging stumps", and started "Blowing Stumps". I have never figured out how in the world so many stumps could have possibly been on that little patch of eighty acres for as many years as it had been plowed, but they sure as hell were there. My oldest sister's husband, Willie, had some experience with dynamite and he offered to do some blasting. Man was I interested in that, particularly since Lucius was not going to be digging any more, and I knew who was going to get trained as his replacement.

Willie came up with an auger just the size of a stick of dynamite, on a long steel shaft about seven feet long, with a thirty-inch bar handle on it. It looked like a giant "T". We would drill a hole at an angle toward the bottom of the stump from about four or five feet away. Then we would cut a stick of dynamite into thirds, bury a blasting cap in the dynamite, and tie wires to the leads from the cap. Next we would take a long straight shovel handle and shove the charge down the hole, pack it with dirt, and run the wires out about three hundred feet away, and hook them to the detonator. All it took was one plunge, and it was majestic to watch that huge stump appear to just lift itself up, out of the ground and slowly fall out on level ground. I finally got to the point where I set the charge myself, and while I was cautious, I always got a little rush when the ground made that muffled "whomp" sound and vibrated just before a five hundred pound stump was launched for just that few feet.

* * *

We didn't always use crosscut saws and dig stumps. We moved into mechanization in getting wood, always looking for an easier way that we could afford. Long before chainsaws, which we never had on the farm, and which had not been invented as far as I know, we started using a bench saw to cut the oak wood for the fireplaces. At first we used a flat belt running from the jacked up back wheel of a fenderless old truck to a flat pulley on the saw. It was hard as hell, make that impossible, to firmly anchor and align the saw and the truck. We spent all sorts of time eyeballing whether or not the saw and truck were "squarrred" [square] to each other. I suppose we only used twice as much energy realigning and resetting the belt, as we would have just axing the wood. However, if we ever got it 'running right', it seemed we almost never had more than about an hour's worth of wood left to saw. My oldest sister's husband, Willie, was pretty mechanical and could weld, and repair engines, and he welded a frame and hooked up a five horsepower engine with v-belt sheaves to the bench saw. That solved the alignment problem; it made it so we no longer had the problem of the belt jumping off every time we started a cut.

Sometimes it would have been best to leave well enough alone, but not us, the last contraption we got was called a 'monkey saw', used mostly for pulp wooding. For one of those things to be safe, it would have taken a four hundred pound gorilla as the operator, and I was way over two hundred pounds shy. Those wonderful tools [translated into stupid tools] had two bicycle type tires, usually solid rubber, attached to a platform, which sported a 5 HP Briggs and Stratton engine with a double v-belt sheave. A five to six foot shaft, which ran through an arching bow, was the driver for a twenty-four inch circular saw blade bolted onto the end of the shaft. The weird bow could be used to cut down trees and then be rotated ninety degrees for cutting up the tree into fireplace length blocks. If you have trouble visualizing it, think about the current weedwackers you can buy with the curving power shaft and make it big enough to require those bicycle tires. Some of those damned things actually had eight horsepower engines, but thank God I never had to operate one with an engine that big.

It never was safe; I didn't like it even in the wagon with me even if the engine was not running. Nobody ever gave me instructions on how to use it, but I was absolutely sure about one thing - as long as I held onto the two metal handles, I was the maximum distance from that damned dangerous circular saw blade. I had several conversations with 'self', where I admonished 'self', if you are still conscious, and you can't cut the throttle off, don't ever, ever turn the handles loose, keep a death grip on them. Why in the hell somebody hadn't thought to put a "dead man" throttle that would automatically cut the engine off if your hand was yanked away from the handle, I'll never figure out. Maybe the manufacturer thought pulp wood sawyers were cheaper to replace than a safe and adequate throttle.

Several times while cutting down oak trees, I would get a little careless and not check the "lean" on a tree as carefully as I should have, and get a pinched blade. More than enough times when it pinched, it caused that weak feeling in my stomach to become downright queasy, and that feeling always came just after that damned saw would lift me off the ground and shake me like a leaf. There are many ways to sweat, perspire, or glow, that have nothing to do with physical exertion, I always smelled like a damned old, make that a very old billy goat from adrenalin, after running that saw.

On one trip ole John went to the woods to help me cut wood with that sucker, and according to what I understood, he had run one before. Hindsight is a wonderful thing, and it would have been magnificent had I given John's 'self' the advantage of my training of my personal 'self' about that saw. He had cut down several trees and seemed to have everything under control, and had turned the blade into the "cut-off" position for the blocks, which meant the blade was vertical. It only took a split second..... He let that huge circular blade, running wide open, dig into the ground. All I could do was watch as it flew up, throwing the handles down to the ground, tearing them loose from his hands.

At that instant the contraption became a self-propelled deadly weapon and that fool was trying to catch it. I was hollering for him to run like hell, but he didn't move quickly enough, even if he intended to listen to me or could hear me. That big blade hit a root or something else to make it swing around and head directly toward him. I thought he was to be the guest of honor in a butcher shop. I was convinced he was about to be sliced like a side of beef, and how it missed him, I don't know. It couldn't have missed him by more than a foot, and then, he did decide to evacuate the area at flank speed. It took another three hundred feet before it wedged the wheels into trees where it couldn't move and I shut it down. When anybody else was running that monkey, I always made it a point to be around some big trees, and at least fifty yards away. Thank God we were both safe, but I never, ever started that damned thing again, and we got rid of it.

I drove the wagon back home but I left the damned saw there. Ole John walked home through the woods and I didn't see him for quite some time...he had "shit his pants" and it must have been loose cause it sure was everywhere, so maybe he was more than a little embarrassed. I suspect that, to this day, if he uses any wood for heating, he buys it all. Ah Yes, it is these wonderful memories that make me regret reading and studying everything I could get my hands on, preparing to get out of sand bed hell. Believe that 'regret' stuff about wonderful memories and I will help you buy some of those sand beds down there!

* * *

Wang doodle eviction. Betcha don't even have an idea of what a Wang Doodle is and how one may affect property settlements. You may want to build one after I tell you about this little jewel. It is not something you can just go out and pick up at the local hardware store. Actually, you don't really want anyone who is a current friend, or even who could divorce you and testify against you, to know you have ever heard of a Wang Doodle. My Daddy told me about Wang Doodles and was willing to supervise the building of one, provided Mama didn't know about it, both for his protection and mine. Since he was so specific about that, it just made me more than positive that I didn't know of any close friend who was close enough to even think I had ever heard of one. You know about fathers and sons having quality time doing things together, well, in this case, there may be just a "tad" of a question about too much time and there is no question that it didn't really qualify as quality time. According to Daddy, it was put in the Georgia Annotated Code as a felony crime just to have a wang doodle. I never tried to look it up, cause the reason I wanted it was going to be more than slightly illegal anyway. It could be called *eviction by fear of bodily harm from ghosts.*

We had a Bubba person who looked pretty much like Junior Samples when he was on Heehaw, except he didn't have a telephone number to forget. However, our Bubba happened along years before there was even a television set, much less before that show. Now Bubba was about forty years old, and was a bunch more than plump. He was what I call "Mo-bile fat", I mean he had the kind of fatness that would surprise you at how fast he really could move. I always thought he was fast for short spurts, but I figured, not too good on endurance.

Bubba had fathered a bunch of Youngens, several boys and three girls. The girls were too old for me, or maybe I was too young for them, but they sure did look good from every direction. They qualified for the same lack of social standing I had, except maybe worse, since Bubba was real trash. I don't think he was into incest, but if anybody back then had known that beating kids for nothing was child abuse, he would have been a poster boy for it. I had seen some of the bruises and broken skin and had heard all about it from his kids. Almost no adults knew about it, and back then nobody would get into a "Pa's" face about it very much. His wife and Youngens had finally left him because of his abuse, and he was at the house alone.

Bubba had some drinking problems revolving around white lightening, moonshine, or stump juice. He usually could be expected to be carrying a full load from Wednesday until Sunday noon. Could have been his 'moonshine still' needed sober attention on Monday and Tuesday. Somewhere along the way, I think from the heavy drinking, he had a "vision" or two that he blamed on Ghosts. Probably the best thing to come from his drinking.

Pretty good bet that he was an excellent candidate to be rousted by the ghost of my Uncle Jim who had died about a year before. Uncle Jim was about six feet four or more, and a huge man in every respect. He just plainly had a general dislike for Bubba going back several years and everybody knew about it, especially Bubba. Uncle Jim had a voice that sounded like a wounded elephant with a sore throat. Not only that, but at nearly three hundred pounds of muscle, he had a general willingness to fight, and he could throw people around like they were toothpicks. Bubba made it a point to 'scuse himself if Uncle Jim was anywhere around.

Now Daddy would never admit that he had any idea about what I was planning, and he didn't get too involved in the building operation, but he surely did help me as a consultant. To build a proper Wang Doodle required a nail keg [a small barrel]. A nail box like we get now just wouldn't do the job. Both ends of the nail keg had to be removed, and green hairless cowhide stretched over both ends, and then tied just as tight as you would a banjo head. After a three sixteenth inch hole was cut, dead in the center of both hides, the barrel had to be left to dry. Either a leather bootlace about six feet long, or some heavy 'seize cord' string was then threaded through the holes. A bunch of rosin was put on the cord that was to rub against the dried cowhide as it was pulled back and forth through the keg. Next you needed to decide where to put the wang doodle, and be damned sure you had enough pull cord to get out of gunshot range and amongst some trees for protection. Bubba's house, and many more just like it, were built on brick or heart pine posts, anywhere from two to three feet off the ground with several fireplaces which started at the ground. The fireplaces made good places to hide things, like Wang Doodles.

After I had everything ready to put in place, I spent several weeks sneaking through the woods late at night, watching for an opportunity to put it under Bubba's house. Just about dark on a Friday night in early October, I got the Wang into place. To do it right, you have to get a brick, sometimes two bricks with holes in them, and thread them on the end of the rosin string coming from the back end of the Wang. Tie the bricks in place so they can't slide, and then tie the end of the rosin string near the floor and between the floor joists. The bricks work like counter weights in a window to pull the rosin string back through the wang. There wasn't much more to do except anchor the Wang Doodle keg firmly on the ground so it couldn't move and then bring the string from the other end of the Wang out to the edge of the house.

It was mighty important that at the edge of the house you made a slip knot, or break joint, so a strong jerk on the cord would break the long cord that you had strung out to the woods. It could be very baaaaad news if you had to leave that cord there and run like hell or somebody found your Wang and really worse, if you were caught with your Doodle puller in your hand.

Anyhow, it was Friday night a week later, and I knew Bubba was just about positive to be sloshed with 'shine', and he was. My only outside help was from Zeke who knew where Bubba was likely to be with a few buddies before coming home. Zeke didn't know anything about anything, except that he was to make it a point to find Bubba as he was getting sloshed and bring up Uncle Jim, remind him how he was not on Uncle Jim's list of favorite people, and how he had heard Uncle Jim had been sort of looking for Bubba just before he died. His mission was to suggest that Uncle Jim might be going to come back from the other side to finish what he had wanted to do to him.

Zeke did find him, and the rest was too good to believe. Bubba got home, and went inside, and the kerosene lamps went out, which most likely meant he was out also. After about half an hour, I sneaked out from the woods to the house and tied my pull cord to the Wang Doodle line, and unrolled it into the woods. I slowly pulled the cord that ran through the Wang and a screaming, mournful sound filled the woods, and all the surrounding area. So you know what it must have sounded like inside. Releasing the tension let the bricks pull it back in the other direction with a resulting screech that sounded like some attack party of banshees on the warpath.

When I told you that Bubba's wife and Youngens had left him, I didn't tell you that all the cats and mangy hunting dogs were still there, living under the house. It was absolutely amazing that when I went under the house to set up the wang I didn't get covered with fleas. Dogs and cats will stay under most any house without underpinning, particularly when not allowed inside, and country dogs and cats do have fleas. Somehow or another those old dogs had never barked at me, maybe they had gotten accustomed to scrawny me as just another big dog when I was working under the house. It was most important to be friends with his dogs, I surely didn't want them barking at me if Bubba was not as sloshed as I thought he would be when he got home.

After the first pull, and release I held off for about twenty seconds and started the second pull, sort of jiggling the string as I pulled to get some variations in the sound. It made Jesse Johnson's old mule sound like an infant or maybe a kitten by comparison. Suddenly, I heard a bunch of really high speed bumping from under the house, and there wasn't much time to deduce that it was five dogs hitting their heads on the floor joists. In a split second all five dogs and about six cats came flying out from under the house, aiming directly for the back door at rocket speed. The sound was not the baying of hounds, but it was the sound of total, absolute fear of something they figured was bigger than anything they had ever heard in the river swamp. It was a moonlit night and it was easy to see that the cats were so scared they looked like they weighed forty pounds apiece since every hair on their bodies was straight and standing alone. The squeal of total fear on their part, mixed in with the dogs made damn near as much noise as the Wang. It was such a comical sight; I had to work hard to keep from losing it entirely. By the time I got control of myself, finished the pull and started releasing the tension, the dogs and cats had hit the screen door, busting the screen wire and were in the house.

I don't know how much stump water Bubba had stumbled into bed with, and I don't know if the dogs and cats got in his bed, or under it, or both. I do know that coupled with Bubba's swearing and screaming at his just found "roommates" he had achieved an alertness, which he did not understand. Neither had there been much time to decide what had caused the invasion. Bubba never was known as a quick thinker, but his abilities were shortly to improve, by a bunch. That was because I pulled the Wang's string again and it let out a wicked, eerie and ghostly sounding noise that was worse than before, if that was possible. That reenergized the noise level of his animals and Bubba's alcohol level was instantly reduced by intense brain activity. In less than fifteen seconds, he went from swearing using every epithet I had ever heard to a little interval of absolutely no sound. I felt like the silence needed to be broken so I quickly started letting out the pull which brought on two new sounds, one was the Wang and the other was Bubba begging and pleading, and making all sorts of promises to God and everybody else who might listen. In particular, he wanted Uncle Jim to know that he just wanted to make everything right, that he was sorry for any misunderstanding, and please just let everything be all right. "Just please don't take me away" was the most clearly articulated phrase by Bubba.

I thought of what a no good son of a bitch he was and started another very rapid pull on the Wang string. That time it was a totally new sound, more of an angry bellow, so I started working the string as fast as I could, hearing more new sounds. I'm still surprised that, given the noise level, somebody didn't hear it from a half-mile away and come to see what all the commotion was, but they didn't. In less than ten pulls, all the dogs, cats and Bubba decided that old house was absolutely not big enough for them. They must have decided at the same time, that whatever that damned thing was, ghost, Uncle Jim, or some demon, it was in the house, or under it, or maybe it could be in both places at the same time.

It looked like some of the comic books I had read. The front door flew open, the back door flew open, and Bubba and most of the dogs seemed to be airborne from the front door, missing the porch and steps entirely and landing in the sand yard. From the back door, the rest of the dogs, and all the cats made just about the same kind of exit. I don't know about the animals, but I would have bet that Bubba was convinced his attempt to converse with Uncle Jim had failed. When Bubba hit the ground, all I saw was a pair of boxer shorts, and a whole lot of skin. He hit the dirt road marshaling all his fat in one forward motion directed toward getting somewhere, anywhere, as long as it was away from there. He was pleading, screaming, crying, and begging, but mostly running.

Yes, Bubba did have extraordinary speed for short distances, however, I noticed he also had a bunch more stamina and endurance than I ever suspected. Don't know what ever really happened to Bubba after that night. To the best of my knowledge, he never went back to that old house, never went back to Girard, and I have never heard from anyone that he ever went back to the county. Maybe Uncle Jim would have been proud, that is unless he knew and had helped a little and really did get him. Bubba's wife went back to the old house and collected what she wanted. You might call the event a "Jawja" sand bed eviction, divorce and property settlement. For sure Bubba didn't have any time to hide any assets, he was mostly interested in hiding his ass.

* * *

CHAPTER III

A WHOLE LOT ABOUT FARM ANIMALS, BIG AND SMALL

Actually this recall is about all sorts of things that relate to farm animals, and just possibly, quite possibly, much more than you ever needed to know. Part of this recall is an amazement that I, or any of my family are alive at all, given what we know now and didn't know then, about animal pollution and contamination of every sort. Some of the events in relation to animals will seem sort of sadistic by today's views, maybe, but what we did was just part of eking out a living from nearly impossible circumstances. Mules can make you get in touch with your emotions.

"A Mule has neither pride of ancestry nor hope of posterity" Robert Green Ingersoll, 1833-1899.

One of my earliest remembrances of anything to do with a mule happened when I was between four and five years old. Mama didn't send us Youngens to do any work by ourselves, if she could, she went and worked right alongside us. She could have left me with Grandmamma that day, except that I had a real 'fit' to be allowed to go with them. She took me, along with three of my four brothers, on the old two-mule wagon and to the "Big Field". It was so named because it was the only big field we had, just about thirty acres. To get there, we had to cross the "Little Branch" and about five hundred yards past that, we had to cross "The Big Branch". I will just expect you to understand that we only had two branch crossings on the old farm and one was bigger than the other, pretty much as you understand about the size of the big field in relation to the smaller fields.

One problem with my going that morning was that I didn't have any clean and dry overalls to wear, so I had to put on a pair of short pants and we carried the damp overalls with us on the wagon. There was a fair amount of dew on the grass when we got to the field, one of the first things Mama did was to look for a place that would get the first sun to dry my overalls. That place happened to be at the head of the big branch. The overalls were carefully put on some gallberry bushes about four feet tall, and Mama and the others started pulling fodder. It was about seven o'clock then, so about ten o'clock Mama told me that my overalls would be dry, and to go get them.

That sounds pretty reasonable to you - maybe, but it didn't do too much for me. I really didn't want to get that far from the working group. I don't really know just how far it was in adult distances, but to a five year old, it was waaaay too far. After considerable cajoling, I walked a little way, looked back a little, did a little crayfish move or two, walked a little farther, and kept that up until I got really into the "waay too far" zone. I managed to screw my courage up a little tighter, telling myself that if I would run as fast as I could the rest of the way, and get just the right angle, I could yank those overalls off the top of that gallberry bush at full speed. That would have kept me in the waaaay to far zone for a very, very short time. Damned great plan. Even at five I was capable of great plans, just sometimes they didn't quite work out the way I intended.

I made it to the gallberry bush, but I had to slow down a little bit more than I had intended. Just as I reached out to grab the overalls, I heard the most screeching, screaming and echoing noise I had ever heard in my short life.....Heeeeee Yaneeeeeee, Heeeeee Yaneeeeeee, Hee Yanee. I never touched those overalls; I thought I was about to be dead for sure. I just guessed that God Almighty and the devil both were just about to grab little skinny me. All I knew was they didn't actually have me at that instant, and I developed a scream that must have been audible for five miles. I was in high speed by the second step. Mama and my brothers at first thought a rattlesnake had bitten me or worse, and they started running toward me. They didn't have much time to get very far, at my speed; I was really covering some ground. In that cornfield, we had drought proof planting, which meant Daddy made the rows five feet wide and sixteen inches between plants. I had to cross about fifty rows of corn — no problem at all — I was moving so fast I don't think I was using up more than eight of the sixteen inches between the stalks of corn. Nobody had to worry about me ruining any corn by knocking it down, but there may have been legitimate concern about whether or not I might be fertilizing it. They understood what had happened when that same "Heeeeee Yaneeeeeee" stuff started again, and they saw me hit overdrive, moving toward a new land speed record for Youngens. Mama had to reach out and grab ahold of me to keep me from running past her. I was crying and screaming when she told me "That was Jesse Johnson's old mule braying." That was my first adult size attempt to put a complete hex on something or somebody. I was wild eyed, crying, and screaming, "I hope that old mule dies." It was dead in a week and Mama tried to make me feel a little bit guilty when we learned the old mule had died. I wasn't even slightly sorry. Never did live that episode down within the family!

* * *

We were what was called a two-horse farm but that was a joke, we were a two-mule farm. I can recall only for a year or two when we had three mules. I swear, I am convinced we spent much more time and effort taking care of the mules as we did each other. The reason was simple, without the mules, we couldn't take care of ourselves. There was more to a mule culture than anybody ever wants to know about in today's world.

We got our mules from mule traders; I can still recall the name of one of them. Most of the ones that came drifting by could be equated with the absolute dregs of our current versions of used car salesmen. There were a few who seemed to be honest, it was just that you had to be careful with all of them. They would file the teeth of an old mule to pass it off as younger than it was, or there was some defect which I never understood that I heard some of the old timers call a "Foundered" mule. It seemed to mean the mule was easily winded, and had no stamina. Younger mules had frequently not been "broken" or properly trained to pull a single plow, a one horse [mule] wagon, or maybe to work as a pair [team] breaking ground. Also, we had to be able to ride a mule bareback. Back then, a good mule would cost a hundred dollars. If you don't think that is a lot of money, you could buy a new Chevrolet at that time for about seven hundred dollars.

* * *

The two old mules I worked most, and remember the best, were Anna and Pet. Both of them were a blackish brown and very even tempered most of the time. I can recall an old red mule we had with a vile temper, and she was just plainly mean as hell. Even the best mule can have a mean streak or a stubborn streak about a mile wide. I want to talk to the liar, who really worked mules, who will say he never had to beat the hell out of them on occasion. Mules had to understand who was the boss, and as a skinny kid, that was something that had to be proven to them. I could take over the turnplow or that wonderful Avery walking cultivator from my brother, Dean, who was five years older, where everything had been going along perfectly, and all of a sudden, everything turned to shit. The difference was he had gotten their attention when they first started plowing probably a few days before, by getting them properly directed with the "plow line".

It was essential that I earn my own status, which meant doing the same thing Dean had done using the plow line. The "plow line" was the same whether or not the mules were plowing, or hitched to the wagon, however if you were riding either a horse or a mule, it became a rein. It was, for us, a twisted half-inch cotton line or rope, attached to their bridle at the edge of the bits that went into their mouth. By pulling on the line, the head of the mule could be moved in the direction you wanted the team to go. When things were going well, and a correction needed which was relatively minor, a firm "Gee" or "Haw" as a voice command resulted in a slight movement either to the right, or the left, respectively. Repeated commands should result in additional turning increments in whichever direction you needed, that is if the mules were into what was going on, and if they were willing to cooperate. If they wanted to be stubborn, they would pretend they could not remember from one day to the next, or from one person to the next, so it meant "Reminder time in Dixie" for them. The plow lines had to be just the absolutely correct length for whatever plow was being used and for the person using them. Each line had to loop around each hand and have exactly the correct amount of slack between the bridle bit and the plow handle. Control was absolutely necessary, you couldn't let a team of mules cause you to plow up part of the crop. After the change over from Dean to me, or visa versa, it wasn't too long before, at the end of a row, whoever had just taken over would become totally enraged. Our language was loud, abusive, and that of a muleskinner, which means that we used every dirty, foul, mouthed cuss word we knew and a bunch made up along the way, if Daddy was out of earshot. Punctuated as frequently as possible with a particular arm and wrist twist that tightened the plow line to pop it along the entire side of the mule that seemed to be the major offender, though it was sometimes both of them. You could see a whelp beginning at the front shoulder and ending at the butt start swelling up instantly. After about five or ten of those whelps, the mules usually decided they were ready to work together and with whoever was plowing.

Daddy wasn't stupid by a long shot, he had plowed mules himself, and he actually could be a prolific swearer, he just wouldn't condone our swearing where he could hear it. I know he would wait sometimes until the corrections were made, and about twenty minutes later, he would walk up to the field to see how things were going. Never heard him say a word about all the yelling and swearing, only occasionally, would he check to be sure the mules had not been hurt badly. He knew there could be no question as to who was in control of a pair of mules and no matter how young the plower was, he had to be in charge. Sometimes those damned animals could make anybody so furious that if a gun had been handy one of the other, or both would have been dead.

Plowing with that walking cultivator was an improved method of torture compared to the medieval rack, for me. However, following it in a cornfield of about thirty acres, when the corn was four feet tall, and pretty, green, and tasty to the mules caused problems. You couldn't let them eat the tops out of the corn. Before tasseling that would have meant no ears of corn on that stalk, so we put a muzzle with one and a half inch openings over the mule's nose and mouth to prevent their eating as they walked. Anna, the larger of the two, would walk along the row and try diligently to get the tops of the corn to pop through the openings in her muzzle. There was a particular head movement she made when she tried it, which resulted in a quick jerk on the plow line from me and that would give her head a twist. That correction almost always seemed to piss her off -big time, so for the next two or three rows you knew what was going to happen. That bitch knew just exactly the amount of slack that was in the line and she would jerk her head forward just enough to yank your hand off the plow handle. Her behavior was just like four year olds' antics, just short of being obvious enough to lay the line on her, but it was very damned obvious that she knew exactly how to steam you up. When that happened, for the next two or three rows, there was again some very blue language. No use in my writing all those words down, you know what most of them are anyway. Anybody who plowed a pair of mules as long as I did and is fool enough to tell me he has never used profane language is automatically labeled a liar and a fool as far as I am concerned and I would be really worried about his mental state if he had plowed mules and was not absolutely proficient in profanity. I'm sure there must be some who are so religious I couldn't stand to be around them who wouldn't swear, but it is damned few.

* * *

Runaway, runaway, runaway, I know most of you have watched the Western movies and television shows where they frequently have the stagecoaches pulled by four to six horses either in a full gallop, or occasionally, be a runaway team. We never had more than two in a team, and never had anything with a seat as high and top heavy as a stagecoach, however, I have been involved in more than enough runaway situations that involved wagons. For that reason, when one of those movies or shows had a runaway, I could get an adrenalin rush in a heartbeat. Most likely it was never possible to figure out exactly what caused the runaway situation, though it seemed to start most often when the mules were trotting along with an empty wagon. Suddenly, something happened and a gallop started before the driver could react, and while not all gallops would end in a runaway, anytime one started without the instigation of the driver, all bets were off.

Whoa!! Whoa!! Repeated about twenty times while evenly pulling back on the lines would pull their heads down toward their chests and get them slowed down. However, there was a particular feel on the lines that told you when there was going to be hell to pay. It was a mutiny by both mules and most often those suckers would put the bridle bits in their teeth so it couldn't be pulled against and into the soft part of their mouths. They would start running at top speed, and I know that was not as fast and dangerous as going two hundred miles per hour at the Indianapolis speedway, but I also know that when you were on an old rickety wagon with steel banded wheels and no springs it felt fast as hell. It even felt faster than I imagined Indianapolis was when you realized that damned wagon was not on a smooth road, rather, it was uneven, from erosion, and you had very little control...make that no control. And it also was likely to cause that instantaneous ability of the mind to recall and replay all sorts of details about wagons that had flipped and killed people, high speed or not.

About all you could do was get to the side of the wagon where the mule with the softest mouth was hitched, brace your feet and use both hands to exert all the force you could on the line to make the damned fools turn. Sometimes, however a turn was possible in only one direction, so you just pulled like hell on that line, and swore even worse. The object was to start the wagon turning in a circle until they tired out. One thing that was not allowable was to have those bastards hit either of the branches [a small stream] where there were big trees to wrap that wagon around. The times it happened to me, I was able to avoid that, and after letting them run until they were tired, I would take the ends of those lines and just beat the hell out of them and make them run until they were absolutely lathered down. I didn't say it was a sensitive, sweet, kind and gentle world I was in did I? I don't know if a beating like that had any preventive aspects, and further more, I didn't give a hooting damn, I did know I felt a hell of a lot better, particularly after I got my scared body to settle down to a regular heartbeat again.

* * *

Animal pollution was something we didn't know much about back then. Outside the old house, off the sleeping porch, about twenty five feet away, was the hand dug shallow well that supplied all the water for what ever happened that needed water. It was about twenty four feet deep to the bottom, and I know that distance from the bottom up, since I spent some time at the bottom, cleaning out mud, clay, and silt. I weighed the least of all of us, so I got to ride the bucket down the well to load every bucket full of mud for them to pull up. Don't ever look up, or a sloshing bucket would fill your eyes with crud. When I got out, I was covered with caked clay, which took about an hour to wash off.

About six to eight feet from the four-foot square brick wall around the well, connected by a trough was the mule lot. At the end of the connecting trough was the water trough for the mules. We always had to keep the mules watering trough full, and if there was any algae, or chicken shit, or bird shit, or anything else that might cause the mules not to drink the water, we had to scrub their trough clean, and refill it.

One absolutely certain way for a yard chicken to become dinner was to be seen on that trough. The sentence was known, it was just how long it would take to either catch that sucker by hand and wring it's neck, or get the 22 rifle. Don't get teary eyed about that chicken, many of them went to the dinner table without ever getting near that trough. Just remember, the mules were picky about having clean water, I think more so than we were.

Twenty feet from the well, there was a mule feeder, about thirty inches wide and twelve feet long with eight-inch sides on it. Twice a day, year in and year out, those old mules were fed unshucked corn and two or three bundles of corn fodder. Part of the mule lot was attached on the far side, to the big barn and the covered mule shed. On the East, and the high side, there was a little bit of dry, well drained sand where they could lie down and roll in the sand, or sleep if they didn't want to lock their joints and sleep standing up. The rest of that lot was the results of all that feed they ate. I often thought how wonderful it would be if they would wait to shit until they were out of that lot. However, I knew they weren't discriminating enough to plan to put all that shit in the lot just so I would have to move it. They also managed to put mule piss everywhere except where they rolled in the sand. In addition to all that mixture, we also got about sixty inches of rain every year in that part of Georgia, I don't want you to stretch your powers of imagination, but can you concoct in your mind the kind of smelly, slippery mess that was just a few feet away from our only source of water!!

Do you remember the stories about Bess Truman just after Harry became President? She was being mildly castigated by the press for letting Harry get away with using the word "manure" as a staple in his language? Her rejoinder was that it had taken her so long to get him to use "manure" that she didn't think she had much chance of improving on that part of his speech. I suspect she knew from shit to manure was about as far as Harry would change. Believe me, it is difficult to talk about mule shit as "manure" and I will regress later on, however, the fact was the mule lot was almost on top of that old well. When it rained for extended periods, as it was likely to do in the spring of the year, the water level in the well would come up sometimes within six feet of ground level. Think about that in relation to the skimpy amount of porous sand between surface water from rain, the water table and our water supply. Sometimes the water would lose it's clear pure look, and look almost like skimmed milk. Understand, no one had much knowledge about pollution down there, but it still caused some concern.... in today's world the health department, the environmental protection agency and probably the Corps of Engineers, as well, would have been going nuts and insisting that the mule lot had to be moved. I can recall one time that we did have the water tested, and it came back with no impurities that made it unsafe for drinking. That could have had something to do with the fact that the sample was pulled when it had been dry for a month. Well, mule piss or mule shit or not, I don't think we ever had any sickness that could have been attributed to the mules. I don't know if the mules would have been as lucky, had we put our outdoor privy where it drained into their water supply!

* * *

Watch out for the biter! When you are brought up around animals, you have an innate sense of when and how to be alert. My oldest brother, Lloyd was married to a gal who was entirely too good for him which has nothing to do with this story except to introduce the situation. When her mother died, her father seemed to be disinterested in his youngest son who was about twelve at the time. Mama and Daddy didn't have anything, but they were much more softhearted than you might think, in being willing to share our "nothing". After some discussion with my brother and his wife, and since they and their two kids, which later became five, were living with us because they were in financial disarray, it was decided that Wiley would stay with us for awhile. You have to understand that this youngen was younger than me at the time, but not by much, and he had lived his entire life as a "townie" in Sylvania, a little town about 20 miles south of us. He had no, nota, for clues as to what it took to survive on a "Po" farm. He was game though, and he tried as hard as anybody could to work and pull his weight. He was a reasonably intelligent fellow, and pretty nice, and he recognized just what a bad situation he had to face. I really don't remember exactly how long he stayed with us, but one of two funny stories that have stayed with me all these years revolved around his not listening completely. Maybe he listened, and just couldn't comprehend what he was being told, I don't know.

I have told you about how mules are a great deal smarter than most people give them credit for. Now "ole" Anna recognized there was somebody around who had not yet slapped her up side the head for something or another, and that did not bode well for Wiley. I told him one day, as he was helping me hitch them up to the wagon, that he was turning his back on the biting end of a mule and that wasn't smart. I went on to tell him that almost any damned mule would pop their head around and quickly take a bite of whatever part they could put teeth to, so to be careful. Now what sort of message would you get from that if you had never been around a mule before? I didn't think about it anymore, and went on about my business.

Nothing happened for the next few days. However, there we were again, hitching up the wagon for whatever it was we had to do that day. Wiley was learning and getting better at the work so I left him to hitch up Anna while I was the other side to hitch up Pet, the other mule. All of a sudden I heard a scream of pain, mingled with terror from Wiley. At first I thought the old mule had stepped on one of his bare feet, so I zipped around ready to pop her behind the knee and make her move her foot. That was not the problem at all, by the time I got around and was able to see, Anna had her head straight forward with what I swear was a smirk on that big mouth.... but she had done it. Wiley screamed, "That son of a bitch bit me, she bit me, dammit she bit the shit out of me." I didn't know where Anna had taken her bite and was almost afraid to ask, but at the same time, I knew I had to know because those suckers can really do some damage if they want to. He turned around and, boy had she laid one on him. There was a big wet outline of her mouth, right on the left cheek of his overalls. After about an hour, he finally agreed to unbutton the gallowses [straps] on his overalls and pull them down. Yessir, he had a great big "purple" coming up that looked pretty much like Anna's dentures. I bet you nobody ever had to tell him to be careful about the front or back end of a mule after that. I swear a mule can assess the risk to them, of either biting or kicking somebody. Once you have established in their mind just how dangerous it might be to them, they suddenly decide biting or kicking is something they just don't really need to do, but Wiley had never established that level of understanding with Anna. Does this story prove anything for modern society? Not a damned thing that I can think of. Except maybe when dealing with stubborn people, it is important to have their undivided attention when trying to have them understand who is in charge.

* * *

I know there was a sidekick of one of the big TV western stars who rode a mule rather than a horse on the show, well, as far a I was concerned, he was just a johnny come lately. I was riding plow mules [bare back] long before he did it for the cameras, and back then there were no cameras to make any comic statements [fun] about it. Occasionally, On Sundays, about eight to ten of us kids would get together and ride the mules along the dirt roads, just being sociable and enjoying ourselves. There was only one kid who had a pony with a saddle to ride. Since the pony was about three quarters horse size, as opposed to being a full sized horse, he could ride with us. I don't think he would have had any company if he had been on a full sized horse. That would have been too much of a "put down" for us, since we couldn't afford horses.

Have you ever been close to a big mule? I knew how big mules were at one time, I don't know now, and neither do I plan to check it out, but I seem to recall Anna was at least twelve hundred pounds, and I think Pet was about a thousand pounds. I know people talk about horses in terms of 'hands', but for my purposes weight was more important, except when you discovered you were about to go ass over elbow toward the ground and then both were important since the more 'hands' high was all about how far you have to fall. That was one time when sand bed roads were not bad, 'cause they were so much softer to land on than gravel or hard clay.

We were all riding on the dirt road by the thicket, down near the little branch, but headed toward the main dirt road [you have to understand the hierarchy of dirt roads]. We were letting the mules air it out in a gallop, just as fast as they could run. Suddenly, Anna stumbled with her front foot, and she went down like a big, big, heavy rock. I went right with her, and it stunned me enough that I couldn't move. Anna's first instinct was to get up, and you couldn't fault her for that, however, she had her left front hoof squarely planted dead in the middle of my back, and the pressure was intense and getting worse. I think I blacked out, but it must have been just for a few seconds, because I was still alive, and I knew her foot was gone. Dean and the others got me up, and checked me out. However, they didn't tell me what my back looked like, all they told me was that a brand new khaki shirt was ripped badly in the back. Man was I in a mess, first, I really liked that new shirt, second, to ruin a brand new shirt when wearing it the first time was not going to make Mama and Daddy happy campers. I was helped back on Anna, and we rode home..... very slowly. Anna wasn't hurt, she had just gotten up and done one of those all over 'shudder shakes' to get the sand off her and she was as good as new. We put the mules away, and I sneaked inside being careful to make sure nobody except Dean knew about the shirt. I took it off, and managed to have it disappear with nobody else being the wiser, but I was so damned sore.

Finally I got off by myself where there was a mirror and got a good look at my back. There was a perfect hoof print, outlined in dried blood, just above my waistline with some bloody scratch marks pulling across my back to the left side. When a mule starts to get up, they always slide their front feet back several inches as they sorta rock them self up. Fortunately for me, when Anna started sliding her front foot back, I was not directly in line with the direction of her foot travel, and her hoof slid off my back. She would have broken my back like a toothpick otherwise. Neither Dean, nor I, told Mama or Daddy about what happened, however, punishment comes at strange times - God does his "Gotchas" whenever he wants to!!

At the end of the school year, and just a few days after the accident, Mama and the mother of the boy with the pony were being grade parents for us at Briar Creek for a picnic and swimming party we always had. I had forgotten all about that big scab on my back, and I had my shirt off, and was swimming in the creek. Mama called to me from a distance of about twenty five feet and told me that I had a big leaf stuck to my back, and you know it,,,, Miz Kate told Mama, "That's no leaf, that's from that mule stepping on him." Mama was not amused that I had not told her, but at least she didn't fuss about the shirt.

* * *

Hogs were an integral part of our survival, and so were cows and chickens. The food chain is well demonstrated by an old story about how the smart and efficient farmer would feed his cows corn, which they promptly processed through their legendary seven stomachs. However, after all that "cud chewing", a good bit of the corn managed to end up on the ground in some of those cow pies. The hogs immediately went through the cow pies to get the all the corn out, and considered that they had just had "proper cuisine", then along came the yard chickens to scratch in the pig droppings to eat what they had 'passed' on. Usually just thinking about that will cause the faint hearted to turn a little green, however, just to make you completely green, I generally add that only one thing would cause a yard chicken to stop scratching in pig droppings. If you had a very bad cold, and harked up phlegm and spit it out on the ground, the chickens would fight to get it. Most of the fast food chicken restaurants, and chicken farmers don't want you educated too well on just how filthy a chicken really is!!

The French are right about eating horsemeat. Horses are exceptionally clean animals. Humans are strange creatures when it comes to what we eat from culture to culture. I don't want to eat horsemeat, or mealworms, or grasshoppers, yet, I go ape over venison, fried rattlesnake, shrimp and oysters on the half shell. Well, not really on the raw oysters, I still would love to eat about a bushel, however hepatitis is not something I'm about to fool around with during the rest of my life. I still eat oyster stew, but contamination of the oyster beds from sewage and God knows what else makes me think discretion is the better part of valor.

* * *

We had "Hog killing time in Dixie", and in my portion of sand bed hell. Everybody who writes about living in the country thinks it is mandatory to have a section on hog killing so I guess it is appropriate for me to do so as well. We would generally kill about four big hogs each year, sometimes more. The process was almost ritualistic. It started about two or three months before cold weather came, with repairing the floored pen, which I guess, was a pretty good comparison to death row at the penitentiary. Actually, there never was any 'stay' from our "pen", and the only way out was through the smoke house. The hogs were selected, and put in the floored pen, which had a slope on it so all the hog shit would flow out the end, into a ditch.

On the other end was a hog's heaven of food in a big trough where there was always shelled corn, and occasionally some bought pig feed. A second trough close by had plenty of water. We also made hominy to feed them as well. I never knew that people ate that stuff as well until I discovered some northern folks thought it was just fantastic food. We made hominy, for hogs only. In a wash pot about half full of corn, and filled the rest of the way with water, we added a generous portion of a can of Red Devil Lye. We let the mixture stand overnight, then started a fire around the pot and boiled the water until the corn swelled and got soft. It was important to make sure the lye water was washed from the hominy so it wouldn't eat the hogs stomach. Then it was chow down time for them. Now if I were to plan to feed it to people, I would really, thoroughly wash the kernels, however, I don't want any utensils for washing the lye out that completely, cause I don't know anybody who wants any hominy.

The feeding continued until the weather got cold, and the hogs' weight just kept on going up. You can readily tell all this was long before anybody ever knew what cholesterol was. We flat didn't know fatback, or "fastback, as one of my Polish friends called it, was dangerous. As the weather started getting colder, and the leaves began to drop, we checked to make sure the fifty-five gallon barrels were "swelled up" and the hoops were snugged down so they wouldn't leak. All the "Gamble Sticks" were inspected, and cleaned and ready. A gamble stick was what we used to hang the dead hog up by the feet to finish the hair removal and for removal of the guts. If we were killing four, or more, we usually would fill the syrup boiler with water when the weather forecast said it was going down to freezing, or below, for at least three days. We assembled all the equipment - work tables, meat grinder, sausage filler tubes, and pulled out every butcher knife. They were sharpened to a razor's edge on the "grinding stone". Then we went to check out the saw grass plants, spotted sometimes as much as several years ahead because they were hard to find. They look like dwarf Yucca plants except the splines are as strong as a rope. We used them to hang the hams and the rest of the meat on the smoke house "sticks" which were put across the ceiling joists in the smoke house.

Everything was ready, and everybody was ready, but I doubt if the hogs would have agreed that they were ready, but who was asking. I can remember hog killings for all my life growing up, and I was actively involved when I was about five or six years old. I recall all my brothers being involved, except Lloyd who was already in the army. Still, there was not much need for others to help us. Mama could, and did, work and do more than probably any of us. Daddy's major role was the overseer. He had been a hard worker, but he had a double hernia for a number of years. That was bad, and really got much worse later on. As time moved on, it got down to just Dean and me, and finally just me after the others left home, as the youngest [baby] son to be involved in "Hog Killing Time in Dixie". What I learned from hog killing has saved me several thousand dollars over the years as I have skinned and processed my own venison. Walt Disney has created such a mythology about Bambi that most people are too squeamish to hunt deer, that is, until they have hit at least one or two with their car, been injured or ruined a good car.

Okay, now it was cold enough for hog killing. It began like everything else on the farm, just after soon and before early, which really meant we got to see the glory of another sunrise over the sand beds. A fire was started under the syrup boiler to heat the water, and once a roaring fire was going, we quickly moved on to dig two holes in the ground for two fifty five gallon barrels. They were slipped into the hole, which had to be at a slope [angle] of about twenty-five to thirty five degrees with the low sides of the open ends of the barrels at ground level. Directly in front of the open end of the barrels, about ten one by sixes about six feet long were put on the ground so we would have a place to get the hogs in the barrels and pull them out after scalding them.

We usually would slosh two or three number three washtubs of cold water into the floored hog pen to wash the hog shit off the boards in the pen. When that wasn't done, the floors were slick as owl shit, and it was easy to slip and fall working around the hog carcasses, because the dead hogs were tough enough to manage without having them as deadweight and half covered with hog shit. Two of us were dipping hot water from the syrup boiler into washtubs, and dumping them into the barrels. Two more of us were at the hog pen. Daddy, or one of us had the rifle, and we carefully lined up that 22, dead between the eyes and just a "tad" above them. It never took but one shot per hog. We didn't have to learn from the mafia about how deadly a 22 bullet to the head was.... maybe they learned it from us.... and there was never an exit wound.

Now we had about four or more dead hogs, and everything started moving rapidly, just as soon as the last one hit the flooring dead, one of us would be in the pen with a ten inch knife, lift the front leg and drive the knife into the heart. Almost instantly we had help turning the hog's head down the slope so he could bleed out. That same process was followed for each hog. Next, the leaders on the back legs were exposed by a quick cut, and gamble sticks inserted to make it easier to pull and carry a more than two hundred fifty pound hog to the scalding barrels.

The dead hogs were put in the scalding water one at a time, head first, then they were turned around and the rear end was put in, the timing was the skill at that juncture, because if they were not in long enough, the hair wouldn't let go, and if left in too long, it would "set" and wouldn't let go. If that happened, the only thing left to do then was to skin the hog, comparatively that was a bad thing to have to do. When one was finished and dragged from the barrel, two of us would start pulling the hair off by hand just as hard and fast as we could. Occasionally we would have to do extra work on little patches of hair that had not been scalded long enough by using the burlap sacks folded over the area like a really thick bandage. Boiling water, poured slowly over the area was usually enough to get the hair to "turn loose". A little scraping to get the last remnants of hair off, and it was off to the hanging rack to remove the guts. Don't get the idea that all that hair just fell out like in a fairy tale, it took two men about forty five minutes to an hour to get each hog ready for gutting.

We didn't eat the kidneys, heart, or lungs, however some people did, and we gave them those parts. We did eat the liver, and made "liver pudding" using it. Actually it was liver sausage, which was very much like polish sausage. We usually had some extra people help clean and scrape the sausage casings, and clean the chitlings. However, I can remember getting tied into that job when I was about seven or eight years old. Want to know what that was like? In the interest of "full" disclosure, I'll explain. In case you think this may be "fuller" than you really want, just skip this next part, but try not to peek to find out what those sand bed fools were doing to be able to eat.

* * *

Cleaning chitlings and sausage casings took place out beyond the syrup shelter about twenty or thirty yards. We would dig a hole about four feet in diameter, and about two to three feet deep, to hold all the "stuff" from the guts and stomachs. We would bring out two good-sized benches and one good sturdy table. The reason for the distance from the syrup shelter, the killing area, and the house was two fold. First, in case the wind wasn't blowing in the right direction, the odor would diffuse somewhat before getting back to the house and the rest of the meat cutting. The second reason was to give all that hog shit and blood and water enough space to sink into the ground. A place to cover it up also required us to be some distance from the house. Again, we had to have a bunch of the "good ole" number three washtubs full of water.

Getting all of what seemed like miles of small intestines and large intestines straightened out and disconnected from the maws [Webster's third choice for stomachs] was a pretty disgusting job. Since we didn't use the maws for anything, we just dumped them in the hole in the ground, full of corn or whatever was in them. While cutting the small intestines loose, we drained all the food from them into that big hole in the ground and, once empty, put them in a tub without water. When the large intestines were cut loose, they were held over the hole and drained of all the shit and put in another tub without water. Then one person for each tub started working on the different tubs of guts, washing the insides with water at least three times.

The trick was to fill each six foot long piece of small intestine almost full of water and hold each end, then run the water from one end to the other several time, and finally dump the water into the hole in the ground. Each washed piece was put in another tub of clean water, and then the tub just emptied of intestines was dumped of dirty water and refilled for the next washing. Buddy if you think its tough just reading this, you should have been there to enjoy the smell, and the "large lady" is not even in tune to sing yet.

When it was time for the large intestines to be cleaned, that was an even more odorous job. The corn the hogs had eaten had been mostly digested in that little chemical plant [maw] so you know what was in there don't you? But, when they were clean and cut into small sections about two inches long, they became chitlings.

* * *

Cooking chitlings the way Mama cooked them for Daddy [who was the only one of us who would eat the damned things] was to par boil them, then meal and fry them in a pan of hot grease until mostly crisp. That was one time it was a blessing to have a house that would let the wind blow through. As far as I was concerned, on chitlin cooking day in the sandbeds of Jawja, open windows in the dead of winter were just fine. I swear to you that was the most awful smell I can imagine, even to this day. Daddy loved them, along with grits and eggs, but as far as his palate was concerned, they were good for any meal. There were some people in Girard who actually had a little money, and still liked to eat them, so Daddy would always save some to share with Miz Anna [not the mule - no way a mule would have eaten anything that smelled like that]. I know Mama passed on eating them, and I don't think any of the other Youngens would go beyond tasting. I generally will eat damned near anything, but not chitlings. I eat some things that would probably repulse you, but Chitlings were too much for me.

One time we had somebody eating supper with us, and Daddy was going to have chitlings that night. Mama always fried up a serving platter full for the table. It was absolutely a sure thing that there would be some 'left overs' as far as the rest of the family was concerned, so it must have been that the guest was there just to have chitlings. I honestly don't remember, however, Daddy always got his chitlings served directly from the frying pan, and his was the first serving. Generally, he didn't go back for seconds, which only meant he had a plate very full the first time.

It wasn't me, so it must have been Dean who came up with a wonderfully sneaky little idea. It was pretty easy since we almost always had creamed corn, boiled corn, or some type of kernels of corn on the table. Needless to say, somehow or another, about three or four kernels of corn found their way into the inside of the chitlings of our guest. He lost his appetite for chitlings forthwith and he never let on why he didn't finish his meal. I knew Dean was laughing too much for some reason that night, and later I learned why.

* * *

Making hog guts into sausage casings was another thrill, and I had to help do that little job along with several others all the years we killed hogs. Pork sausage, properly seasoned and cooked, is one of the best breakfast foods in existence. It is even better when it is in a casing. Now for us, the casings did not come from a little salted box from the store. It was all part of the hog killing and butchering process. The reason we had that table out where we were cleaning the guts was so we could cut the chitlings and clean the casings for sausage. We would each get a teaspoon, and a short piece of board on which we would start scraping the outside of the small intestine cleansing it of all the solid matter in the lining by oozing it forward inside the intestine, ahead of the scraping.

That scraping was kept up until the intestine became a transparent casing. Then the casing was washed again, and put in a dishpan ready for filling with sausage meat. Remember, there was no cooking or germ killing done between the scraping and filling it with sausage meat. Even today, when I cook link sausage you can bet your sweet ass those links are fried - well done - in a good amount of fat, or thoroughly cooked in the oven.

Now while the wonderful job I have just been describing was going on, a bunch of us were doing other fun things. Just understand, I was right in the middle of a slaughterhouse, and everybody, no matter how big or how little was wielding big, sharp knives. On what I think was my first year to be given a knife, at about age five, I nipped a good slice on the end of my left index finger, in telling and showing my wound, I learned my left hand from my right! After the hogs were gutted, the heads were cut off, washed and put on a table sitting on the jowls, snouts to the sky. Let me tell you, they looked pretty ghoulish, particularly if the hogs were old enough to have tusks hanging from their lips.

The next move was to cut the jowls off and put the meat in bowls, sometimes as much as twenty pounds of meat per hog. I know you have heard of that perennially favorite food for New Year's Day of hog jowls and blackeyed peas. Well half of the combination was right there in those bowls. Another use of the jowls, along with the rest of the head, was to make what was called hog's headcheese and souse meat. It really did taste pretty good served cold with one hell of a lot of black pepper and vinegar on it.

* * *

Pork Brains and Pickled Pig's Feet and..... After taking an axe, and splitting the head open between the eyes, being careful not to be too reckless, the halves were spread apart, and the brains were scooped out. Now you may want to throw up, but pig brains are not much different from calf brains when they are mixed with eggs and fried for breakfast. Then again, you may not be ready for that much enjoyment either! I ate them, but I have never had any rushing desire to go to the supermarket and buy any pork brains. Maybe because as "coping" as my wife and kids are, I don't think they could really handle that one. The hog's heads, in halves, were put in huge pots, with water and lids on the pots and cooked for several hours at which time the meat was slipped off the bones, and the tongues were taken from the water, and skinned. Tongue meat was good, whether beef or pork, but most of the people who make a creme sauce wouldn't begin to start the saucepot if they had to cook those tongues in a big pot like we did.

Since I'm into it, you need to know about the feet. We scraped, cleaned, and split them up into small sections, then cooked and pickled them. But to be truthful, we were never able to get them to be as tasty as the pickled pigs feet in the store. When I insist on having pigs feet now, I have to go to the store either by myself, preferably in another town, but at least, at an absolute minimum, in a checkout lane as far away as possible from the one my wife is in. We both pretend we don't know each other. Some people are just plain intolerant of "haute cuisine", and are more than slightly culturally limited. Ah well, the finest nectar of the gods go to the true believers. Just these little gems will surely cause those who know that I am Spiritual Adviser to the Brotherhood to completely understand why I was divinely selected!

* * *

What age I was determined what place I had in the hog killing jobs, good or bad, however, it didn't take too long to learn how to cut off the feet, and get started on cutting off and trimming the shoulders and the Boston butts. The Boston butts were ground for sausage along with the trimmings from the streak of lean, and fatback, also known as sowbelly. How the hog was cut up depended on whether we wanted pork chops, or pork loin, and usually we wanted some of both. The hams were the last cuts.

Some of the sowbelly was the kind of fat that could not be fried to eat as fatback, so it went into the tub for lard along with trimming from other parts. All the lean meat trimmings were kept in another tub for grinding into sausage. When the loin was taken out, and the streak of lean was cut off the backbone, the backbone was put in another pot on the stove. The liver, cut into pieces about two by three inches, and it was boiled in the same pot. At the same time, an oven full of sweet potatoes was being baked. The backbone, liver and baked sweet potatoes were our traditional supper on hog killing day.

We had a smoke house probably twenty by twenty five feet, where we kept what we called a meat box. Before it got cold enough to plan this fun little festivity, we bought a 100-pound bag of salt. After all the hogs were cut up, all the meat except the loins was brought to the smoke house, and we “rubbed it with salt”, and then “salted it down.” Rubbing it with salt was just that, trying to pound salt into every exposed crevice in every piece of meat. Then it was “salted down” when we separated each layer of meat by pure salt. The object was not to allow any meat-to-meat contact.

Man did we pray for cold weather because without it, we would lose all the meat. At that time, there was no electricity, which meant no refrigerators, no coolers, no way to keep the meat from spoiling [a.k.a rotting]. That would have been a disaster for us. After about one to two weeks in the saltbox, the meat would be removed, piece-by-piece and with a sharp knife, two small holes were cut in the big pieces so we could feed pieces of saw grass through them. The saw grass was knotted and slid on one of the smoking sticks. Generally, we had enough meat to fill all the space left over from the sausage in the smoke house.

Speaking of sausage, the meat grinder we had was a big’un but it was a hand-powered jobbie. If you think you are a badass, I bet I can cure you of that faster than you would believe by just hooking you up to that grinder handle, and not let you loose until about eighty to a hundred pounds of sausage was ground. It was okay to switch from the right hand to the left whenever you wanted to, and to switch again as many times as you needed to, just don’t stop grinding!!!

When all the grinding was done, the seasoner’s job was the focus, that was usually Mama, with significant prodding from Daddy. Mama would put a lot of salt, a lot of black pepper, a lot of red pepper flakes and a lot of sage and then “test fry” sausage patties for us to taste. The expected rule was that Daddy would fuss and fume that they weren't hot enough. After an appropriate amount of establishing his male dominance, he would grab the salt and pepper cans, and lay some more seasoning on the meat, until we were likely to have really too much salt, really too much black pepper and way, way too much red pepper. Another fry test was in order. Sometimes they were just too hot, other times, just be careful not to fart because they were so hot you might self ignite.

Remember I told you hog killing was a ritual? Well, ritual or not, thank God and all the Arch Angels, we were on the downhill leg, Just as soon as we ran all the meat back through the grinder and the filler spout. The sausage filler spout was an aluminum funnel like spout thing attached to the grinder, and after threading one of the newly scraped hog gut casings on the spout, it was sausage filling time in the sandbeds. It took two people to do it right, that meant getting the correct amount of sausage meat into each casing. It seemed like filling those sausage casings took another lifetime. Just writing about the process will make me sleep well tonight, hell; I'm tired just remembering the work. Your arms felt as if they could drop off from that filling operation as well as from the grinding. Finished..... Man what a relief!! All that was left to do was hang each piece from eighteen to forty eight inches long on the sticks in the smoke house.

After the sausage was in the smoke house, it was time to start the smoking process. We started by using hickory chips and small round wood, which smoldered for a long time, and we kept it smoking for twenty four hours a day for up to six weeks. In later years, we got a little sorry, or lazy and took the hams to a meat packing plant where they did a 'sugar cure' on them. We did avoid some spoilage that way. Rancid ham would probably kill me today, but I sure ate more than my share over my growing up years in Girard, and I never was sick from it to my knowledge.

While that grinding operation was being enjoyed so much by up to four people, some others were "rendering" the fat by cutting it into properly sized pieces, about one by two inches. The "fat" is the same type blubber many people carry around. Hogs do it too, except we never liposuctioned the hogs. From the hogs, it was cut from the belly section, and over the rib cages, along with the fat, which was all around the chitlings. All the pieces were put in the wash pot for cooking.

Chances are most of you have never seen or used a wash pot. They were various sizes, known as little wash pots, good-sized wash pots, and big wash pots. I know you need to ponder that sizing code some, however, they were the same cast iron vessels we used to put work clothes in after washing, and boil the hell out of them. I never remember that we had but one little wash pot because everything we did seemed to demand the big'uns. I suspect the little wash pot was found abandoned at a burned out house. I just don't believe Daddy would have bought a small one. Money was too hard to come by for decorator pots!! Every one of them, all sizes had three little feet about three inches long neatly spaced on the bottom. The feet allowed the flames from the fire built around them to suck under the bottom and heat whatever was in the pot quicker. You could get a feel for how much the pot was used by the amount of soot "build up" on the outside, and how high it went up the walls. Now you know everything about wash pots you always wanted to know, but were afraid to ask!!

It was usually getting about four in the afternoon when this was happening. A hot fire was started around and under the wash pot, and kept that way most of the time until after supper. By kerosene lantern, and the light from the fire, we would pull the "cracklings" from the pot to see if they had 'dried out' enough. What that meant was, had all the fat been given up by the tissue solids? When the decision was made, usually by Mama, and with a degree of caution since nobody could eat food cooked in "burnt" lard, all the fat was dipped and poured into five-gallon tin buckets. Once cooled, it became as hard as "store bought" lard.

Cracklings are the solid tissue and they look pretty much like the fat part of slightly overcooked microwaved bacon. They can be used to make bodacious and sumptuous vittles called "crackling bread". What you did was make oven-baked cornbread with a generous portion of cracklings added to the batter and baked slowly until it browned on the top. While it was hot, you served it for breakfast with some good cane syrup -not - repeat, not with Maple Syrup, either real or fake. There are no pancakes or waffles that can compare. That is unless you corner me and find out the details about my own invention of crackling bread waffles!

We used those cans of lard all year and if any of it got rancid, we would put it back in the old wash pot, melt it down, and make soap. Some of that stuff would take the skin off your hands even if you had gloves on, which we couldn't afford anyway. We had a dozen recipes for soap, and most of them worked, however, they were not for really sensitive skin. Whatever, after using our soap, you either had very, very sensitive skin, or you were tough enough to never be bothered by any homemade soap, and absolutely never bothered by "sto bought" soap.

* * *

Sex and animals from a country boy's perspective, I guess means I knew more about animal sex than I really needed to know. Watching the roosters strutting around among the yard hens made me wonder what he was bragging about. First, the hens never really did run as fast as they could to get away from the rooster, so catching them was a put up job on their part from the beginning. Second, when he caught the hen, he jumped on her back, and most often grabbed the back of her comb, jiggled his feet about twice and jumped off. Mr. Rooster then acted like everybody should applaud, and then he raised hell, crowing every morning like his deeds with the hens were what caused the sun to come up. Come to think about it, a lot of men are more like roosters than I thought at first.

Cow sex was never much to watch, they were just big, heavy and clumsy with a little bit of mooing by the cow, and bellowing by the bull. I always thought that a cow had to really be driven by some horribly strong forces for reproduction to put up with the weight of some of those huge bulls. Still seems that the cow's back should have been broken, but it wasn't. There wasn't any after the act posturing done by the bull, and they didn't get a cigarette either. Only the dominant, main bull ever got the girl unless Mr. Main Bull was just completely worn down from too many demands for his services. Well, maybe there are some parallels again, what with the serious questions about the safety of that little girl cow and the hulking size of that bull. Wonder what would have happened if they had used the missionary position and the bull had fallen. Watching the Less Than "main bull" get his strokes with the girl cows made me think about how it seems that some men seem to get too heavy to get aroused, or work so hard that they are too tired to take care of their homework. Then Mr. L. T. Mainbull [Less Than] takes care of the job, just as a neighborly gesture.

Obviously animal behavior can be translated to humans, however, much to my sorrow I never learned how to emulate the hogs on this one. We had a sow in heat, or season, or whatever you want to call it, anyhow, she was ready to be bred. My brother in law was down at the hog pen where the two interested parties were just getting it on, and he called to advise things were happening and to come look. He was from the farm as well, so it couldn't have been the first time he had noticed. Anyway, I saw for the first time what he was talking about. That male hog was up on the back of the sow, and his weapon was ready for insertion, what was weird to me was that it looked just like a loosely twisted corkscrew, and that damned thing was rotating in what looked like complete circles, and at what I considered pretty high speed. To this day, I don't know if that was a left or a right hand rotation, or if a boar can reverse rotation or not. Maybe it depends on whether or not the pig was right or left handed, go figure. I must tell you I made it my business to be around for the next few years, watching for that rotating tool. They all rotated, I have been envious all my life, and seriously wondered what the secret was!!!

Sows ready for breeding [in heat] were interesting. If you put a male hog in to service her, and he was noticeably smaller, there was likely to be trouble. True, if the sow was not quite ready to accept any male, things just were not going to happen. The sow wasn't much at saying no, but she was damned good at showing the male hog what "no" really meant. However, even when a sow was ready and the male hog was smaller than she was, there was likely to be one hell of a fight with the sow just trying to beat the hell out of the male by biting, and ramming her snout under the male and throwing him "every which a way". That behavior was likely to catch the male hog off guard, and he would get battered a bit until he came to understand that his hormones for screwing were getting their shit stomped. He had to get serious about getting the sow under control, and to flat dominate the sow by tearing into her in a mean fight. I never saw a male hog lose, however. I guess there was some point to be made by the sow that said the preservation of the species was in danger if the male couldn't win a fight. Maybe, just maybe, those old sows knew how and when to throw a fight and let the male win!

* * *

I never heard that pigs were born, but that the sow had "found" pigs or "that old sow has dropped her pigs". The problem was that when it was "her time", no matter how much hay straw, or pine straw you put in the pen, most likely she would go to the branch and search out a gallberry bush patch and "find" her pigs. There was one thing about the tamest old sow, and that was when she had just dropped pigs, she forgot who in the hell you were, most especially if she went to the branch for birthing. I don't know if you have ever seen wild hogs, or wild boars or not, however, let me tell you one thing - they can be ferocious and will attack anything, and those sows reverted to the wild. The problem was, you wanted to get the pigs back to the hog pen as quickly as possible to be sure bobcats, or whatever, didn't eat any of them. Also, you could not trust a male hog to be left alone with the pigs either.

Once Clifford, an older brother, went looking for a sow and her pigs. He had an old single shot sixteen-gage shotgun with him as he plundered around the branch with his best buddy, a dog-named Popeye. The name Popeye had nothing to do with the comic strips, rather, he was solid white, except one of his eyes was black in an almost perfect circle making it stand out. Popeye was about half pit bull and half pointer bird dog. Neither of which are noted for placid tempers. He was a pretty good hog dog in that when you really needed him to manage hogs, he would go for their ears and either bite them, or force them to go in the direction we wanted.

Clifford heard the old sow snort about fifteen or twenty feet ahead of him in a really thick area, and she startled him enough to cause him to jump backwards and in the process, he hung himself up in some vines. He couldn't get the shotgun up to shoot, and she was in a full charge heading dead for him. He said he didn't even have time to scream, when all of a sudden, all he could see was a white blur completely airborne, fly in front of him. He didn't even know Popeye was that close to him but he could never do enough for that dog after that. Ole Popeye beat the hell out of the sow, and Clifford got untangled from the vines. He didn't kill the sow, maybe because he was shaking so badly he might have hit Popeye, I surely don't think it was because he knew it would have been costly. That episode changed the way we looked for sows after they had dropped pigs around the little branch, and that's for sure.

* * *

Working on pigs was another way of saying, castrating, though some old timers said, "Well, it is time to cut them pigs, I reckon". The decision was purely economic. Most farms did not need more than one male hog, and some didn't even have one, instead they would put the sow in a box on a wagon, or in an old pickup truck for an excursion to a farm with a male they thought had the blood lines to best suit their sow.

That reminds me of a story about a sow who was in "heat", and since the only way to carry the sow to the farm with the male hog was by wheelbarrow, they put the sow in the wheelbarrow. Sad to say, the breeding did not work, so the next time she was in "heat", the farmer put her in the wheelbarrow and repeated the process again, with the same outcome, no pregnant sow. When the sow came in "heat" the next time, and the farmer went out to put her in the wheelbarrow she was already sitting in the wheelbarrow and ready to roll!

Had all the males been left with their "nuts" they would not have fattened up anywhere nearly as rapidly, and even if they had, the meat would have been too stringy to eat. Not only that, after cooking it would have smelled like a stale, overheated whorehouse. Not that I would have any first hand knowledge about such smells.

Believe me "cutting them pigs" the way we did it was not a sterile operation. When the male pigs were about 6-8 weeks old, we shut them up away from mama sow. Now understand that the sow was still protective of the pigs, so we always were sure to do this little deed in a very sturdy pen. I have seen a two hundred fifty pound sow run head on into a fence at full speed and do it several times trying to get to where we were when one of her pigs started squealing. We would catch the pigs one by one and the squealing started and got progressively more shrill. Good buddy, you would have squealed too.

One of us would put a knee on the neck of the pig, and then hold the front legs with one hand and the back legs with the other, Daddy would take his pocket knife, sharpened so it would shave you, and grab the testicle sac. He squeezed the sac enough to stretch the skin over the nut [testicle], and with one quick cut, the testicle would pop out. He would pull it a little further, and cut the cords off, and throw it over the fence to the dogs who knew what was coming. A second quick cut of the sac just over the other nut, and cut off of the cord, and we then had what we called a "barrow" [a.k.a. a nutless pig].

The only medicine we used, benzene, was later said to be environmentally unfriendly. We put it in a pint whiskey bottle, with a properly sized corncob as a stopper, with slits on the side to act as a dispenser. It was liberally applied to the exposed flesh, and on top of that we used an open bottle of what we called "cold tar". It was sticky, and smelled, and seemed to seal off any bleeding. On some occasions we would have as many as twenty pigs to "cut". I know some people talk about eating "mountain oysters" from that little operation. None of us could ever begin to even discuss cooking or eating them. Frankly, I have never known anyone down there to do any more than talk about it.

It was then, and is now, amazing to me that we almost never lost a pig from that nut cutting operation. On some occasions, we could see by just a walking inspection that two or three pigs were puffy around the incisions and we would catch them and reapply some benzene and tar. On fairly rare occasions, flies would get past the benzene and tar and get on the open wound, lay eggs, and maggots would hatch. That involved some serious cleaning of the wound, and several applications more of benzene and tar to cure the problem.

About every two years, we would save about three males to make sure we had at least one good healthy pig with good conformation to become our male hog. When we were sure which one best met the requirements, the other two were "worked on". Now that became one hell of a lot more of a job than just working on little pigs. But, it was something that could be done, however it did take an extra person or two. However, the real problem was when the "big male hog" was about to lose his job of servicing all the sows. At that time he was between four and five years old and had to be denutted. That sucker's testicles would each be about the size of a quart jar, and he usually weighed more than two hundred seventy five pounds, including tusks, which were pretty sharp. We weren't interested in removing the tusks, we just had to be careful he didn't get to use them on us. "Working on that hog" was something that could be done just like the others, but it required some serious help, like one person for the head, and another person for each leg.

An example of what we encountered was after I started us in the Berkshire hog business, which resulted in our having a Berkshire male hog. That was the biggest hog I have ever seen in my life. He was more than six feet from nose to tail, and strong as a mule. He was so hard to keep in the hog lot that we had to build an eight foot high, peeled pine pole pen, with notched joints to be sure there was no way for him to climb out. When he got mad, he was madder than hell and he would root dirt over into one corner, and stand on his hind legs with his head over the edges of the pole pen. We used him for our sows, and also let him have his pleasure with many sows from surrounding farms. No body ever even thought about charging a service fee for their male hog. Maybe that's why when we it was time to "retire" the bigun, we had so many to help us "cut that ole male hog.". That was the damnest fight I have ever been in with an animal. I still marvel that we, all seven of us, got out of the pen without getting hurt.

* * *

First Hog...I turned on Television recently, early on Saturday morning and quite by accident saw the farm report. Some young kids were getting their pigs and calves ready for showing. They were members of a 4-H club in southwest Georgia. The Cooperative Extension Service, administered by The University of Georgia, in Athens, Georgia the first land grant institution in the United States was in the business of "diffusion of innovation." They knew the best and maybe the only way to get proven facts about farming to many of the Georgia farmers was through their children. The Burke County Extension Agent had an assistant county agent, and he was always in charge of the 4-H clubs. I have many good things to say about the huge role that club played in my learning.

Each member always had at least one project every year. One year an offer was that for our club, there was one registered Berkshire "guilt" [female] pig available and I was the lucky one who got her - FREE!! The stipulations were that Daddy had to agree to my doing it, and for me to keep it away from the other hogs. He also agreed that when she was ready to breed, we would use a registered

Berkshire male. I worked on an acre lot next to the mule lot. I repaired the fence, built a little house, put in the water trough, and everything was ready. Mr. Logue, the assistant county agent arrived with my pig in a wooden box, stuck in the back of his 1935 Chevrolet coupe.

I had to keep detailed records of everything. What I fed her, both corn and bought feed. I had to weigh her every week and really make her a friend. Let me tell you that pig did well. She gained a pound a day, maybe a little more, and Daddy was getting a little green since his pigs, just a little older had already been passed by her weight gain. A Berkshire hog's head has a short snout, slightly turned up, and it almost resembles a bulldog's turned up nose. She was a little short tempered, but she was one pretty hog, and all mine. We let the first "heat" pass, as we wanted her a little older for her first litter. On the second heat, she was too big to get in that little box in Mr. Logue's car, so we had to put her in the pickup and take her nearly twenty miles to Waynesboro for breeding with a registered male. Then it was just a matter of waiting.

When she dropped her first litter, they all looked just like her, solid black, with a blaze of white on what looked like little bulldog heads. I seem to remember she had eight teats and 10 pigs. Even with two more pigs than faucets, every one of them lived and were really healthy. Daddy was watching closely, and I was documenting every pound of corn, and hog feed the sow ate. When the pigs were weaned, I gave one "guilt" back to Mr. Logue to pass on to another 4-H member, and I was on my way. I was now keeping a record on her first litter and weighing them every week. Daddy was even greener with envy because the mixed breed he had just couldn't keep up with the Berkshire pigs. He worked out a trade with me for the "gilts" so I didn't have to pay him for the corn I had fed my hog. By the time my sow was in heat for the second litter, he was ready to be in the registered Berkshire hog business and he bought a male hog from a different bloodline. That young hog became the biggest hog I have ever seen, and he serviced our rapidly growing herd of Berkshires. I kept my sow for nearly three years and then sold her to Daddy.

Anyway, I wound up with some cash money and something more important, I had been able to weasel about a three-acre plot [even if it was the absolute worst land on the place] to plant my own corn. During the first planting season that I had the pig, I made some corn but not much. I doubt if I made 75 bushels total during the two seasons I planted it, but I sold it for about a dollar fifty per bushel. That, plus the money I had made on the hogs, made me a multi jillionaire...a kingly sum of $252.00 in a bank savings book. Actually it was a little less, but that was what it was worth when I closed the account. Best I can recall, interest was between one and two percent.

Things were changing rapidly for me, it was 1950, I was a senior in high school, and I knew I was getting ready to escape from Sandbed hell shortly. Dean had graduated from high school in 1945, and had been at ABAC junior college for one or two quarters. He was working wherever he could, I sure at about fifty cents per hour. But, he dropped out because he was so far in debt he was sure he would never be able to pay the money back, he owed a whopping fifty dollars to an older brother. So he had joined the Air Force on an eighteen-month enlistment, and when he was discharged he got the GI Bill. He graduated from ABAC, transferred to the University of Georgia, and finished in June 1950. He had a job as an Assistant County Agent in Wilkes County, but it required a car. That was to be his first car. I knew he was between a rock and a hard place so I just handed him the bankbook. I had already taken the tests for the Air Force, and knew I wouldn't need it since I was to leave for Lackland

AFB, Texas the first of July. Dean has returned that favor many times.

* * *

Cows and more damned cows...No kid who ever grew up in the country should have escaped the delight of cows. Most folks as "PO" as we were and with no more land than we had, could ever maintain more than three or four cows on a regular basis. We always had a least one milk cow, sometimes two, and usually one heifer going on two years old, and one, or two calves. Have you ever milked a cow? I don't mean with a milking machine, I mean by hand. It is a miracle I can still look at a glass of milk. Do you know what it is to have to milk every morning and every night, seven days a week, rain or shine or hot or cold? We used aluminum milk pitchers most of the time. Sometimes we used a bucket, but as I recall, the pitchers were used for the simple reason that we had to share the teats with the calves until they were weaned. Sharing with the calf was an ongoing battle. Every calf was thoroughly convinced all that milk was theirs, so considerable jostling was going on most of the time. That coupled with the fact that cows have this innate ability to know when it was the absolute worst time to kick you, for no reason always created an uncertain situation about being able to stay steady for any length of time.

The absolute worst time for a solid kick was when the pitcher, or bucket was about full, and you spilled all the milk as it went flying from the kick. That action made all of us mad as hell. The milkee [cow] was aggravated from the milking and the sucking by the calf, the milker [me] who had just had at least a half gallon of milk splattered all over, and Mama [who used it to cook everything], and the rest of the family because it shorted biscuits, butter, and just about anything else imaginable that was cooked. Unless the cow had an exceptionally good record for not kicking, we would put on a pair of "kicker chains". If you got them on just right, the cow couldn't kick, however, even when they appeared to be on just perfectly, quite often an unexpected kick could still knock the hell out of you.

The cow's head was tied to a post with the kicker chains on and positioned so the calf could get to the left side, between the cow and the fence to suck his share. With the kickers on, a five gallon bucket turned "bottoms up" to sit on, and your knees under the cow, everything was ready for milking. The pitcher flared at the top, allowed the legs to clamp just under the flair with your thighs anchoring it in place. Using both hands, you gripped a teat in each hand and did a squeezing motion, which resulted in a stream of milk going into the bucket [once you learned how to aim]. There you would sit, alternating between the four teats, pulling two dry and shifting to the other two when the calf was no longer there, until there was no more milk. Usually the pitchers would be filled two or three times, and dumped into a milk bucket.

The milk was taken into the house, poured into several big bowls, and put in the milk safe. No, there was no combination on it, just screen doors. There it cooled, and after about twelve hours, the cream would rise, and we skimmed it off as sweet cream. We collected that for several days, and then made butter. Sometimes we would use a hand operated glass butter churn with wooden paddles which rotated, other times, we would put the cream in a half gallon or a gallon glass jar and just shake the hell out of it until the butter separated from the cream. The separation left butter as a solid ball and buttermilk, which, could be used to make biscuits, or for drinking. We always had sweet milk, sour milk, buttermilk, clabber, and butter. Sometimes we used clabber to make whey, and cottage cheese. Most folks today don't have a clue about what clabber is, so for the uneducated, after the raw milk turns sour, if you don't put it in the refrigerator, it will become entirely solid and by spooning it into a bowl, you can add anything or nothing and eat it.

One thing I absolutely hated was the odor from milking. The odor on your hands after milking was pungent, though not particularly offensive, it could not be washed off, scraped off, sanded off, or any other way that I could find. I tried lemon juice, onion juice, and everything else I could think of and nothing worked. If there was anybody else in my entire class in school who had to milk a cow before school, they must have milked with gloves on. My hands, I think, were the only ones with that particular stink and while it was gone about two p.m., school was out at one thirty! Get around one of those coal-fired stoves we had in school, and warm your hands, and the odor got one hell of a lot worse. I had cold hands most of the time. Given the up close and personal time I spent massaging those big cow mammary glands, and the disgust at the smell of my hands, it is a wonder that I maintained my fascination with well shaped and gracious breastwork endowments of young and not so young women!

* * *

If this tale were not so sad, it would probably be considered funny, but in any case, it is still ludicrous. Cows are more sociable than mules, hogs, or chickens, I think. It always seemed to me that our old cows would jump a fence, or break down a fence every so often for what appeared to me to be absolutely no reason. Of course if the cow was in "heat" you could bet the farm on her going through fences to get to a bull.

One night, our cow didn't come home. You can miss one milking, but more than one, and the cow will engorge or whatever and it will cause problems with her udder. So "when the cows don't come home", a search must be started. We searched with no success. In our neck of the woods neighbors made it a point to come tell you if they recognized your cow at their place, but no one came to tell us our cow was at their place. The next morning at about ten o'clock, the damned cow just showed up, and she had been milked. We had noticed she came from the direction of Uncle G's house, but we hadn't heard a word from him and we expected that he would tell us if he had milked her. Daddy started getting hot under the collar, and he started back tracking the cow.... right to Uncle G's barn. Fortunately, he wasn't home and Daddy came home, mad as hell. You see Uncle G had a semi-dairy, which meant he had about five or six cows that he milked and sold the raw milk to ten or fifteen people in Girard.

Daddy arranged for us to have all sorts of "business" at the thicket, near the turn off to Uncle G's house. So when Uncle G came down the road about noon, I knew what was going to happen. Daddy made me walk back to the house but I could see him stepping in the road to stop Uncle G's car. Uncle G. was the youngest of all Daddy's brothers and sisters, and wasn't a mean person by any stretch of the imagination, but Daddy could be, and was on occasions. I was too far away to hear what words were said by Daddy, but I could tell he was hot as a firecracker. I kept trying to see through the trees and couldn't be sure, but I think Uncle G. was about to be pulled from his car for major modifications when apparently he got the car in gear and took off.

Daddy came home muttering and swearing that Uncle G had milked the cow and sold the milk. I don't think the two of them passed a civil word from that day forward, for nearly twenty years. They lived just across a field from us. Finally Uncle G moved about twenty miles away, to Waynesboro and I was glad to see him go. There had been a lot of tension. I liked him and he would speak to me, and we would talk, just not as much as before the blowup. I probably didn't see him but four or five times after he moved his family away. Right or wrong on whomsoever's part, two brothers became enemies over less than two dollars worth of milk because a dumb old cow just wanted some company, and two silly old men weren't smart enough to settle the problem.

* * *

Any old cow can start a fight under the right circumstances. It was another cow, with another reason for tearing the fence down, this one was in heat, and nobody had noticed it. Mr. Bonnie Dixie was a big landowner, and his land joined ours on two sides of our place. He also owned a cotton gin and had fifteen or twenty 'hands' or tenant families living on his farm. One of the "hands" [workers], on a horse, herded about fifty head of cattle every day. The cows were herded to a different field every day to scavenge corn or anything else that may have been left on the ground. On that particular day, the cows were just beyond the 'thicket' when our old cow decided to find the best bull in the herd. We didn't know about it until, when we expected the cow to be ready to go into the pen for the evening...no cow. We did the usual search thing, but had no success. I had checked with Uncle G. since I could still talk to him, and she wasn't there. Later on in the evening we began talking about where she might be, and one or another of us recalled seeing Mr. Bonnie's herd up by the thicket.

Daddy would drop us off at school sometimes, on his way to the fire tower when he was working as a seasonal forest fire fighter. Just as we got into Girard, he decided he would swing by Mr. Bonnie's barn and see if his cows had been taken out, or not, and whether our cow was there. She was. Daddy got livid and even way past that, as I have said he also was mean as hell sometimes. I know he belonged to some pretty bad organizations. He worked as a marshal in Girard pretty regularly, and as a superior court bailiff in Waynesboro, a part time deputy sheriff, and with "revenoors" pretty often. Back then almost any of those jobs could be right tough. He carried a 38 revolver with what almost looked like a rifle barrel on it. I never could figure out how he kept that damned thing in his back pocket since the barrel was so long. He never carried it in a holster that I knew about.

Anyway, he cut the steering wheel on that old car, and we careened into Mr. Bonnie's drive way and slammed to a stop right in front of his house. He was on the porch at mach speed, beating on the door. Mr. Bonnie would have been one hell of a lot better off if he had let his wife answer the door. Before he could open the door, Daddy was calling him every type son of a bitch either Dean or I had ever heard, and he had a bunch more names that related to activities that the independent counsel just recently investigated the President for. He tried to get him to just unlock the door and come out, cause he was going to "drag his ass off the porch and remodel it."

In one respect, I wanted him to open the door, and in the other, I was afraid he was, because Daddy was so out of control, he might kill him. I can't remember exactly how Mr. Bonnie got a chance to get Daddy to understand that he would have the cow cut out of the herd and delivered to the house by the time he could get back home. Daddy never mentioned the episode to us again, and the surprising thing was that Mr. Bonnie and Daddy seemed to get over it, and get along.

They did have an argument later over a landline where some of Mr. Bonnie's workers decided to do a little "midnight surveying", that meant moving the property line about twenty feet onto our land. That argument was not as vicious, and ended peacefully. I must tell you though, more people have either been killed, or badly hurt in that part of the country over just a few feet of that sorry sand bed land than you can imagine. Damned if I know why, you can still buy land down there for about four hundred dollars per acre. I don't need any of it or want any of it, and furthermore, you couldn't give me any.

* * *

Cows and Wolves, four legged cows, but not wolves. When you were less than 10 years old, did you ever really know what blackheads were? I surely didn't, but I had heard from some of my older brothers and sisters, that they were worms. They knew better, and they were just messing with my mind. Actually, when a "fully growed" black head was popped from a pore, it did look much too close to what a baby maggot looked like to suit me. Somehow or another, I had gotten a small, three legged adjustable magnifying glass, and I spent an inordinate amount of time observing the largest ones I could get, waiting to see them move. They never did, of course, but it took me a long time to decide that they had not been killed when popping out. Now with that introduction, maybe you will understand why I kept one other reason to myself, about why I was concerned about whether blackheads were alive or not.

A cow lot is home to massive amounts of cow shit and all the associated bugs and whatever else that might survive in it. Back then we would walk in the mule lot or the cow lot barefooted and think nothing about it. However, it did give me some reason to worry about that practice, when one year I noticed some hair coming off the cows up near the backbone and all the highest parts of the cow from the shoulders on toward the rear. It also looked like there were several infected "boils" just about ready to pop open. I don't remember who told me what the boils were, and what to do about them. I was told they were "Wolves" [never did learn their real names] that got into the cows through their hooves in the cow lot. They worked their way up through the legs all the while developing into full-grown larvae, and finally escaping when they were able to break through the cowhide. The way we got rid of them was to get a coke bottle, position the mouth of it perfectly over the boil, and slam the bottom of the bottle with our fist. The larvae would come flying out of that hole and explode against the inside bottom of the bottle. Sometimes we would take out fifteen or twenty per cow during a year. I don't know if there was a treatment for the cow shit that would kill those things or not. Now popping wolves may be amusing, but it surely can't compete with Disney world. Those suckers did look "right much" like huge blackheads and that was the reason why I was concerned about whether the blackheads were alive or not. By the way, I always managed to break those particular returnable soft drink bottles. I didn't know just how well those bottles were really washed and I was afraid I might get that Wolf catching bottle back from the store.

*   *   *

CHAPTER IV

COUNTRY DOGS AIN'T ABOUT TO BE CITY DOGS

Country dogs ain't about to be city dogs. In the country, dogs come and dogs go. We had special dogs, and some not so special. A dog that I could barely remember had central billing at our house for years. His name was Dash, and I never understood why, and as a matter of fact, many of the dogs' names had no rational explanation. So what, nowadays many children's names are worse than absurd, I think the only rational explanation is that the parents must have a significant amount of air space where their brains should be. Anyway, Dash was a dog that had reputedly been fed gunpowder, which was supposed to affect the mean cells of the brain, and make a dog vicious. He was just that to anybody he didn't know.

One day a peddler came up to the fence at the house and he called out, being sensible and wary, since Dash was on the house side of the fence, growling and barking. He was letting it be generally known that he controlled the territory inside the fence. The peddler was selling cookware, and as soon as Mama came out the door she told him "Stay out of the yard, its not safe for you to come any closer.” Being a bit pushy and maybe pushy had worked for him in other places, he swung a leg over the fence and started towards Mama. She started to tell him, “don’t do that”, only thing was, she didn’t get much more out than... “don’t do”... before Dash DID. Dash was about twenty feet away from the peddler and growling, when he dropped his head and got to attack speed forthwith. Mr. Peddler saw him coming, and he really did try to make that fence, but Dash took a bite of his leg, and tore his pants, just before he managed to hit the fence. Mr. Peddler also had on white under drawers, because Dash, with his second bite also took the seat out of his pants. Needless to say, however he got there, by car or buggy or whatever, he used the same way to get the hell away. Mama didn’t really want any more cookware, but I know she didn’t “set” that dog on him.... well, I don’t think she did!!!

* * *

Eskimo Spitz and brogan shoes can come to an understanding. I have never been able to understand why dogs have never frightened me, but they haven’t. Occasionally, I have been confronted with a dog that started growling at me like an attack was imminent but all my life my usual reaction has been and is to point my finger at the dog, arm outstretched, and in my deepest and meanest voice, start hollering at him. If he doesn’t back down, I start swearing at him full voice, calling him every dirty word I can think of as I move toward him. If I have a gun with me, I swing it around, dead at him as I continue moving toward him, because I know he is a dead son of a bitch if he doesn’t drop his tail and run. Frankly I don’t give a damn whose dog it is, I’ll kill him on the spot. The dogs that live seem to know that instinctively.

I don’t always have a gun on me, but I have also gone through mental imaging on what to do if one attacks.

That is, I fully expect him to get one forearm in his teeth, and then he will be one dead bastard, because, he is going to be flipped over and I'm going to try to tear his guts out. I decided this was the best way to attack after I had an encounter with an Eskimo Spitz when I was about fifteen. Fortunately, it was close to November and cold enough for me to be wearing brogan work shoes. I was on my way walking to school and as I got close to Cousin Mattie's house, which was almost across the street from the school, I heard her dog barking at me. She had a Spitz with a bad reputation, but it had never concerned me.

However, I knew he was coming up behind me, so I turned to look at him. He was about thirty feet away, and he started showing his fangs and growling with his hair up on his back. I didn't have time for more than about two or three of my verbal attacks before the bastard started his attack run. I timed my kick perfectly for his lunge at me, and since I moved forward toward him about one step, he was still low and my foot got him right in the chest. He hit the ground like his wind had been knocked out a little bit. He was barely on the ground before I was on top of him with my "brogans" stomping the living shit out of him, all the while hollering that he was dead sure as hell. The only mistake was that he was fast enough to get away from me, but he was hurt and badly. I didn't have a scratch, but I couldn't catch him. So I went on to school. Know what? He lived, but every time I saw that "mother sucker", I was looking for a way to kill him, but he would see me and tuck his big curly tail and not walk, but run like hell away from me. He was a pretty damned smart dog after all. About a month later, I saw Cousin Mattie and she asked me if I had beaten her dog, now you have to understand she was about forty five years old, so I had to be somewhat polite. I told her that her dog had tried to attack me, but I had serious doubts that he would ever try it again. I never did know if she had seen it from her house or if somebody had told her. I think she knew there was a good chance she might have to get another dog if I had ever met up with him again. I don't recall hearing of anybody else being attacked by him either.

* * *

Whistles with the right person can do wonderful things. I wish I could claim to be able to do what I'm about to talk about, but I can't. Daddy was one of the best shots with almost any gun I have ever seen. He loved to hunt quail, and when the season came in, he was in the field almost every day rain or shine. He was so good, it was disheartening to us ordinary mortals. It was unusual for him to go out and not come back with at least one bird for every shell in the box, and most of the time, he would have shot so many doubles that he would have four or five more birds than the twenty five shells in a box. Understand, we bought shells by the case, and that was just like buying food. We were meat hunters, plain and simple. To this day, I don't hunt anything that I won't eat, and I must confess, that doesn't leave too much that's safe.

Daddy trained quail dogs for hunting, he wouldn't train dogs for field trials, even though he did once or twice. His reason was that Burke County may be known as the Bird Dog Capitol of the world, but you couldn't eat the trophies. He trained dogs for himself and other people. I think they paid him something like $100.00 per dog, and for that time, that was like a ton of money. He was pretty inflexible, first he tried the dog to see if it was "gunshy", if it was he told the man to take it back, because the dog was not likely to ever be cured. He always told the people to be sure before they brought the dog, but he fired a few rounds, as if he were hunting over the dog before the owner left. If the dog was skittish or worse, and the owner still wanted him to try, he would tell him how long it normally took, and he would do his best, but the money was payable up front and no refunds

Daddy must have worn out at least one pair of 15 or 17-inch lace up boots every hunting season. He would take his hunting vest, load it with a box or two of 12 gage, number 8 shot shells, and a piece of flour bread and cheese and walk off in the morning. Depending on how the day went, he would be back anywhere from noon, until night. When he was training, he usually would take one of his good dogs along with the trainee. For the first while, he kept the trainee tied to him and let him observe how the "professional" bird dog worked.

Once he got to where he wanted to hunt, he used his copper police style whistle to start the trained dog working. It was a thing of absolute beauty to watch Daddy and his dog cut that field up and search for a covey. He had a certain number of blasts to make the dog go straight, or turn right, or turn left, or come home. Coming home meant wherever Daddy was. I started to say standing, but he would start the dog hunting, and he would keep walking, so by the time that area was hunted out, he either had shot a covey or two, and some singles, or he was well on the way to the next place.

You never wanted to go hunting with that man unless you had shoes that weren't going to cause blisters or slow you down as he would walk off and leave you two or more miles from home. That was one reason few non-country boys ever wanted to actually hunt with him. Hunting was serious business, and we ate better because of that perspective. I watched him train dogs, and he was good at it. Generally he used a rolled up newspaper when a trainee had made a mistake, almost never was he mean to a dog with potential for training. But, he would "drop" one of his own dogs in the woods in a heartbeat if he had tried as hard as he could, and the dog was just useless.

He told me about one dog of his that somebody had bet him he couldn't train to point birds. The reason was the dog was half bulldog and half bird dog. Daddy told me that he had more trouble winning that bet than if he had been trying to train six dogs at one time. He finally did it, but he allowed as how he wouldn't make any more bets like that.

* * *

I told you about Popeye earlier and how he had saved Clifford's life by attacking a sow that was coming at him at full speed. Well, this is a happier story about a dog that got much more than he bargained for, or wanted. Popeye was somewhat the king of his little domain around the house when any other animals were concerned. Only problem was he had never had a monkey in his kingdom before. Lloyd, my oldest brother was always up to something, and you never knew exactly what might be going to happen next when he was around. This particular visit, he brought his pet monkey. I don't know how he got that monkey, don't care, and if he had told me, I most likely wouldn't have believed it.

He had put what looked pretty much like a dog collar around the monkey just in front of his hind legs because according to him the monkey's head was so close to the size of his neck, he could slip out of a collar put around his neck. Looked a little strange, but it worked. I had never seen a monkey up close and knew nothing about them, and I was amazed when Lloyd had the monkey demonstrate just how strong they could really be. After awhile, the monkey got settled down and Lloyd said he was going to take him off his leash, but not to worry he was well behaved. So far so good, except now that the monkey was loose, and Popeye was upset that some strangely built animal, about his size, was just jumping and climbing around everywhere. Maybe he was a little bit more than upset, maybe he was between angry and really mad.

That was going to bring some real grief to Popeye. When he started growling and circling the monkey, you could tell the monkey was keeping an eye on him, but it didn't seem like he was paying much attention. Popeye started moving in on the monkey and sounding like he was about to attack. Daddy or somebody, told Lloyd he had better get his monkey out of the way. Of all of us, only Lloyd knew that monkey was perfectly safe. Popeye sure as hell didn't know it, cause he started his attack. That monkey jumped straight up in the air and came down on Popeye's back, facing forward. With his hind feet holding a hand full of hair and skin, he was using his arms to pull hair, pinch and just flail the dog shit out of Popeye.

It happened so fast I had to do several replays in my mind to really see it all. Popeye didn't have a clue about what to do, but instinctively he made the correct choice. That old house was about twenty inches off the ground and Popeye headed for it as fast as he could run. I guess he was about twenty-five feet away, and he didn't slow down. That damned monkey was just tearing the hell out of him and Popeye was howling like death had a serious grip on him. The monkey acted like it was an everyday event at the horse track, he just stepped off Popeye's back about two steps before Popeye got to the house. We could hear that dog's head hitting floor joists with a popping thud until he got far enough away to be sure whatever the hell that thing was, it wasn't following him under the house. Popeye didn't come out from under that house until the monkey left two days later. I think it took about 2 months for him to regain his composure, and even then, I think he kept popping his head around, looking to make sure that damned thing wasn't slipping up on him.

* * *

Another monkey story that happened in Sandbed country was funny to me, maybe because it didn't happen to me. Lloyd had a light blue Nash Ambassador car, and it was really nice. It must have been about a 1939 or 40 model two seater, but the back of the rear seat was hinged at the top so it could be pushed out as a pass through from the trunk. The back windows had both a standard roll up and the kind that would push out something like wings. Lloyd tried to keep the monkey in the trunk some of the time and we were riding down the road, monkey in the trunk and the wing windows pushed out. We heard the monkey pushing the back seat, but Lloyd didn't worry because he wasn't going to jump from a car moving nearly fifty miles per hour.

He was right about that, but what he didn't know about was that the monkey had spotted two Youngens walking along the road, each with a stalk of sugar cane about five feet long. Both of them were chewing one end of it for the juice. The end they were not chewing was on the roadside rather than the ditch side. Bad, Bad choice for one of them. The end was just about exactly the height of the wing window, and I saw, first hand, how fast that monkey really was. With his long arm he grabbed the end of a cane stalk and held on. The kid went ass over elbow, the monkey yanked the cane in the car and very calmly started chewing cane. The kid wasn't hurt cause we could see he had gotten up, but Lloyd wasn't about to stop. No telling how many teeth had been loosened or pulled out. I have often wondered if he lost some teeth and how that youngen had explained to his Mama that some really ugly dude with a big toothy grin and a really hairy arm had snatched his stalk of sugarcane. Now, if you had been his Mama, would you have believed a story like that from a twelve year old?

* * *

We had some other dogs, one really distinguished himself enough to have his own special recognition in a newspaper story, and another which didn't actually too much, except he managed to "integrate" the old house by spending some time inside. "Tap" was the first dog I know of that ever had house privileges for short "day visits", never any "overnighters" of any sort. "Tap" was what we called a Fice dog, and I think that meant he was some kind of Rat Terrier. He was pretty good at treeing squirrels for us to shoot, however, other than that, except for being a best buddy, he wasn't worth much of anything. After Tap just dropped over dead one morning right by the washbasin on the sleeping porch, we got "Rattler", a dog of the same type as Tap. Rattler was what I liken to many Blacks of today's generation who really don't have a clue about what they owe Martin Luther King, and he had no concept of just how much he owed to Tap for being the first dog with house privileges from birth. There was a country music song written and one of the lines was "Call ole Rattler from the Barn, hear Rattler here" I don't know if we stole the name from the song, or they wrote the song about our dog or somebody else's dog, but it made us feel pretty proud, don't you know! He wasn't as good as Tap at treeing squirrels, however, he was special to two of my older brothers, Herbert and Clifford. They were smoking without Daddy knowing, or at least he didn't say anything about it. They had been stripping the butts to make sure there was no evidence, and then they hit upon a clever plan that actually worked for a while. Rattler was trained by them, to jump on a lighted cigarette butt, knock the fire out with his feet, and then eat it, paper and all. That was fine and dandy until Dean and I got the smartass idea to send that little trick to the Atlanta Journal - Constitution magazine section where, at that time they had a section about unusual and dumb pet tricks. It was published and we earned two dollars. That was my first co-authored publication, however, I think we could have gotten a lot more money from Herbert and Clifford if we had let them bid on not sending it!!! Daddy did read his Sunday paper from cover to cover as well, so their little scam was out. He was not happy with them, but he never congratulated us on our story either.

* * *

Snowball, the quiet one was the "other dog" during the time Popeye, the one who had saved Clifford from the sow, was the King. Interestingly enough, Snowball had been the result of Lloyd's general ability to never be able to say "no" to anyone. Anyway, he came home with a cute little puppy about 2 months old, and the upshot of it was that Lloyd really had no place to keep the dog, so, guess what!!! Snowball was one of those "opposite" names. He had long hair, and except for a few white hairs on his chest, he was the blackest black you could ever imagine. He was a shy, quiet dog, rarely ever barked, minded his own business, and was always willing to be sure he wasn't underfoot. He never challenged Popeye, and he was a loving dog. Except for one time.

Snowball had a trait that was unusual. Even though he weighed about forty pounds, he had stealth ability like I have never seen before or since. He was quieter than a deer during hunting season. Moving through leaves or whatever, any time of the year, day or night, you could not hear him coming.

As I told you, we didn't have electricity, no windmill, and no pump system to get any water pressure. Without that, we were limited to "drawing water" from the well and I just presume you understand that meant no indoor bathrooms. Translated, that meant you could use either an outdoor privy, or the woods to piss or shit. I never ever remember seeing the "old man" go to our WPA privy, he always went to the woods. Most of the time he would take a crap near the head of the little branch, that is, except when he had to dump before daylight. Then he would head out beyond the pecan trees into some plum trees near a fence row. Since he knew where he was going, he didn't need any light.

On this before daylight morning, as he told it, he was all alone, in the dark, and it was particularly quiet. I suspect he was just enjoying the solitude, and taking care of "business". Then, all of a sudden, without any warning, he felt something cold, right on his bare ass, and according to him, he couldn't remember if it pushed him forward, or if he jumped forward. He was not somebody who scared easily, but he said he thought he was going to have a heart attack. He had not a single clue as to what had sneaked up on him. Somehow he got himself under control, and then he felt Snowball rub his head against his pants leg. He had relieved himself before the dog nosed him, the only extra relief apparently was a deep exhale. He said he wanted to kill the dog for scaring him so badly, but he was so happy it was just a friendly old black, black dog, that he let the urge pass. What amazed me most of all was that he would tell that story on himself.

* * *

Licking Dogs. I know this post script is something you probably will think should just not be added, but it will tell you why, even though I like dogs, you will never see me getting too friendly with them. I'm sure some of you, well, maybe many of you have never heard the expression that someone was, or is, "a shit eating dog". For those of us who really understand the expression, it means that any dog I have ever seen, when presented with the opportunity will eat human shit. Yes, you got it right, the feces of homo sapien sapiens. I don't care if the dog is the fluffiest and cutest little Poodle, to the biggest Great Dane, they all do it. Aside from that, every dog I have ever seen takes an inordinate amount of time publicly licking all those parts of their anatomy that we call "private parts". I must admit I do admire their ability to twist until they can clean their ass with their tongue, and then work on around to do the same for the rest of their privates, whether male or female. But the twisting ability is all that I admire about that feat, and so far, I haven't met anyone who has bragged about eating shit.

I have heard so many people say, just after letting their dog lick them on their lips, and what appears to be in the mouth, "Of course you know a dog's mouth is cleaner than a human's." That may well be, however, I have not seen very many humans capable of licking their own ass, and if they could no matter how beautiful, I don't want to kiss either him or her. I will admit that I just have to get up and leave when some intense animal lover starts playing mouth to mouth with a dog. I have always felt I could sit on a dead cow full of maggots, and eat a bowl of rice, without throwing up, but I can't and won't be around shit eating dogs licking people in the mouth.

* * *

CHAPTER V

FECES, EXCREMENT, MANURE AND ALL THINGS ABOUT SHIT

Feces, excrement, manure and all things about shit in Sand Bell hell. Since all this is about being PO, be advised an important part of that situation had to do with shit, or the more polite word *manure*. Believe me, when you are PO, you try to avoid spending what you don't have, namely money. The careful management of manure [shit] from mules, cows, pigs, and chickens to fertilize plants was one way to make things grow without spending as much money for fertilizer. I want you to keep the word management uppermost in your mind for a while. Maybe you'll see later it really means the manual labor part of spreading shit, cause that's what a lot of management really is.

People have a real problem when it comes to anything to do with the excretion of waste fluids from our bodies, or from animals for that matter. It's crazy as hell, we spend godzillions of dollars aggrandizing the intake of food, and drink in the very best places, and the presentation of food, and fancy restaurants with various "courses" for a meal. You are really supposed to be somebody if you go to the fanciest of hotels and restaurants, dress for dinner, and have wine before dinner. A sumptuous ten-course meal with acres of silver, along with the very proper finger bowl, a liqueur after dinner and finally the best of all things - being seen by the right people. So many people spend way too much time simpering, "Dahling, I haven't seen you since we ran into you in Montreal at that lovely dinner party." All of that is about the intake for that little chemical plant, also known as the belly of mammals.

Contrast that with the effluent, or the discharge, from that same little chemical plant. First off, the restrooms in those fancy places, while they are better than the local convenience store, have never been planned for television cameras. Further, I doubt you will ever hear someone say, "Gosh, I haven't seen you since the men's room at the Astoria and God, you were really smelling up the place!!" The restaurant is a social place, however, if you were to attempt to be friendly in the crapper, most likely someone would call the police. The first word that comes to mind is "That degenerate!" Particularly among males, it is unlikely you will ever look very many people in the eye in the bathroom. It would be harder to have a conversation in the crapper than in the elevator. It may even be worse to really let loose a loud fart in the crapper than it is to belch in the restaurant. It is funny that a statement about flatulence would be much more socially acceptable than a discussion about farting.

Have you ever stopped to think that there is no animal, that I know of anyway, that hides to shit, piss, or have sex, except humans? Now I confess, there are better things to do than watch a person or animal defecating. Want to really ruin a "romantics" day? Have him or her visualize the most sexually attractive person they know broken down like a shotgun, taking a crap in the woods. That will just kill most any sexual urge for more than a moment. For years, I have used something similar to that for people who have problems speaking in public. I tell them to either mentally undress everyone, and pretend they are speaking to an entirely nude audience. If that doesn't work, and I know the group extremely well, I suggest they think of everyone as sitting on a commode, or just finished, and wiping their asses. If you can't talk to a group of asswipers, then you had better get a job where you don't have to talk to groups. God deliver me from a group composed of people who aren't asswipers!!

* * *

Most often about March, we would get the two mule "turn plow" and begin 'breaking up' the field from last year's harvest. Naturally that was after we had used the stalk cutter to chop either the cotton stalks, or corn stalks into small pieces so they would rot quicker. One thing about row crop farming, even when you are trying to get rid of last years left over and dead stalks, everything has to be done by the row. Every row that you planted so carefully, and cultivated so diligently must be done again, only this trip is to cut the stalks. However, the one saving grace was that a stalk cutter had a seat on it. You got to ride to cut stalks and even that little bit of good news was tempered by the reality that stalk cutting was usually done in February, so you froze your ass off riding on that metal seat. It was "sissy" to even suggest a cushion would make a softer ride and a much warmer ass. Yes, Macho did live among the PO in Sand Bed Hell.

For years, when we started to "breaking up" the ground we would divide the fields into what we called 'lands' which really meant plots that were small enough to fool us into thinking there might really be an end to that job. Try using a two mule "turn plow", cutting one single furrow, which would actually turn over a six to eight inch cut [furrow] and repeat that on the next trip around the "land". Then do that furrow over and over and over again. You knew you had a ten-acre, or a twenty acre or thirty acre field, and every damned inch of it had to be turned over that way. We are talking about days, and weeks. Want to talk about desperation!

Anyhow, finally that part was done, and the March winds had blown some of the top soil [sand] through the house, or into South Carolina, and then it was time to spread manure. Wet or dry, rain or shine, usually in a pair of rubber boots with hard rubber soles, we would first put the wagon in the mule lot, and with pitchforks start loading mule shit. Fork after fork full, until there was as much on the wagon as the mules could pull. Then it was out to the field where just the opposite took place. Unload the damned wagon, one pitchfork full at a time. The only difference was that we had to spread it by throwing it as hard as we could where it would scatter over a pretty broad area. Working from daylight to dark, it was possible to get about four to five loads per day. We were done with the mule lot when we got back down to the underlying sand. We knew the mules were going to start replenishing that mother lode by depositing more shit for our benefit for next year as soon as they were in the lot.

The exact same process was followed for the cow lot. There was a slight difference in the smell of cow shit, however, neither the mule nor the cow shit had any aroma that was even slightly pleasant. Hog shit was never a big fertilizer item, thank fortune they usually spread theirs around so much that it never accumulated in piles large enough to make hauling it practical. To this day I can drive down the road, and if there has been a concentration of farm animals, I don't have to see anything, I know instantly what kind of animal was there by the stench of the excrement. Great God, such a talent and no way to make any money from it!!

When it was time to go to the chicken houses, that was a problem of a different nature. We had a three-tiered system for chickens, there were "yard chickens" who found a place to make a nest and lay their little hearts out, and we found the nests and took the eggs. They roosted in a huge privet hedge bush that had grown to about twenty feet tall. Something happened to the droppings from that place, it never seemed to accumulate. Actually what happened was that they shit all over the yard, just whenever the urge hit them. Part of being PO was going barefooted, so I really do know where they put it. Mushy chicken shit squeezing up between the toes does have a special feel, but it feels about the same as hitting it with the heel of your foot. The second tier of chickens were all laying hens, and they had a chicken yard, and built in individual laying nests inside the chicken house. They roosted on about eight to ten wooden sticks, about ten feet long across the chicken house, starting about three feet off the ground, and spaced about every eighteen inches. The roosting sticks kept going up toward the back wall of the chicken house like a set of steps, until they were about five feet off the ground at the back of the chicken house. Every night all the hens went on the roost, and they must have shit all night. We had to clean the chicken house out about every two months. Not only did we have the penetrating ammonia odor of chicken shit, we also had the great fun of knowing we were going to have to take off our clothes before we went into the house so we could get rid of the fleas. When we were thinking clearly, we would sprinkle some salt on the manure in the chicken house before we moved it to either kill, or run the fleas off. It took some skill since too much salt would kill the plants we put it on.

The third tier of the chicken shit kingdom was between one hundred to one hundred and fifty day old chicks, started in a brooder, and later allowed to spend all their days on a "run" made of hardware cloth. Their feet never touched the ground, but their shit did. It fell through the hardware cloth and we had to use a hoe to pull it out from under the run about once a week. We would pile it up and take it wherever we needed it. A few of those chickens made it to the layer house, but most of them were what we called “fryers”. One good thing about the chickens in that pen was that when we wanted to have fried chicken, running them down to catch two and wring their neck was much easier than dealing with yard chickens. I sure do wonder how many Kentucky Fried Chicken customers would eat as much chicken as they do if they had to wring a chicken’s neck, dump it in boiling water, and pick all the feathers off. Naturally, just getting the feathers off was just a precursor to gutting and cutting it into pieces for the frying pan.

Chicken shit was the most powerful of any shit we had, it would burn the plants if used too freely. For that reason, it was used for our gardens, which were about an acre, maybe more, depending on a bunch of things I never really knew about. Sometimes it is better not to ask too many questions, there was enough work canning everything we made anyway, so I was afraid Mama and Daddy would decide to make it bigger if I got too nosey.

The part of my life spreading shit was just another thing that made me much more aggressive about my schoolwork, just like many of the other “fun” things in my life. That job would really increase your attention span. Can you imagine how hard it was to bore me with any subject in school, about anything, after a week to ten days spreading shit? The odor alone was a motivator, not to mention mucking around in the shit lots!!

* * *

The WPA privy. President Franklin Delano Roosevelt’s plan to get us out of the depression was also involved in making it possible for us to get an almost proper shit. He did it by instituting a Privy Program under the auspices of the WPA. It is not that I am trying to be vulgar, and I can guarantee, that no matter how prim and proper you may pretend to be, there's not one of you who has been reading, or will read what I have written who can't identify with some of the things here. If you need to hide from the indelicate side of humanity, mores' the pity for you. Some may have difficulty believing it, but it is possible for me to go for extended periods of time and never break into crude or vulgar terms. Surprisingly enough, I am capable of being so erudite you would have difficulty believing I ever have need for a commode, which of course would mean I am really, terribly full of shit. This book is about "when I was and where I came from before I became who I am now."

The WPA, which was part of the Public Works Administration and a cornerstone of President Roosevelt's great society. It was a means of putting people who were worse off than we were [God only knows how] to work. Even though we had thunder mugs and slop jars in every room, we didn't have a shit place in the house, all we had was an above ground, outside, two-seat privy. A fence was on the backside to keep animals out, and sometimes it actually did keep animals out.

Do you have any answer to why anybody would build a "two seater" privy? It takes real love, or stupidity to have a partner in an above ground, outdoor crapper with you. Do you hold hands or noses? After pondering the question about multiple hole privies, I decided to ask someone who really knows their shit and I was advised that the multiple holes were of various sizes for children, up to very big ass adults. I guess that was really important when the WPA started digging those whopping deep privy holes. Since there was no way for anybody who slipped through one of the holes to get out.

One day Mr. Will Powell who lived about a thousand yards down the road told Daddy we qualified for a free privy. It wouldn't cost us anything, that was good, we could definitely afford it on that basis. Mr. Powell and Daddy decided where it should go to be convenient to the house. By today's standards, he had not been well trained. He arrived with a crew of about ten men with shovels, and all the materials. A hole was dug in the ground about four feet by six feet, and about eight feet deep. Meanwhile, the men who were not digging were cutting, sawing, and hammering. They built a one-hole privy, with a door that had a hook on it, and it also had a luxury cover for the seat of southern yellow pine, and which weighed about twenty pounds. The idea was to let it down to stifle odors. Obviously they had built a few before since just about the time the hole was completely dug, the privy was ready to be pulled and pushed into place. It had a nice tin roof, and man, we were almost into the 1700's!!

Thank God for Sears and Roebuck, their catalogs were wonderful, and the slightly more absorbent newspapers served our needs quite well too. I had almost no contact with expensive toilet paper, it seemed pretty flimsy to me anyway. Another interesting thing was that before the WPA crapper, we had kept corncobs in the above ground privy. I don't ever remember corncobs in the new privy. One reason was Sears and Roebuck catalog pages and the newspaper scraps would have blown all over the world from the above ground crapper. With the hole in the ground privy, paper couldn't blow away. A second reason we didn't use corncobs was that they didn't breakdown as well as paper. Ah, Progress, how sweet it is!! It is only fair to tell you that one hell of a lot more people in Burke County had outdoor privies than indoor bathrooms at that time. If you don't believe me look it up in the 1930 and 1940 census reports.

Earlier I mentioned that Daddy never used the privy, and that he, like the other older males mostly used a spot down near the headwaters of the little branch. It was about a hundred and fifty feet from the old cow barn, and well hidden from anyone at the cow barn, or anyone walking the wagon road. When the urge started to build, we would walk over to the corncrib, and pick up three red corncobs. One old story said that a person needed two red and one white corncobs and the correct order of usage was first a red, then the white to see if another red corncob needed to be used. Who would bring a single red corncob back to the barn anyway?

We just had red ones. Then we walked down to the spot, unhooked the galluses on our overalls and dropped them, along with our underwear, just far enough for our ass to hang out, and then pulled the overall bibb and galluses into a position to be sure nothing got on them from either source and squatted down. After having done it for years, it was a fairly restful position. After using the corncobs, and stepping forward a bit to make sure nothing got dragged through anything, the galluses were hooked back up and life went on. What I have described was a real "country shit".

* * *

Crude toiletry, yes, but that was a necessary part of living on a PO farm, and in the woods. Not everybody knew how to "assume the position" and ole Wiley, the "townie" was a good example of that lack of knowledge. After he had learned about mule biting, he had another lesson to learn that was funny as hell to those of us who had been going to the 'branch' with corncobs for years. Actually, it was something of a "rite of passage" to be able to head for the branch with the men. He had not been to the branch before, but he thought he understood what to do. He left, and was gone for what seemed like much too long. I walked down to check on him, and what I found caused me to almost fall down laughing, however falling down at that particular location would not have been smart. He had finished doing his business, all well and good, however, he didn't have on a stitch of clothes. The only way he could figure out how to squat down to take a crap was to take all his clothes off. After I quit laughing, and he had put his clothes back on, I had him take a couple of practice runs to be sure he would be able to head to the branch if he needed to later on in the year. I didn't think the way he was doing it was very good for cold weather crapping!

* * *

Privies and fig trees may seem like very different topics, but in my case they were related. I mentioned one of the purposes of the privy location was to make it convenient to the house, however, it surely wouldn't have made it on today's standards. It didn't hit me suddenly, in fact it was years later when I realized we had dodged or missed being hit by a pollution, environmental or health bullet, and it was quite by accident that we were missed. There was the most prolific yellow fig tree I have ever seen growing just about fifteen feet from the back door of the old house. It had so many figs that we made all the fig preserves, and what ever else could be done with figs, and we still had sacks full to give away. For some reason, I never really like figs much, but nearly everybody seemed to think they were exceptionally good. The risk we had all taken was pretty simple, the path to the privy went between the smoke house and the fig tree right to the privy. As that fig tree grew and prospered, the limbs from it reached right to the door of the privy. We weren't from Japan, but in looking back, it sure seems to me we were using 'honey buckets' to grow figs!!!

* * *

CHAPTER VI

HUNTING AND FISHING

Hunting and fishing were as natural as breathing to our entire family, it was something the males did, and the females benefited from. Living where we did, and under the circumstances of being PO, there was every reason to both hunt and fish. I can't remember when I did not have permission to shoot a 22 rifle. As I mentioned, Daddy bought 12 gage shotgun shells by the case to hunt quail. He also bought 22 bullets in small cases of ten boxes at a time for us boys, which was five hundred bullets at a time. On weekends in the Spring and Summer, Dean and I would spend some time sitting with the rifle, on the front porch, which faced the county road about twenty yards away.

We had some Oleander plants [poison as hell] in the yard that attracted bumblebees and as they would fly from one bush to another, they were in a "No fly zone" as far as we were concerned. If you know anything about bumblebees, they tend to fly along for a few feet, and for no apparent reason, they just stop for about two seconds, in mid air. What they do is somewhat like a helicopter or a humming bird. That was a very poor choice for them since Dean and I sat there with the rifle, following the bee, and when it stopped, about fifteen feet away, we blew the bee from the air. In retrospect, that was a mindless thing to do, but what the hell, on Sundays after church, we didn't have much else of great importance to take up our time.

One thing did come out of it, with all that practice, we became much better shots. We also had to concentrate and listen very carefully for cars coming down the road. It would not have been such a good thing to get the bee, and also get a car at the same time. There was no doubt the bullets were going across the road, and landing in a field, but we never did even come close to getting a car.

In the fall of the year when we had time to get away from work, Dean would usually take the rifle, and I would take the 410 shotgun, and we would head for the woods to hunt squirrels. "Rattler", our squirrel dog, was almost always with us, and we separated at the branch, Dean on one side and me on the other. We ran the dog between us from one side to the other, either the dog, or one of us would see a squirrel, and if the tree was not too high, I would get him with the shotgun. However, some of the big trees were too high for the shotgun, and Dean had to use the rifle to bring him down. He always accused me of just missing, I never recall him admitting the tree was too tall for the shotgun. When we had three or four, we would walk home, skin them and have fried squirrels for dinner or supper. We never really made too much of hunting rabbits, however the ones that jumped up when we were just walking along hunting squirrels made their way into the same frying pan.

* * *

Killing rats was another form of hunting which had nothing to do with anything to eat, even though a squirrel is a rodent. A rat shooting at the barn was in order when they started eating too much of the crop. Mice were not a problem in the house because of a large cat population in and around the house. The same cats also tried to patrol the barns, but there were rats in the barns, not mice, and the cats had more of a problem with them. We had rattraps, and other major trap surprises which worked well, but not to perfection.

The really major rat surprise was to take a washtub and fill it up within about three inches of the top with water, and put about one inch of cotton seed on the water surface. Cottonseed floated nicely, however, it took just about no weight at all for the rat to break through the seed and be in one large pool of water. Even big rats never could figure that one out, and we drowned bunches of them. I have heard East Indians believe even rats deserve to live, maybe so, but not from the corn I had to plant, plow, and plow and plow, and then break [harvest] and haul in that old wagon to a barn. I took it personally; I was not willing to be a caterer for damned rats!

However, I digress. Every so often, when all other ways seemed to have lost ground to a growing rat population, we scheduled a rat killing. We would move sacks, cotton sheets, and everything possible out of the corncrib to flush the rats out. Most of the time, we would be able to kill them with sticks, but sometimes those suckers were pretty cunning. They would get on a beam, or somewhere up high and we just couldn't make them get down. We had two approaches, the first was to take a slingshot and kill them with a high-speed rock, and that worked pretty well.

The second approach was for the really tough places and we used what is still called "Rat shot". It is shot that is just about like really coarse sand in a 22-rifle rim fire bullet. You can buy the same thing today and also in a 38 casing in case you have a poisonous snake where you don't want it. Some of the biggest and toughest rats would jump from the barn to the limb of a huge old sycamore tree that overhung the roof of the barn and play squirrel. That brought about a 22 short bullet in the rifle, and his only remaining trip was to fall to the ground dead. The cats ate what they wanted, and the rest were thrown down the hill for the wild animals to eat that night. That food chain stuff works.

* * *

After the corn was in the barn, mourning doves would start flying in, usually it was getting fairly cool, about October, and that was a fun time. Well, almost fun. It is one thing to be able to hit quail "on the rise" and quite another to be able to successfully "wing shoot" doves. I became much better at it as an adult, but I never could justify the cost of killing a dove on the basis of the meat. I like the meat, but it is nowhere nearly as good as quail. Since they were so hard to hit, we started going to get them where they came in for water. They were flying lower and slower, so we went home with enough for a meal more often.

During Quail season however, we would have chicken fried quail and smother fried quail at the same meal, along with doves. I have dressed so many quail so many times that I wanted to figure out a way to keep Daddy from carrying so many shells. He let me go with him some, but I didn't really want to push too hard. I was afraid he would expect me to walk the entire day with him. I may have been a bit crazy, but I wasn't stupid.

Given my background around guns, I have major difficulties trying to understand gun control. From the time I can remember, in that old house with all of us there, we had enough guns to start a small war. We had Daddy's 12-gage semi automatic, Daddy's 38 long barreled revolver, a five shot 410-bolt action shotgun, a single shot 20-gage shotgun, a single shot 16-gage shotgun, a single shot 22 rifle, and most of the time a semi automatic 22 rifle. They were stacked in their specific locations in designated corners in various rooms, and there was never even a glimmer of a thought that anybody was about to misuse any of those guns. Generally, I support the National Rifle Association position that people kill people, even though I have never been a member of the organization. I part company with them though on any sensible rationale for me or anyone else to own some of the assault pistols and rifles on the market today.

We could inventory our shotguns just walking by them. Three of the guns were left loaded at all times, they were Daddy's 38, his 12 gage shotgun, and the 410 shotgun. Loaded, meant with shells in the chambers. The only misadventure I can recall was when Herbert, who was about eighteen, went in to get Daddy's 12 gage, and it went off, shooting a hole in the ceiling in the corner of Daddy's bed room. There was a terrible argument between Herbert and Daddy. Daddy swore Herbert had taken the safety off, and Herbert swore the safety was off when he picked it up, and somehow it went off. To this day I believe Herbert was right, even so he should have checked the safety, no matter what. That hole was still there until the old home place burned, and it was a stark reminder to all of us to be even more cautious than we already were. For us, at that time, those guns were just another piece of equipment we needed to feed our self.

* * *

From May to October, we went down to Briar Creek to fish in bateau's. Don't ask me how we got a French, or Creole designation for what we used to fish from, I plainly don't know. We usually had at least two of the little fishing boats, one was Daddy's and almost nobody else ever got to paddle it. The boats were particularly well suited to

Briar Creek. They were built locally, from plans in the head of Fulcher Ward, who among his other talents was barbering, and I really don't know what other talents he might have had. I do know he didn't build enough boats to put much food on the table.

Those little boats were made of one by twelve inch clear heart cypress boards. At the stern, they were just wide enough for a twelve to fourteen inch ass. The gunnels flared out to about thirty-six inches amidship, slightly canted outwards from the bottom. A "wet well" fish box was part of the bracing which went from side to side in the middle of the boat. The fish box was about eighteen inches wide centered in the boat and, the rest of the space on both sides was used for storage of bait boxes, and the cooking bucket. At the bow, the gunnel boards were tapered from twelve inches amidship down to about seven inches. The seat for the second person was attached to the cross bracing on the front of the fish box, and running toward the bow about sixteen inches. With the tapered bow, and two people, the bow usually rode about a foot above the water. That made it look something like an Adirondack guide boat on the stern end, and a barge on the bow. Irrespective, it was a jewel for the tree and 'snag' infested Briar Creek.

We did two kinds of fishing; I guess you could call one type 'local fishing' and the other "long distance" fishing. When we were doing local fishing, we could go to many different landings [places] to 'put in' [launch the boat]. For example, Heath's Bridge was just a local name for a bunch of Heath's who owned land where the bridge was built. There was some time spent discussing and deciding whether to fish upstream or downstream. Depending on such important variables as how recently we had fished from that location before, and which direction had we taken, and what the catch had been. I never understood what the critical variables were according to Daddy's system, and since I was going to be fishing with him, you can bet his choice of direction was the one we were going to take.

My choice was to go upstream because paddling against the current, we would tend to fish the best places carefully. Past behavior told me we would keep going up stream until we were tired from fighting the current, and it was getting late. When we acknowledged it was so late we had better get moving to get the boats back to the landing, that strong, swift current moved the boat rapidly with just a minimum of steering. I can still remember when we fished downstream, and had to paddle like hell, fighting the current, from what seemed like five miles downstream to get back to the landing before night.

Dean and Herbert would fish together, and after Herbert left home, Dean would fish by himself most of the time and I fished with Daddy. I can tell you we were all pretty accomplished at fishing, but there was never a time when I could even begin to understand Daddy's ability. It didn't matter if he was using July Flies [katydids], Catalpa worms, meal worms, earth worms, yellow jacket larvae, wasp larvae, or dough balls, he would catch more fish than I could. We used bamboo cane poles about ten to twelve feet long, and while everyone was convinced he had the best pole, the fact was they were all about the same. If you wanted to really start some 'bad karma' all you had to do was accidentally break about six inches off the flexible tip of somebody's "most favorite" fishing pole. Bad karma my ass, it damned nearly would of started a fight, or cause you to be exiled from fishing for God only knows how long. I guess you might think such a minor thing couldn't be that bad, but it ranked right up there along with breaching conditions of surrender in a major war.

The long distance fishing trips were the greatest. Somebody would drop us off about 6:00 a.m. at Heath's Bridge, and they agreed to meet us at about 5:00 p.m. or later. We would drift and paddle down to Ellison's Bridge, an all day trip. We knew most of the best places to fish, and just exactly how the boat had to be positioned for the best chance to pull a few bream and red bellies and occasionally a "stump knocker" from each place. We were not fishing for Bass, catfish, mudfish, jackfish, or any of several other occasional varieties that might pass by. We didn't refuse them, we just didn't rig for them. On rare occasions, we would put out "trot lines" which meant a piece of what we called 'seize cord' with big baited hooks in the water at different depths, tied to a limb above the water and left overnight. The next morning, we would 'run the lines', which meant checking each line to see how many fish we had on the fifty or so hooks scattered down the creek. Another way of rigging a trotline, especially in lakes, was to make up a line about a hundred feet in length, and tie a short eighteen-inch lines with a baited hook about every two feet. After anchoring it off and marking it with buoys, it was time to put a hex on anybody who might come in the area and cut the line somehow, or steal the fish before you could get back to get back to check for fish. Let me tell you a "body" who would steal fish from someone else's trot line just didn't want to get caught at it. That was a flat and absolute invitation to get an opportunity to see if a new record could be established for swimming with a log chain wrapped around your body. As we 'usta' say "Zeb should have known better to steal more log chain than he could swim with!"

Getting back to the all day trip, Daddy seemed to try so hard to keep from giving me any basis for bitching about him always taking the best spot to put his line, that he was willing to agree to almost any thing I wanted to try. He almost seemed a little embarrassed that he caught so many more fish than I could, and he really wanted me to learn how to fish. Sometimes I would tell him I wanted to put my line in first and just where I wanted it, then he would put his line in, and dammit, he would start pulling in the biggest, hand sized red bellies, one after the other, and I was not even getting a nibble. On other occasions, I would have the same hook size, sinker size, and have everything set up exactly like he did. And I would put the tip of my pole within four to six inches of his, and he would catch three or four, and I might get one. I watched him closely, he didn't put any "mojo" on his bait, and he didn't spit on it either. Never could figure it out. On some days, the two of us would catch about a hundred big pan fish, he would get about sixty to seventy, and I would catch the remainder. My luck seemed to improve if I was in a separate boat, can't be sure though, since I never caught more than fifty to sixty in one day.

As we made our way down the creek, we had to watch for what we called 'snags'. A snag was nothing but a tree limb about four to six inches in diameter, in the bottom of the creek which was anywhere from two inches under water to about three inches above the water. To get surprised by one of those puppies often meant you stood a good chance of flipping the entire boat, or the person in the front seat could get flipped into the creek. Daddy didn't cotton to the idea of little surprises like that, so I was pretty vigilant.

There were numerous trees, which would be completely across the creek, and if it was less than a foot above the water, we would both start paddling furiously to get up speed and just before we hit. We knew to stop paddling and as the high riding bow slid up on the tree, I used the forward momentum of the boat to quickly step forward and jump out on the tree. Daddy was moving just a split second later, stepping out of the boat on the other side of the tree to keep the stern from going underwater. If we timed it right, and we generally did, we'd take on no water as we slid the boat across the log. I would get back in, while he held the stern, then he stepped in, and away we would go.

* * *

Cooking on the banks of briar creek during our long distance fishing was about the most enjoyment a youngen can get. I never could have been happy with Boy Scouts, hell, I camped out all my life. Sometimes we would be fishing with some others and there may be as many as six or eight of us. It was purely routine to us, we had a ten-quart Chalmer's Coffee bucket with a recessed lid. That recessed lid perfectly accommodated our cast iron frying pan, and in the bucket, we had a one-quart can filled with salt, pepper, cornmeal, lard, and coffee, along with other supplies.

About midday, we would start yelping and hollering for any other boats with us. We usually were the last boat, so when we started getting answers, they knew to start looking for a high and dry place to cook. By the time we got there, they usually had already located two logs, about four inches in diameter and three to four feet long, put them in the creek to get them wet, and positioned them properly to hold the frying pan to cook fish. We started the fire, took live fish from the fish boxes, scaled, gutted, mealed and had them in the pan with orderly speed. When the first pan of fish were frying, we would mix corn dodgers [a.k.a. hush puppies] in a can with corn meal and creek water. Another quart can with coffee in the bottom and filled with creek water was started for coffee. Everybody knew to bring a number two can in their boat to use as a coffee cup. I don't ever remember anybody having a plate except Daddy, who always got the lid from the bucket the frying pan sat in as his plate. I always used the blade of my paddle to put my fish and corn dodgers on. Fish will never ever taste any better.

After dinner, we would go out to the bushes to take care of any other necessary "business", and then all of us would talk awhile, and after that, start back fishing. I also had a great amount of time while in the boat to do "man talk" with just Daddy and me, and also a great amount of time learning when it was appropriate just not to talk at all. Sometimes, whether you are rich or PO, the best experiences just plainly don't require a lot of verbal communication.

I can tell you one thing though, it still seems to me that the 'old man', as we referred to him when he was out of earshot, got a fiendish delight in putting my end of the boat in, or under the bushes when we were pulling into a place to fish. I'll bet you have never seen somebody in the front of a boat take their paddle, and start beating the bushes like they were "killing snakes". Well, if you have, just maybe they were either running snakes off, or killing snakes that might be sunning, and waiting for a nice juicy boy like me to come along so they could fall in the boat and bite him. To the best of my knowledge, the snakes were generally water moccasins or black snakes, both of which were non poisonous. Hell ... if they scared you to death, they didn't need to have fangs. I wasn't afraid of snakes then, and I still am not, but to have one drop in the boat with me was something I just didn't need. I don't think I ever had but one to drop in the front of the boat with me and he wanted out as much as I wanted him out.

That's not to say that we didn't have plenty of really dangerous snakes in that area, because they were there. I think it is a tribute to God taking care of, or having mercy for the PO, the dumb, and the crazy. Sometimes I think we had combined streaks of both dumb and crazy which would come and go. We knew we wuz PO all the time, so we qualified all the time for two of the three reasons we shouldn't have been bitten and sometimes all three. Rattlers, copper heads, pigmy rattlers, and cottonmouth moccasins were plentiful and if I could see the snake, everything was just fine. What I didn't want was to step on one. Most often, after it got fairly warm. I went barefooted and it was not smart to step too close to any of those "slope shouldered " little snake fellows I just mentioned.

About mid afternoon we started to keep fairly close tabs on the time since somebody would be at either Ellison's bridge, or Hankerson's landing to meet us. Sometimes, we would just lock the boats to a big cypress tree rather than load them on the truck to haul home. We always put the fish either on stringers, or in big tubs of water. At the house, we would start scaling and gutting fish, and to this day, you had better be pretty skilled at getting fish ready to fry if you think you can even begin to work at the same scaling table with me and not get shamed for being inept.

* * *

Fish Fry. Everybody loves a fish fry where I come from. A fish fry at Hankerson's landing on the banks of Briar Creek was something we did about twice a year. That was plainly country living at its best. Rather than just Daddy and us in two or three boats, there would be about 15 men and Youngens fishing either in boats, or from the banks of the creek. We would start just after daylight, and either fish down Briar Creek from Heath's bridge, or put in at the Hankerson's landing. The women, and kids who were too young to fish as well as some men who liked to eat fish, but didn't like to catch them, or who just couldn't take the day off to fish, would arrive about noon. They brought all the cast iron cooking frames, buckets of iced tea, and whatever cooking supplies were needed. Along with that, there was potato salad, deviled eggs, cakes, pies and every thing guaranteed to add blubber to anyone who tried to eat their own weight. Depending on whether or not it was watermelon season, you might have to punish yourself by having to eat watermelon too.

As quickly as they arrived, in wagons, or old trucks, the non-fishers started about two or three wood fires, getting some really hot coals going. When there was a hot bed of coals, the cast iron cooking frames were put in place. Each frame could hold about three or four deep frying pans. As the fishermen started coming in about noon with their catch, about eight or ten people would start scaling and gutting fish. Mama was always there, and she and the others were mixing corn dodgers and salting and mealing the fish. About four inches of lard was put in the pans, and heated to boiling, and then the fish were put in and fried until they were golden brown.

The fires were kept stoked, and the frying kept going on until probably two hundred fish had been fried, and God only knows how many corn dodgers. It took some serious cooking to feed nearly fifty people. The reason was that most of the men either had been working like hell in the fields, or wherever, everyday, and we expected to eat three big solid big meals each and every day. Even with all that food everyday, the men there were not "fats"!! Many of the women didn't work as hard as Mama, and while she wasn't skinny, most of the rest of them had a tendency to be something more than 'tidy sized'. During the cooking and eating we talked and discussed whatever seemed to be topical. I don't ever remember anybody ever getting into fights, or yelling matches. There was almost always lots of singing, mostly hymns. About the only thing that happened as a direct demonstration of faith was a blessing before dinner. Many of us down there went to churches, but very few were religious zealots.

I don't ever remember any moonshine being at any of the fish fries, just lots of iced tea. At about 3:00 in the afternoon, we started loading everything up to go home. That may sound to you like a boring day, but to be lucky enough to even get a chance to be involved in something like that today, is about slim to none. I have doubts that many of you could find forty to fifty friends who are close enough to be involved in a good ole fish fry out in the open with good clean wholesome family fun in this day and age.

* * *

Don't stand up in the boat, especially if it is underway in a stream like Briar Creek. I had a cousin, I don't know if he was a first or second cousin, or just slightly related, who came for a two or three day visit with another of my brothers, Herbert. One of the reasons was to fish. But I think the most important one was that his mama wanted a few days rest from him. Herbert didn't really like Wright at all, but he tolerated him, since he was related to Mama. So, it was no secret among us that fishing that day was going to be under strained conditions. One reason Herbert didn't like Wright was that he had lived in town all his life, and in addition, he felt he had all the answers to all questions, even if they hadn't been asked. Stated another way, he knew too much about everything to take any instruction from us country hicks. Anyhow, the fishing commenced with Daddy and me in his boat, Herbert and Wright in another, and Dean and a buddy in the third boat. I don't think we had gotten to the second fishing spot before Daddy and I heard Herbert yelling at Wright to sit down...."You don't stand up in the boat while we are moving."

Shortly after that there was some more hollering by Herbert because of some dumb move by Wright that almost turned them over and then we rounded a bend in the creek just in time to see our highly intelligent cousin refuse to sit down again, and almost instantly he seemed to just fly from the boat into the creek. He was pretty wet for the rest of the fishing trip, but he was willing to stay seated after that. Herbert was never asked by Daddy, or anyone else, what happened but at least three of us, including Daddy knew that those little boats were pretty "tippy" and all it took was just one fast, quick jiggle of the paddler's ass in the stern of the boat to make the bow jump nearly two or three feet. Herbert always had something of a mean streak at times, however there was unstated agreement among us that one fast "jiggle" had definitely been in order. Wright was lucky to be allowed to get back in the boat.

* * *

Fishing at Shumake Lake and maybe dying was not high on my list of things I wanted to do, but I sure felt like it might be close at hand on one trip there. Fishing in a lake was something we seldom did, but occasionally we went to Shumake Lake. I never really felt comfortable about finding that lake because it was deep in the woods surrounded by nearly eighteen thousand acres of swamp. Every tree looked just like the others, and if the sun wasn't out, getting off the nearly nonexistent trail would have meant wandering around lost until there was some sunlight to get a direction. We didn't believe in compasses, which really meant we didn't have one. Shumake Lake was near the Savannah River. In fact, when the river was at flood stage the lake was flooded too, which didn't happen, according to what I remember, more than every six or seven years. Irrespective of that, the woods were always pretty swampy and wet, and man was that old mud slick! That was another time when being barefooted was a good thing, you'd be surprised just how much traction you can get with ten long skinny toes working to help you keep your balance.

Usually there were two or three old boats left at the lake. I never knew who owned them but we could use them if we got there first. I guess that was the way it worked, nobody ever forced us to turn the boat we were using over to them. The thing that made it interesting was that it was a majestic lake, probably about ten acres, and in the early morning fog it was so quiet and tranquil, just a thing of absolute beauty. We caught plenty of fish there, and it surely wasn't over fished since it was in such an isolated place, and a long and muddy walk to get to it.

I can remember one visit to that lake that had me convinced it was probably going to be my last. Ever been afraid you were dying from some dreaded disease, but you didn't know what it was? In hindsight, and with the aid of years of maturity, I think I know what was wrong. Anyway, for reasons unknown to me, I had started having some burning sensation every time I took a piss the day before, and then between the old truck and the mile or so walk in to the lake, I started having to piss about every 20 minutes. One time it would be white, like chalk had been added to it, the next time, it would be slightly bloody, and then a mixture of the two, and it burned more than just a little. I was scared to death that I was going to see a stream of bright red blood the next time.

Even though the bright red blood never happened, I had a terrible backache that really had nothing to do with the hard seat in the boat. That surely didn't make me any less frightened. I lied like a rug and told Daddy that I wanted to fish some from the bank so he let me get out of the boat. What I didn't want him to know was that I was pissing continuously. Looking back, I now figure I had some relatively minor kidney infection. I lived, but I also had been scared as hell for another reason, I kept worrying about how Daddy would get me out of that swamp if I passed out. Sure was dumb as hell not to tell him about my problem. Sometimes, years later, and, too late - we get smart!

* * *

CHAPTER VII

FARMING AND THE "FUN'OF IT

Farming and the "fun of it", and that's a joke son. Some of the less than fun things about late 1800's farming [but done until nearly 1950] have already been mentioned in relation to mule stories, however, there was much more involved, aside from mules, even though mules were usually involved somewhere along the way. One of the things mentioned was what was called "breaking ground" and the way the March winds would blow off the topsoil. Everybody I knew used some form of 'turn plow' to break ground, unless they had a tractor. I assure you, it would have been very easy to recruit me into the mafia if a tractor had been the payoff for just one contract for a hit.

Daddy almost lost the farm during the depression, and if Grandmama hadn't been willing to use what little money she had, he would have lost it, so I was told. Funny thing about bank failures in a depression, it only seemed to work one way. The puny deposits Daddy had seemed to have just evaporated. However, it was mysterious that the mortgages hadn't disappeared in the same way. There is a sound reason why bankers have kept their bad reputations over the years.

Anyway, Grandmama's money was enough to pay off the loan, and if you don't think that $400.00 was a princely sum in 1933, think again. The terror of almost losing the farm back then instilled a fear in my family that has affected the way I look at risk even to this day. It also did something else, it meant there was no way in hell to ever get Daddy to go into debt enough to get even a small tractor. When everybody else was getting little one-row tractors, for about eight hundred dollars, including equipment and cultivators, all he could see was a damnedable mortgage. In the last two years before I left home, we did get some custom land breaking done by some of the people who had bought tractors. In fact, part of the way they planned to pay for them was by breaking land for people like us. The going rate was one dollar per acre. In one day, with a two-disc plow, they could plow at least four times the amount we could do with a pair of mules and when they went home at the end of the day, they hadn't even halfway sweated.

It was plainly impossible to talk to Daddy about the extra corn we could grow and sell by having a tractor. Logic and reason couldn't get through to him, the fact that the rows didn't have to be far enough apart to have a pair [team] of mules walk between the rows, which translated into more corn per acre and would have meant more corn to sell. Second and most importantly, we wouldn't have to feed the corn to a tractor either. Gasoline for the tractor was about sixteen cents per gallon at that time. One of the biggest reasons was one we didn't dare use it, was that pulling fodder was one thing we wouldn't need to do since tractors wouldn't eat fodder, either. Even if we had gotten a tractor, I think he would have made us pull fodder just to make sure we didn't get spoiled and have time on our hands. He had experienced what I later learned was called a "significant emotional event" with the near foreclosure of that mortgage, Anyway pulling Fodder builds character, you know. My opinion was that I already had way way WAY too much "character."

After breaking ground for planting, either Daddy or Dean would 'layoff the field' for corn, cotton, peanuts, or peas. The row width was variable for each crop, however, corn rows were sixty inches apart, and two wooden measuring sticks [poles] eight feet long were used to be sure the rows were the right distance apart and straight. A mark was made on the sticks to show the appropriate distance between the rows by using them as a ruler on the ground. The first measuring stick was laid with the mark at the middle of the previous row, and by gently standing the stick up, you would have the correct distance. The measuring stick was jammed into the ground, as straight up as possible, about one third of the distance from the beginning of the row, and the second measuring stick was used to set the row width in the same way as the first on and placed about one third of the way from the far end of the row. The object was to keep the "middle buster" plow and the mules in perfect alignment with the stakes. As you plowed up to each stake, you had to stop the mules, walk around them and move it and measure for the next row. Some really white cloth was wrapped around the measuring sticks to make them stand out so they could be easily seen. Want to go nuts, if you did that for about twenty acres and there was an excellent chance you would get a free trip to "Sylum City" which was where the Asylum was in Milledgeville, Georgia. Back then, when you went, you didn't get to come back most of the time [EVER].

It takes a much better "eye", and more control of that plow than you might think. I know that a person who has not done it for awhile will have rows that are so crooked it is hard to cultivate them without plowing up half the crop. Generally, with corn for instance, enough rows would be 'laid off ' for a day's planting. Then, it was a one-mule operation to pull the fertilizer distributor and another mule to pull the corn planter. There were two skills in this deal, one was to set the guano [fertilizer] distributor where it would 'put out' the correct amount - say one half ton per acre. That means you have to know about how many rows there were per acre, and how many feet of cornrows were involved, and then how many pounds of guano were being put on each row. Now that was the smart way to do it, we just 'had the feel', and guess what, we were seldom wrong!

Where the corn planter was concerned, we knew each seed of corn was going to be somewhere between 14 to 18 inches apart, or as we said, 'in the drill'. That was pretty much a "no brainer" since we had various cogs [gears] which when matched with different 'plates' would regulate the distance between the seed. Each available plate had a different number of slots, which would hold exactly one kernel of corn. The drive wheel on the ground caused all the gears and plates to rotate and a single kernel of seed corn would drop down a little chute to the ground just ahead of the drive wheel. The kernel was promptly covered by the compression of the wheel. While I said it was a "no brainer", maybe it really wasn't, since I recall rolling that old Cole Planter on the hard ground by hand, measuring the distance between the seed it dropped. I hope you will understand that I observed the operation for a number of years, following that mule's ass up one row and down another, day after damned day. Damn being "PO", Damnit, Damnit!!!

If you should have had the misfortune to have selected the ears of seed corn poorly, or the misfortune to encounter a flock of marauding Crows or Brown Thrashers, there was always the fun of 'replanting corn.' Again, really rocket science stuff, you fill your front overall pockets full of seed corn, take a hoe, and start following each and every row. Everywhere one or more kernels had not sprouted and resulted in a pretty little corn plant, you replanted it. Where you might see what had been a pretty little corn plant that had been pulled up by Crows or Brown Thrashers to get the kernel of corn, your assignment was to dig one edge of the hoe into the ground and plant another kernel of corn. Yes, I know the Brown Thrasher is the State Bird of Georgia, and they are pretty, however, they were an endangered species when they pulled up corn that I had to replant. I damned sure killed them, and I hope the statue of limitation has run out.

By the way, I forgot to mention, during the spring and Summer all the wonderful stuff [work] was done barefooted. First, you only had one pair of shoes [brogans], and second, that dirt "just plain felt good to the feet." When summer was in full heat, the ground would get so burning hot it would blister your feet, so when you plowed, you always made sure to walk in the newly plowed ground. It wasn't air conditioning, but it sure made 100 to 105 degree Fahrenheit days "cooler all over" for the plower. In short, we went barefooted unless it was cold as "a well diggers ass in January", or we felt we had to dress up and wear our shoes for social reasons.

Planting cotton, peanuts, and peas followed the same boring routine as planting corn, except that the rows were close enough together that we could lay off the rows by judging the distance from where the dirt rolled off the plow for each row and that made for a pretty field. We had to adjust all the planters and guano distributors for each crop and the same process went forward for replanting cotton as for corn, but somehow or another we never had to replant peanuts or peas. Thank you Lord for peanuts and peas!!!

One aspect of "tending" cotton was what we referred to as "chopping" cotton which mainly meant cotton seeds were sowed, about every two inches and after they came up and got about three inches tall, we walked every row. Again, the tool of necessity was a hoe. One width of the hoe was to used to thin the plants by "chopping" out that width. We would leave about three cotton plants, and chop again, just don't ever make a mistake, and cut all the plants out and have two hoe widths without any plants. Try doing that when the rows are twenty four to thirty inches apart, for about ten acres of cotton.

Notice I said one aspect, there was another that was just about the same and about as much fun, known as "hoeing cotton". After chopping, and the first cultivation using 'sweeps', we had to hoe every row again. Carefully getting out every blade of grass, and when it couldn't be done with the hoe - guess what - you had to get down on your knees and pull it out by hand. I almost had nightmares from being so afraid I might accidentally chop down some cotton plants. Usually we had to hoe each crop at least twice. Have you counted? That meant going up and down every damned row of cotton in that field at least three times with a hoe in your hand. There are some other more ribald usages of the word 'hoe', but to me, the only thing I can think of is pain!

I have gone into some detail about this process to be sure you understand just what PO really meant when it came to dirt farming in Georgia. There is no way you would ever last through all the details for every crop we planted. Just understand about the same amount of "hoeing and tending" was done for all of them. Remember when I said we used "sweeps"? That had nothing to do with television ratings week. Those were little plows that look a little like a boomerang, basically they were designed to go under the surface of the soil, and cut the roots off grass. That stopped the grass from using the fertilizer, which would have reduced the crop yield. The sweeps were usually used three, and sometimes four times, mounted on an old Avery walking cultivator, pulled by the pair of mules. Handles were attached to two "feet" to which the sweeps were bolted. Those two handles were offset so the plower could walk alongside the row. Again, it took one trip on every row, every time the grass started showing itself in the crop. A special trip was made just before one of the plowings to put out nitrate of soda. That was done by toting a bucket and by hand, throwing out just the right amount of fertilizer along the side of the row of plants. I didn't know nitrate of soda could be used as an explosive until years later and that was probably a good thing, well maybe it didn't matter since it wasn't but just a few years later I was using dynamite to blow stumps. What you have had described to you was nine to twelve trips through that cotton field, and that was before the hell of cotton picking started. But it wasn't just cotton that was back breaking work, it was every damned thing we planted.

There was a time near the end of the summer every dirt farmer looked forward to with glorious anticipation, it was called "Layby time". What that meant was that the final plowing and hoeing had been done, and everything was left in the hands of the rainmaker. Most of the time there was no concern about too much rain, only would there be enough to mature the cotton bolls, the ears of corn, the peanuts, or peas or whatever else we may have that year. I don't have many occasions to hear "Layby time" in my world today, but if I just happen to even think I hear it, I have a feeling of "Thank God, Thank God." Which loosely interpreted means, thank God, I'm not in that PO Sandbed hell anymore!

* * *

Harvesting, to me, was just another word for a different kind of killer hard work. Whoever romanticized the end of the growing season with a harvest ball was sure as hell not anybody who had to work like we did picking cotton and peas, shaking peanuts, pulling fodder, and breaking corn. There was enough stooping, bending, crawling and aching as to be mind boggling, and all that was before you got into the really fun stuff like putting up peanut poles, stack poles for fodder, tying the fodder into bundles, sledding peanuts, running the thrasher, baling hay, and other wonderful little jobs that had to be done to keep hide and hair together and put food on the table.

In many respects the details I have given could seem to be just too much, however I have never read anything that told quite enough about just how brutal and hellish the work was during that era. Before you castigate me too much for my detailing, I have tried to give major examples, glossing over others, which were really just repetitions of already explained aspects. I know many readers do not like to have every labor pain painted in vivid detail. But, since most people never have first hand birthing experience, vivid detail is frequently the nearest they can get to truly understanding either "PO" or birthing.

Part of what may be accomplished by writing about this is that you will have the opportunity to become more understanding and sensitive to what was an important platform, or starting point, for many people who grew up in a rural, and economically deprived circumstance. Notice I did not mention deprived in all aspects, I still marvel at the fact that we were able to find some things to be amusing, happy, or downright gut busting funny. Some of that 'humor' will never be totally understood by the nonparticipant. The cement that saved us was a healthy and strong family with a powerful structure, no matter what our faults might have been.

* * *

Picking cotton was not a racial thing, it was a qualification for the condition of being PO. Recently there was a big outcry about the insensitivity of planting some cotton in the median across from the public library in Milledgeville, Georgia, the small southern town where I live. Some wonderfully politically correct people were just wringing their hands about how it was an intentional degradation of Blacks in the community. How damned dumb can some ass holes get? I considered it as a monument of great significance. I will gladly watch anybody plant it, but I won't help, I will gladly look at it growing, and I will talk about cotton, but I have no intention of ever picking one 'lock' of it. I still have the scars etched deeply in my mind of too many summers stooping in a cotton field, dragging that damned cotton sack. Maybe we should consider that cotton patch across from the library as a symbol of emancipation for all people who had to pick cotton. In fact, I suspect that most of the Blacks who joined in the caterwauling about the 'horrible thing being done' had never even been in a cotton field. There is no doubt in my mind, that if even one of the "I can feel your pain" whites had ever walked in a field of cotton it would have been totally by chance, or to develop their sense of moral outrage. Picked a sack of cotton - never!

Let me tell you something - my mother, brothers and I picked cotton right alongside Blacks, both male and female. Talk about envy. I was green with it. I had to work longer hours everyday, both starting before they did, and finishing after they did. My pay was one major goose egg, at least they were getting paid anywhere from one to two dollars per hundred pounds. An additional insult to me was that they only stuck around for the first picking. After the first picking was done, the few slowpoke bolls would open, and we had to do what was called 'scrapping cotton'. All that meant was we toured every row of nearly bare stalks, and for that we got the last 500 pounds on a ten-acre field. That would "gin out" to less than two hundred pounds or about forty dollars worth, if we were lucky.

When it is cotton-picking time in Dixie, just MOVE, especially if you are talking about before the 1950's. The song about "When them cotton balls get rottin" never meant shit to me. What meant something to me was when the cotton field turned white with more than half the bolls opened, because it was time to get all the burlap cotton sheets out and make sure they were repaired. Depending on whether Daddy was going to try to hire some day laborers to help, we would need from ten to twenty cotton sheets.

Cotton sacks were hundred pound burlap guano bags, to which over the shoulder "straps" were attached. We would use a walnut, or a rock the size of a walnut to loop a string from the shoulder strap to the cotton sack. Want to know about an instrument of torture, that sack was one calculated to break a person's back. Everybody started picking cotton by stooping over to get all the cotton locks from the bolls on the stalk from the ground up. After stooping over as long as you could stand the increasing pain, pulling an ever increasingly heavier sack of cotton, the pain would get so excruciating that any cotton picker would choose an even worse "condition", just for a change. That worse condition was to get on your knees and crawl over burning hot sandy dirt, with occasional small clay pebbles. Even with what we erroneously or stupidly called kneepads, it was common to have heat scalded and blistered knees at the end of the day. Our "knee pads" were about four to six thicknesses of burlap bag made into a six-inch square and tied above and below the knee to blunt the trauma of the pebbles, heat, and force needed to pull a fifty to seventy five pound sack of cotton up and down the rows.

When the sack was so full of cotton it could no longer be packed in, even shoving with our feet, we 'went to the sheets' laid out at the end of the cotton row and emptied the sack. That brilliant operation continued from "can till can't", all day, every day, from Monday morning until Friday night. Damn, can't you just imagine the fun and hilarity of everybody involved? Everybody's pickings were 'weighed up' at the end of every day. Generally only the best cotton pickers could 'weigh up' with 250 pounds every day.

Some considerations as to how much a person could pick depended on just how good the crop was, and whether or not an acre would produce a bale. Back then, the best cotton was usually no more than a bale an acre, and most crops were not that good. Another aspect of what a person weighed in with had to do with how much trash, in terms of cotton leaves, and stems, and plants were stuck in the sack. The last considerations were whether or not anybody had put rocks in their sheet, or had been able to pour a gallon or more of water on the cotton. Sometimes, the most industrious pickers would try to save back a little bit from the day before, and get an early start with moist cotton from the night dew. Believe me, except for trying to establish some sort of record for the day, there was no reason for any of us in the family to do anything to kick our weight totals high, we weren't going to get paid anyway.

I'm sure I knew, at one time, how many pounds of picked cotton was supposed to be on the wagon before we took it to the gin - I don't remember, and if luck holds out, there will never be a reason for me to look it up. Going to the gin was another aspect of humiliation for me. I knew it would either 'cower' me for life, or make me so blasted disgusted with every thing that I was damned sure going to find a better way to live, and I was not going to "cower" never, damnit, never. Getting on that wagon, and being about the only person on the road using mules to pull that bale of cotton was bad enough, but what was worse, was to have to pull over to let a person who had a tractor pulling a trailer pass by, leaving me in the dust. Even worse was to have several trucks pass you on the way to the gin. That always led to another wonderful opportunity, to be on the ass end of a line waiting for a chance at the suction pipe for the gin to remove the cotton from the wagon. Mules were never placid when hitched to a wagon, let alone standing and waiting, sometimes for up to two hours. That meant I had to spend all that time at the wagon to keep them settled while everybody else with tractors and trucks were able to walk around wherever they wanted, or talk with each other. It was unlikely anybody wanted to form a group discussion at the head of a damned mule. God, it sure makes me sad to know I gave up all that character building, all that fun!

Remembering how much I enjoyed going to the gin also makes me remember just how great it was to be in that damned cotton field which was usually bordered by at least one county road, picking cotton in hundred to hundred and four degree temperature without a lick of shade and obviously sweating buckets. I would look up to see a huge cloud of dust being kicked up by one of my classmates running up and down the road in their car or truck. That really burned and roasted me in a fashion that the sun couldn't. I knew they couldn't even begin to compete with me in the classroom, and while that was some satisfaction, it was damned poor consolation. I still almost boil over with rage when I hear somebody say, "I think the most awful sin anyone can have is to have the green eyed monster of envy." Any son of a bitch who says that is either a total damned liar, or they never were PO and on the farm like I was. WAS I ENVIOUS - HELL YES, WAS I MOTIVATED TO GET THE HELL OUT OF THERE - HELL DOUBLE HELL YES!!!

* * *

Pulling fodder was another of the tortures of the PO farm in Sandbed Hell. I have mentioned pulling fodder as partial feed for the mules, which had such a dominant part of my whole "PO" life until I left home. When the feed corn for the cows and mules had been plowed and plowed and plowed, and it had tasseled and the ears formed, and the middle buster had been run down the rows for the cowpeas, it was time for something else. At that time it was possible to say nothing you could do that would affect the corn yield. Guess what! It seemed there was always something else for us to eagerly wait for. Now was the time to proclaim, its fodder pulling time!! That was such a thrill, it almost still gives me chills, and in some respect it was even more of a pain in the ass than picking cotton.

We always tried to get at least three or more people to help, that way at least some conversation could take place, though in retrospect it is hard to understand how. Each person got his own row of corn to strip of leaves, and it was your very own all the way down that row, for about three hundred yards. That was, by my count, three times the length of a football field - not that a football field had a damned thing to do with it. You would address [that means face, not talk to] a stalk of corn likely to be between six and seven feet tall, and lifting both your arms put one hand on each side of the stalk, grabbing the next to the uppermost blade [leaf] of corn. Don't ask me why, we just always left the single highest blade which was usually rather small, to wave around in the breeze. For all I know it was some sort of artistic statement. Then we brought our hands down on each side of the stalk and about two inches away from it, stripping all the blades or leaves off as they tore away from the stalk. Since we were using both hands, we were collecting the blades in each hand. You now know all the technology of "pulling fodder", just multiply it 20,000 times for each fodder puller. One of the important aspects was that as soon as both hands couldn't hold anymore of the blades, say after "pulling" about three stalks, you got to make what was called a 'hand' of fodder. Don't even think about going there - just like I never knew why we left that pissy assed flag at the top of the stalk, neither did I know why those little blades about to be tied together with two blades of fodder were called a "hand". Know what, I don't care about 'why' either.

After tying the hand, a stalk that had already been stripped would be broken off about a foot or two above the ear of corn, and the hand of fodder was impaled on the stalk and left to dry, along with the ears of corn, in the hot August sun. Hey man, I learned all about strippers long before I left for the Air Force. I also got to know what a cornfield looked like with a massive number of nude stalks just standing there with ears of corn at attention. I must confess, some ears of corn did droop down and, hanging there like that, they looked like very depleted, or disinterested young male studs - or maybe lovers after the act.

Normally it took about a week for the hands to dry, and then, bless us all, we got the great privilege of working at night after the moisture had 'risen' [about 9:00 p.m.] so the dried blades were moist enough not to shatter in the "hands" and they could be used to make bundles. Again, it is the hundreds of repetitions that start to bearing in on you. Walk the rows, and pick no more than five hands, then take two of the moist blades in one hand, and two in the other from one of the "hands of fodder", and with a flipping motion, squeeze the other four hands tightly, and at the same time, tying a tight knot so it wouldn't slip out, and then throw the bundle ahead of us and down the rows of corn, about twenty feet. Of course, two or three or more people were walking the adjacent rows, actually one person was usually working two rows by walking between them and tying the hands of fodder. That fun could go on until 1:00 at night. Somewhere along the way some of us would start gathering the bundles we had just tied by grabbing a few blades of fodder from each bundle in our hands.

When we had so many we couldn't hold any more in our hands, we would hoist the bundles up on our shoulder, and head for the stack pole. It really looked comical, to see a pair of legs seemingly coming from a huge ball of fodder stumbling along in the night toward some mysterious destination.

A fodder stack pole was usually about twenty feet tall with a couple of sticks nailed across about a foot off the ground to keep the bottom bundles from getting wet and rotting. A good stacker was an absolute necessity, cause nobody wanted to get a stack up about twelve feet, and have the whole thing come loose from the pole and wind up as one huge mess. Daddy most often was the pole procurer, and the stacker - why not - we had to do all the damned walking. All he had to do was stand and catch the bundles and put them down as they were thrown to him, and walk around and around that pole, getting higher and higher with every layer. When he had filled the pole, he would 'cap' the stack of fodder so rain couldn't get in at the pole and rot it. We had to worry about rot from the bottom and the top. After that he would slide down the side of the fodder stack and we went home. You knew daylight was coming early and just because we had been having so much fun, it wasn't right to think we could lolly gag in the bed until some late hour like 8:30 or 9:00.

The only really good thing I ever remember about that operation was that one night I was so tired I couldn't go anymore so I just fell to the ground and rolled over on my back just resting. It was a gorgeous night, with every star just showing off, when I saw something streaking across the sky. I don't know what year, or what time of the night, and to this day, I don't know how long that display lasted. I recall telling everybody to look at it, and everything stopped until it was over. I suppose it was a meteor shower, no matter, it was my first, and I was in awe of something so impressive. I think I was inspired because I had been permitted to be a spectator to such a magnificent show. The display didn't frighten, alarm, or cause us to think of impending doom - cults weren't in our vocabulary.

* * *

Shaking peanuts was another of the fun jobs we were allowed to enjoy more than we wanted to. Shaking peanuts had nothing to do with palsied ground peas [peanuts] rattling around in their shells, however, it had everything to do with how those mothers were harvested back in the time of PO. Put another way, there were no mechanical harvesters for anybody, rich or poor or PO. I recall seeing a prototype harvester, which was under development by some Yankee company at a big farm outside Girard, but it never worked very well during the time I knew about it.

Thank God peanuts were an "acreage control" commodity, which meant we could plant only a limited number of acres to sell at subsidized prices. I don't think we ever had more than seven or eight acres and that was more than enough, given the way we had to harvest them. Depending on how they graded out, the three fourths to one ton per acre was pretty good since they sold for about $200.00 per ton. Too bad, I never got to see any of it except in the form of another pair of overalls, or some other equally exciting and rare "store bought" items.

When the plants were ready to harvest, the "Boy Dixie", a one-mule plow was brought out. It was a 'turn plow' except that the turning wing was removed, and the "point" was used to loosen the sandy loam the peanuts had made their home in. The intent was not necessarily to make our work easier, rather the jostling was to be sure the peanuts did not come off the vine and stay in the ground. One person plowing could keep ahead of five shakers whose sole job was to grab as many plants as possible in each hand, and shake all the damned dirt off the peanuts. As you were doing your shaking, you were walking toward the stack pole, and putting them on the stack. I still can't believe it, but before we got to shaking and walking, we actually had to pull them from the ground, shake them and sort them out so all the tops were aligned and put them down in a row. Then we went back, picked them up and took them to the stack pole. Innovation is a magnificent thing, finding out that the peanuts didn't grade out any worse even if they were ass over elbow, was not as important as discovery of the electric light bulb, I don't think.

Everybody shared the same stack if you in the non-payment group [family]. If you were day labor, you were in a special section of the field where the number of stacks you had done could be counted, since pay was based on the number of stacks you completed. I seem to recall the price varied between $0.20 and $0.30 per stack, there was no real reason for me to be too interested because it was a lead pipe cinch there was no money in it for me. If you ever stack one peanut stack, you will certainly understand the job does not require a GED certificate to keep your position. Just to make sure even the slowest learners could really get proficient, we had to keep stacking those damned things for sometimes up to two weeks.

By the way, where do you think the stack poles came from? The tooth fairy did not cut the damned things, haul them out in the wagon, and throw them off every fifteen to twenty feet. Neither did the twinkle-toed fairy dig the holes in that sandy land, nor furthermore did I ever see a tooth fairy with a hammer and nails put the stacking strips about a foot off the ground. I know who it was, and I sure as hell didn't fly through the peanut field, I was grounded in Sandbed hell, don't you know. Anyhow, I didn't have any pointy-toed shoes.

Picking Peanuts. The peanuts [a.k.a. goobers] were left in the field on the stack poles, until dry enough to rattle in the shell. Meanwhile Daddy was looking for someone who owned a peanut picker [thresher] and hay baler and who would charge a reasonable price to strip those little suckers off the plants. We were busy building new peanut sleds, or repairing the old ones, and getting ready for the great fun. When the person who owned the tractor, peanut picker and hay baler arrived at the field the picker was placed in a central location in the field. The picker was disconnected from the tractor, and the tractor was then jockeyed around so the flat belt drive wouldn't jump off. At least part of the operation was ready. At that point the hay baler was pushed into alignment behind the discharge end of the picker and lined up to a flat belt drive from the picker to provide power for baling hay..

The only 'good' jobs in this whole operation were the ones around the 'picker', the most difficult of those usually took two people with pitchforks to keep it fed with the dried plants. The "candy ass" job was running the peanuts into tubs and throwing the full tubs into the truck. Somehow or another that never got to be my luck. The totally worst job was feeding the hay baler, that was because all the dust, dirt, stems and leaves from the picker were being blown out the ass end of the peanut picker by a fan. Guess where the person feeding the baling machine had to be, right where all the crap landed. No, I don't expect you to find it too hard to guess where I was. Hell I think I actually got to put the wires on the bales one year - for about 30 minutes. Being the youngest sure as hell didn't get me any seniority on what job I had to do. Talk about crud, I always had a bandanna over my mouth and nose, or I would have died of peanut lung disease as a teenager. What was amazing was that there was no place on your entire body that wasn't caked with crap, and sticks and leaves, about the only thing you could see was the whites of eyes after feeding that damned baler.

The way to get the peanuts to the picker was to take a mule pulled "sled" out to each stack, stand the sled on its end against the stack, and loop a wire from the sled around the top of the six foot stack pole. Then the mule pulled the stack pole and the sled to the ground. The driver's main job was to be sure the peanut stack didn't roll off, and to get it to the picker as fast as possible. Usually we had to have at least three neighbors help us, which meant, we weren't really through with the damned peanut picking season until all those helping had been repaid by helping them with their peanut picking. Makes me feel exhausted just thinking about it.

All the peanut hay was baled as the leaves and sticks were blown from the picker. It took two six foot long wires quickly slipped through slots on the bale divider while the hay was being compressed and formed into a hay bale by being pushed through the machine. The hay was still in the field and had to be hauled before it rained, hell no, we didn't have anyway to cover it, so if it rained the hay rotted. Every bale of hay weighed about eighty pounds, and no, that isn't so heavy until you have loaded about six to eight loads a day on a two-mule wagon just as high as you can get them up in the air. One other little point, every wagon loaded had to be unloaded and stacked in the barn.... Do you wonder that the delight of peanut picking time in Dixie was just about as much fun as cotton-picking time in Dixie?

* * *

Picking peas and velvet beans and breaking corn were some of the other things that provoked much excitement among people like me. And if you believe that...... We planted peas under contract for a canning plant for several years. Picking peas was the same thing as picking cotton, except the sack got heavier and fuller much faster, but your back and knees suffered the same as in cotton picking. They were dumped on the same 'sheets' used for cotton, and weighed on the same balance scales, and dumped on a truck to be taken to the cannery. I got paid the same amount for picking either peas or cotton, or shaking peanuts - notta.

Velvet beans were one of the cruelest things we ever planted or that I have ever been exposed to. Generally, they were planted in a special field and planted in the same row as corn, that means one corn seed, then one velvet bean seed. The cows were turned into the field to eat both beans and corn in the fall after they had both dried. The corn stalks were still standing with the ears of corn on them, and the velvet beans would wrap around the corn stalks with the beans just hanging everywhere. Believe me, turning the cows in to eat that fool stuff was an ideal choice. Just remember, the pigs followed the cows after a few days, and you know why!!!

The "fun" in picking velvet beans was that they had hairy fuzz over the entire two to three inches of the bean. Picking those suckers guaranteed that you would itch all over from the top of your head to between your toes. We always had to pick enough beans for seed for next year. I didn't know for years that the way to avoid most of the itch was to wait until after about three hard frosts had fallen and most of the itchy, hairy fuzz was gone. Can't understand, to this day, why it was necessary for us to endure an itchy hell for something we couldn't eat. I guess it was more of that character-building thing!

'Breaking corn' was just that, after the corn had air-dried on the stalk, and it was late October, we went back to those wonderful sacks mentioned first in relation to cotton picking, except this time, we turned down a wider flap and attached the strap so that we used only half the burlap sack. We traveled down each row of corn, grabbed the ear with one hand, and put the other hand near the stalk. We would 'slip shuck' it, and put it in the sack. Slip shucking means that you leave only a few layers of husk on the ear of corn and no long stem. Doing that meant less to haul, and made it much easier to handle. Every time the sack would get full, you would walk about twenty feet up the row, beyond where you had "broken" the ears off the stalks and dump that sack full on the ground. That was the collection point for about eight to ten rows of corn, and after you passed that corn pile, you would walk back to it every time your sack got full, until you were about twenty feet beyond that pile, then it was time to start another.

The "almost final" fun episode was picking the corn up from the piles, putting it in woven white oak bushel baskets and dumping it in the high body on the two-mule wagon. That sounds a lot easier than it was. Loading baskets with corn, and then lifting the full basket up above your head, dumping it over the high wagon sides was no easy job. That motion was repeated time after time until the entire body of the wagon was level full with corn. Now you could rest on the ride to the corn barn, where the reverse process took place, basket full by basket full. One person loaded the baskets, and handed them to the person who was just inside the barn door and who took each basketful to the back of the barn, dumped it, and returned to exchange the empty basket for another full one. We kept at it for about four wagonloads each day, until all the corn was in the corncrib, about a week later. Afterwards we were all just mentally exhausted from the intense, focused concentration required, so naturally we looked for some type road race, preferably a marathon to enter [lies, lies, and more damned lies].

* * *

CHAPTER VIII

COUNTRY EATING

Yes, we were PO, but eating well was something we knew about. From what you have read so far, you won't expect us to ever have eaten lobster or other fancy culinary delights, and you would be correct. However one thing was for sure, we ate better than most people who had many economic advantages that we didn't even know how to imagine. Just how could that happen? First, we had to do long range planning, and make the plan successful the same way we did everything else - the hard way. Everything that could be saved by drying, or canning, or curing as a long term food supply was considered with the same native intelligence so many people have, but frequently don't use. Always keep in mind that we were working just as hard as the mules, and the family seriously outnumbered the mules. When you work like we did, there was no appropriate time for a light meal. I still remember the derision we focused toward people who talked about having "Lunch" or a sandwich. Anybody who had managed to get away to Savannah, Augusta, or any other large city, often adopted the manners of the city, and returned on visits to use "having lunch" or a "sandwich" would be mimicked with serious intent to make "fun" of their "Putting on airs". We had three big meals each and every day, including Sunday. How did we do it?

Many of our stocks of food were stored, without any refrigeration from season to season, and what we kept had better be enough to last, otherwise what we had to eat would have been just what was in season at that time. The first thing we started, just after what we expected to be the last frost, was our patch of red Irish potatoes, and for a slightly longer growing season, we started the white potatoes. We generally bought the "seed" potatoes and cut the "eyes" for planting about March 1st. Usually we had about a half-acre of both kinds, and the red potatoes had to be ready by Daddy's birthday on April 26th. It was a seriously bad situation when we couldn't dig a 'mess' of new potatoes by then. Though we usually let them mature for a few more weeks before digging them, the goal had to be met, even when they were not much larger around than quarters.

When the "taters" were mature, we used the two mule middle buster, which had a turning 'wing' on each side to throw the dirt and potatoes out so they could be picked up and put in bushel baskets and carried to the wagon. Depending on the harvest, we had one hell of a lot of potatoes [probably 600 pounds], which were taken to one of the cribs, and spread out on burlap sheets so they could be kept fairly cool. Usually they would last until about December.

Sweet taters were among the earlier considerations for planting because they were such an important crop for us, not particularly for selling, but for us to eat. From the previous year's supply, about thirty pounds were saved back and planted in the "Potato bed". That meant we had to dig a five foot by five foot hole in the ground about a foot deep and spread the potatoes out, and liberally mixed either mule or cow manure and the dirt, and put about three inches of the mixture back on the top of the potatoes. The "bed" was kept watered, and it wasn't long before, there were little potato plants everywhere. When they got large enough, they were transplanted to about a half an acre that was devoted to them. As always, we had to put manure in the row first, then use a turn plow to "bed" the row to take the plants, and cultivate until they started "running" all over the ground and putting down roots for the potatoes.

If we ran short of plants, we would cut "slips", which were little pieces of the vines one the ground called "runners" off the healthiest plants about two weeks after putting them in the rows. The slips would grow roots and make more sweet "taters." Diligent cultivation was expected to result in enough sweet "taters" to allow us to sell a few, but most importantly "bank" one hell of a lot. Five "banks" were what we considered the minimum requirement for the next year. Most people have never even seen a potato bank, and if they have, only very few knew what they were seeing. More about the banks after the happy harvest.

The harvesting of the sweet potatoes was done the same way as for the red and Irish potatoes, except that the sweet potatoes ran all over the ground and we had to really dig a wide swath of dirt about three feet wide to get all of them from the ground. The same mules and wagon hauled them to where we planned for the banks to be. On a sandy site where any rainwater would drain away quickly, we would dig five or more round holes about four feet in diameter and about twenty to twenty four inches deep and line it with three inches of new pine straw. The sweet potatoes were unloaded off the wagon and stacked up in a cone shape just as high as we could get them and still stay within the size of the base of straw. When that was done, a tepee sort of covering was done using one by six inch boards, leaving about one inch between each of the boards, followed by about three to four more inches of straw on the outside of the boards. The straw was promptly covered with about four to six inches of sand. That would keep them in good condition for cooking until we "opened" the bank. One little secret was that we always made a board lap in one particular place, which worked like a door where we could remove the dirt and straw and start pulling out the "taters" as we needed them. I don't ever recall our losing any to freezing. Baked sweet 'taters, fried 'taters, 'tater souffle, and sweet potato pie were most of the things we used them for. It took me a long time to recognize that old sweet potatoes were yams to some people.

Gardens were an absolute necessity, we usually had at least two. They probably wound up being nearly two acres. One garden was in a damp, boggy place where we planted turnips, cabbage, rape, kale, and mustard greens. We didn't plant collards greens, even though we did eat them. For some reason they didn't seem to grow well for us. Willie, a brother in law, found a source of absolutely lush collard greens, and the old woman who had grown them gave him some. Thank good fortune he didn't share with us. He started trying to get her secret on how she made them grow so beautifully with no insects. She finally divulged her secret, she told him she sprinkled them with "chamber lye", which is another name for urine from a slop jar. Willie didn't beg anymore of her collards!

In the other garden location, we planted five hundred tomato plants, which we generally grew from sun-dried seeds from the previous year. We were cautious not to over fertilize, or over manure, the tomatoes or they would have just grown beautiful vines and nearly no tomatoes.

I have always loved vine ripe tomatoes, and since I was a well-qualified overeater, I ate fresh tomatoes until itchy blotches started showing up on my arms and stomach. It was a yearly occurrence for me. We picked tomatoes by the washtubs full every morning. They were used in everything we cooked. However, we never made tomato jelly or preserves, a delicacy I have recently grown to appreciate and make every year or so. More about those mountains of tomatoes later.

The garden also had about three hundred or more onions bulbs, and at least one row of scallions about a hundred feet long. During the season, onions, tops and bottoms, would be cut up in one half-inch sections and smother fried in grease very slowly. Pretty scrumptious eating though now, at my age I have to really be sure it's early in the day when I eat them!!! Back then, I would grab a small brown paper sack and mix some salt and pepper and head for the garden. I'd pull up fresh radishes and scallions and clean them and after a final wipe on my overalls, douse them in the sack with salt and start eating. We also had alternating, or staggered, planting times for turnips, and other greens to carry us through the summer and into the fall. You can't match good garden fresh radishes, beets, speckled butter beans, garden peas [green peas], okra, squash, cukes, peppers, corn on the cob, and the list goes on.

There was a watermelon patch, which had a place for cantaloupe and muskmelon. Sizes varied on the watermelons up to about sixty pounds, cantaloupes were about the usual sizes you would expect, however, muskmelons got to be so large none of us could eat more than half of one. The muskmelons were nearly sixteen inches long, and about eight inches in diameter. We would haul them in by the wagonload, and have a watermelon cutting with friends standing around and eating until we were stuffed. It would have been an insult to offer anyone less than half a watermelon at a time. We made watermelon rind preserves, some of which found their way into fruitcakes at Christmas.

Canning, and preserving and anything that would go in a jar was just a way of life and one of our homilies was "Don't salute it, can it". Remember we were in a place with no refrigeration, and long term planning, to us meant particular ways of doing things that would last for at least a year, and doing it safely. To this day, I can spot a spoiled can, or jar, of almost anything by the look of the can, or the look of what is inside either the jar or can. Does it have a foam where it shouldn't, does it have an appearance that is "off standard", and is the odor just slightly wrong? I don't recall being wrong, however, being right doesn't mean much, except you either don't get sick as hell, or maybe fail to wake up because of a sudden case of death by botulism. Some folks who have virtually no experience will throw out perfectly good food.

* * *

For a number of years, we had three different ways of canning available to us. One way was the hot water bath method, which we didn't trust too much, however, done carefully spoilage could be kept reasonably low. Since some spoilage was likely to happen, that made the ability to spot a jar that had not sealed properly mighty important. A second way was our sixteen-quart "Presto Pressure Cooker." A scary sucker in the hands of folks who should know better, but sometimes didn't. Last and the best way for us for years was to go to the schoolhouse where there were huge commercial size cookers, available through the agriculture department.

Canning at the schoolhouse was a social event. Certain days during the week were set aside each year, usually Wednesday and Thursday, and everybody who wanted to can would put their names on the list a week ahead. About ten families could work any particular day. We would buy cases of number two steel tin cans. Depending on what we were canning, for instance tomatoes, we would start picking tomatoes about 2:00 p.m. the day before and have washtubs, sacks, and white oak bushel baskets full. We would be at the schoolhouse by 8:00 a.m. when the door opened. Somebody had always gotten there much earlier and fired the hot water boiler.

Anywhere from three to five of us would start scalding tomatoes, dipping them into the boiling water in white broadcloth sacks, dumping them out, and reloading for another batch while others started slipping the skins off the tomatoes. The next job was to core the tomatoes, and put them in a big dishpan. When all the pans and tubs were filled, the cans were filled and sealed by an electric can sealer. After cooking in the pressure cooker, by about 3:00 p.m. everybody went home with about two hundred and fifty cans of tomatoes ready for use through the next year.

When the canning corn was mature, and 'filled out', we signed up for another session of canning at the schoolhouse. A similar process got underway. We picked, or pulled, or broke the fresh yellow corn and put it in burlap bags to be ready for the next day. When we got to the schoolhouse we started shucking from five to ten bushels, silking it and rinsing it and getting ready to cut it off the cob. We always canned cream corn, so after cutting the kernels into dishpans, we scraped the cob for the remaining juice and put it into the pan with the cut kernels. Then came filling and sealing the cans and the pressure cooker, and we went home at the end of the day with about three hundred number two cans of creamed corn.

During the times when the cannery was not working at school, we had to can at home. Even though it was slow, and we had a hand operated can sealer, we still used up one hell of a lot of tin cans on corn and tomatoes. Also, there were many other things that we canned at home even when the cannery was open at school. For instance, blackberries grew wild on the fencerows and the edges of the fields and woods. When they started ripening, we hooked a milk pitcher, or anything that had a handle and a fairly large mouth to a belt and wore it on our overalls. We could strip blackberries off those sticky, thorny briars like you wouldn't believe. Put about six of us around blackberries, and we could pick a bushel basket full faster than B'rer Rabbit could beg B'rer Fox not to throw him in the briar patch. Some people did a lot of hollering and fussing about the briars sticking them, but not us, we were fast and slick berry pickers! .

I was always involved in some aspect of canning, but for some reason or another, we had done most blackberries using the hot water bath process. That was, until we decided to use the recently acquired pressure cooker, using glass quart jars. The first year everything worked well, however, on the second year I was again helping can blackberries. All the jars had been packed, and cooked for fifteen minutes at ten pounds pressure, so it was time to take them from the cooker. We waited for a while, and Mama suddenly went over and exhausted the last five pounds of pressure. I went ballistic because it was so dangerous. She got upset with me for being loud with her. "After all, it was only a very small amount of pressure in the cooker," she said. I tried to explain to her that the pressure inside the hot jars was going to be much greater than the five pounds, which had shown on the gauge. Anyway, I got her to leave the lid locked into place, and finally convinced her to get out of the way and let me run the risk that she didn't think was even there.

I waited about fifteen minutes, and slowly unlocked the lid, removed it, and cautiously put my hands over the edge to get a hold of the handles on the basket. I lifted it about an inch when I heard a sound that I learned later, while in Korea, was the thump sound of a mortar.

I was instantly covered with purple, scalding hot blackberries and juice all over my chest. I was wearing PT shorts and didn't have a shirt on, which was probably a fortunate thing in retrospect. What I don't understand to this day is how all that scalding liquid missed my face entirely. A scream, the likes of which I had never heard came from Mama as she started rushing toward me. I hollered "Get out of my way," and with a sweeping motion, grabbed a big pan of cold dirty dishwater that was sitting there and flailed it against my body - to hell with the floor, Saturday scrub day was coming anyway. This was the year we had gotten electricity and we had a pump, so I made record time to the outside hose at the pump house, and started spraying my burning body with cold well water. Yes, man, oh yes, it did feel good!!! In 1950, the burn treatment theory did not include cold water as a treatment method. Fortunately for me, my desperation caused me to make the best choice. I had only a minor peeling of skin, and I was left with no deep scars. The scariest part of the whole thing was that Dean came home about twenty minutes later, and when he saw the pain I was in, he made me get in his new Studebaker, and we took off for the doctor's office. About five miles after we got to the paved road, I tried to get him to slow down. I had survived the exploding jars and the burn, and damned if I wanted to get killed on the way to get some medicine.

Mama was all upset, that it had been her fault, and it had been, but I had never seen her so out of control. The truth is something like that could have happened to anybody, and I tried to tell her that, but I don't think she ever believed me. I have always been so grateful that I was there to see what she had done, and thankful she didn't get that hot juice and blackberries all over her.

We also canned butter beans in quart jars and tin cans, along with okra and also a soup mix of okra and tomatoes. We pickled cukes in jars and in big five-gallon crock jars, both sweet and sour, as well as relishes. Pickled peaches and pickled pears were fantastic as a side dish for the table at any meal, however, we also canned about fifty jars each of peaches and pears to make pies during the off-season. In fact, if we could figure a way to get something in a jar or a can, you would see it later in the year, on the dining room table.

Another something we did that was also a good source of “fixings” for biscuits was to make blackberry jam, strawberry jam, pear, peach and fig preserves. Just to make you understand that PO ain’t necessarily stupid, or even ignorant, we also made as much jelly as we needed from about anything we could add pectin to, when absolutely necessary to augment Mother Nature’s own.

It must be pretty evident to you that we never went hungry even if we didn’t have much store bought foods. Loaves of store bought bread, which we called “Light Bread” was a last resort for us. I’d bet I didn’t have two full loaves of it until I left home at seventeen for Korea. We had a pantry just off the kitchen that held a few ordinary supplies. Ordinary, that is, to the typical dirt farmer in Burke County. First and foremost was a flour barrel. At first it had been rough-cut boards both inside and out, but after all the years of use, it became as slick as an onionskin. That barrel held about ten bags of self-rising flour at a time, and that is the way we bought it. Given the way we used self-rising flour, it didn’t last but about six weeks. Mama made one to two big pans of biscuits every meal, three meals a day, seven days a week. It there were any extra biscuits, we usually ate them cold as syrup biscuits. Poke a hole using your little finger, fill it with syrup, or slice it open and put some barrel cheese in the biscuit, and a better than average snack was ready to eat. Once or twice a week, she made flour bread, which really was nothing except one huge biscuit, spread out over an entire griddle and cooked on top of the stove, just like you would cook hoecake corn bread, or a big pancake for you city slickers. When the flour bread was about done and while it was still steaming hot, it was pretty common to take a knife and slice it open to insert a slab of sharp cheddar barrel cheese. It was even better if you left it on the griddle until the cheese melted, and talk about something that was "Sho nuff fit to eat", or as some said "fitten to eat", man, that was it.

Biscuits could be used for other things as well, and one way, which was years ahead of the time, was to slice a biscuit open and insert a good slab of country cured fried ham. Another good use of biscuits was to split open a link of fried smoke cured pork sausage and slap it between two pieces of biscuit. I bet you have never thought of trying a piece of fatback or 'streak of lean' with a little mayonnaise and a thin slice of onion between two pieces of biscuit. I guess had we been smart enough to start a biscuit shop in Savannah, or Augusta with Mama's biscuits, we would have become multi jillionaires many years ago.

Another barrel in the pantry was for cornmeal, which we took to the mill and had ground from our own corn. Remember all that corn we hauled? Well, on rainy days we got to see some of it again, up close and personal. Like, "You boys don't have anything to do, so go to the corn crib and "shuck and shell" some corn for the grist mill." That meant taking all the husks off about four to six bushel baskets of corn, and then running it through the hand operated corn sheller. Each ear of corn was inserted into the sheller, to face the continuously turning, hand powered sheller, one at a time, and all the kernels were stripped off the corncob. The corncobs fell outside the box to which the sheller was attached and the corn stayed in the box until we scooped it out and put it in the meal sacks. You do remember all those corncobs I mentioned in the hygiene section and how they substituted for toilet paper, now you know the rest of the story on how they became available. We had to shell at least four bushels of corn, that is, after the corncobs were out, for the old water mill. When it comes to going to the mill, don't talk to "nobody about nothing" except a gristmill powered by a water wheel, at an old millpond. Something about the grinding stones moving more slowly and not 'burning the corn'. Anyway, we usually would get one-bushel ground for grits, and three for cornmeal. The miller kept an eighth of every bushel he ground, so we brought the rest home and put it in the meal barrel.

While I have talked about biscuits with every meal, the same was true for hoecake cornbread. Besides cornbread, we used it to meal fish for frying, make hushpuppies [corn dodgers] to fry along with the fish. Oven baked cornbread was another use for cornmeal, but we didn't make it very often. Another fairly frequent use was for "crackling bread" which was drenched in pure cane syrup for something that would stick to your ribs for a while. Crackling bread was the same as oven baked corn bread, except the dried up solids from rendering lard were added to the batter. Making hoecakes was the main use of cornmeal and it was pretty simple to make. Just get a pot or bowl, and slap about a quart or two of meal in it, and start pouring water and stirring until it was like a light cement slurry. Add a little salt and cook it by pouring the mixture onto two hot well greased griddles and after turning, both sides turn brown, and little holes have formed to show the dough was cooked. You could just sit and eat cornbread, along with anything else on the table until stuffed. If you wanted to be different, milk could be used in place of the water in making the batter.

Hoecake cornbread was eaten occasionally with syrup even though biscuits were the usual choice. Cornbread was good with just about anything else, like breaking it up in little pieces, and putting it in clabber, buttermilk or in sweet milk, or spreading it with butter and some extra salt and just eating it with nothing else.

Cornbread was also good with just about anything, including meat.

Nobody could weigh less than four hundred pounds if they ate like we did, unless they worked like we did. Our dining room table would seat about ten, and sometimes we squeezed in a few more. I still remember when we had benches on both sides, and chairs at the ends. When we went "uptown" and were able to get individual chairs for everybody, things were a little different. They were homemade chairs, which is another story. There were no questions about where leftovers were because they were on the table and covered by a white tablecloth, except for the last almost two years I was still at home. They couldn't be in the refrigerator, since we didn't have electricity, there wasn't one. For us, dinner was in the middle of the day, and it was common to have fried ham, boiled ham, two fried chickens - including the feet and necks, chicken and dumplings made from a whole fryer, a roasted hen with dressing, smother fried round steak with onions, and maybe about fifty fried fish. The rest was either garden fresh, or from what we had canned. It was likely to be turnip greens, butterbeans, field peas, macaroni and cheese, fatback, rice, boiled potatoes, potato salad, baked sweet potatoes, boiled eggs and deviled eggs. We thought ourselves as "civilized" so we always had dessert for dinner and supper - make that plural, we usually had many desserts. It was not the slightest bit unusual to have Mama's "Sho Nuff Good Pound Cake", just to smell it was a minimum of thousand calories, and three thousand fat grams. Along with that cake, there was likely to be a chocolate layer cake, backed up by such things as banana pudding, lemon pudding, cocoanut pudding, chocolate pudding, apple or pear pie, and blackberry deep dish.

If somebody was visiting, no problem, it made no difference, there was always plenty for a few more. One of our major splurges, in terms of cost, was keeping a fifty-pound block of ice in an old wooden icebox, so we could have iced tea. We drank that stuff by the gallons. When I think back to that table, it is with total amazement that we could marshal that amount of food every day and keep what wasn't eaten from spoiling. That white tablecloth cover was used no matter whether it was winter or summer. We just knew when leftovers had become 'goneovers' and were unsafe for eating. Funny thing about it was I can recall very few instances where we threw anything out the back door for the dogs because it had spoiled.

There were so many ways to say milk wasn't spoiled it wasn't even funny. The biscuits could be made with buttermilk, sour milk, or sweet milk. If we didn't use up the sour milk, it became clabber, which was very good with cornbread in it, furthermore, if we really wanted to save it, we just made whey, also known as cottage cheese by putting the clabber in cheesecloth and dipping it into scalding water. By squeezing out the juice, it became a whole new product to be eaten. PO people in the country knew lots of ways to keep from starving and most had the training and the mastery of the necessary skills.!!!

* * *

The first absolute necessity around that big old table was that Daddy had his particular spot at the head of the table, which I never -never ever- saw him abdicate to a living soul. The second absolute was that, just don't even think about sitting in Daddy's chair. When we went from benches to chairs, made by Jimpson Oglesby, they all looked alike, well almost, but he wasn't really an accomplished artisan. Actually in one way I guess he was. He made them from white oak wood, and the ones I still have could be used to bludgeon an elephant and they would come through without a mark on them.

Daddy discovered the chair that according to him, had the feel his ass deserved, even though he didn't express it exactly that way. At first only he could tell which chair it was, and at times, I think he couldn't be sure he had gotten "his" chair. One thing he was not about to do was make a mistake, and have some of us snicker about it.... So he decided to make a mark that would be easy to recognize by feel. I just about fell out laughing when I saw him take a one quarter inch bit, and with the hand brace drill a hole through the top slat of "his" chair. Now that was an identification mark to stop all questions and end all disputes. Well not quite, since the hole was small and not easily felt, his next move was to take a coping saw and just above the hole, make a three eighths inch deep cut and split it out. "By God, don't give any excuses that you couldn't tell that was my chair." I still have that chair in my mountain home in North Carolina, sitting on my side of the bed, and every time my hand hits that broken out piece, I have to laugh about that episode. Another absolute, you had better have found a "place" to land at the table and be seated. Nobody dared touch a plate, or lift a fork until the blessing was said. The one exception was that Mama's place, right to Daddy's left, and closest to the kitchen could be vacant if she was still putting the final touches on something for the table. It was sorta like the starting line when the drivers had to stand outside their cars before a race. When quiet descended, Daddy slightly bowed his head and said his lengthy weekday blessing - "Thank The Lord For Breakfast, [or Dinner, or Supper] AMEN".

After the blessing, there was no foolishness going on, just the serious business of eating. Believe it or not, we were required to have excellent table manners. No hats were allowed, and you had better not come to our table with dirty hands, unless you could prove a mighty close association to God himself, because you would be leaving for the washstand. Yes, there were things we didn't know about such as what to do with forty eleven dozen forks and spoons, individual butter plates, or finger bowls, but so what, I have since seen some elitists embarrass themselves about what to do with finger bowls and really fancy table settings!!

* * *

Cooking and kitchen cleanup along with dish washing was some job. I have told you about the food, and while lengthy, it left out much about the entire process of preparation. I want to say something here, I can cook anything, and frankly anybody who can read can cook and a bunch who can't read are damned good at it. People who tell me they just can't cook a thing either are tacitly telling me they think I am stupid enough to believe it, or they are yelling from the house top just how stupid they are!!! I will concede, however, that a person may not be the best of cooks because of insufficient time in the kitchen, or they won't work at it for whatever reason. Of the five brothers, every one of us could cook, and better than just average, two brothers were cooks in the military, and the rest of us avoided it with a passion as far as the military was concerned.

For years, Mama had just one cast iron cook stove, with the wood box just to the left of it. Neither God, nor Mama forgot if one of us didn't fill that wood box with stove wood every night. God wasn't likely to seek immediate retribution if we failed, but Mama was. Refilling that box every night was one thing, however, if anybody was around the house at any time of the day, and it looked like it might rain, stove wood took precedence over just about anything except diarrhea - and you'd better be able to prove that.

In 1948 or 49, we got an electric stove, and while it didn't use wood, Mama just didn't trust electricity, and certain cooking plainly couldn't be trusted to anything except the wood stove. Therefore, Mama had two stoves, and much of the time, they were both going full bore for dinner and supper. Since I can barely recall my older brothers and sisters being at home, most of my recall was of Dean and me cooking with Mama, and as long as Grandmama was healthy, she as right in there cooking as well. Now listen, with at least four cooks in the kitchen, we could take care of at least one army, any day, anytime!

K.P. country style, or the cleanup detail was something else. You know we didn't cook in disposable pots, or eat from paper plates. To this day, my wife gives me hell, saying I cook just like Mama, by getting every pot in the kitchen dirty and never washing even one until absolutely necessary, or the meal is over. There was some solid reasoning for that, not that it has been accepted by my wife, and it all goes back to that old well and the difficulty of getting water from it to the kitchen. Another reason was that you couldn't wash those pots, pans and bowls without good hot water. Now you figure where in the hell anybody was going to find space on just one or two stoves to heat water. You had to wait until the stove was free of the food being cooked to heat water for washing dishes.

We washed dishes in a big dishpan, loaded with soap and water, and rinsed in another dishpan, then they went to a drying rack, occasionally, but most often directly to the hands of whoever was doing the dish drying at that time. Hell, by the time I went into the Air Force at seventeen, I had logged more K.P. than anybody except a twenty-year veteran screw up. They didn't have to get water from the well and boil it on a stove.

* * *

Woman's work was and is just a plain damned bad joke, and a pretty stupid one at that. I think I have told you that of the seven of us Youngens, only two were girls, one was seventeen years older than me and the other about fifteen years older, so by the time I can really remember, they, along with my oldest brother had left home. As a result, where the girls may have had to do all the 'girl work' when they were home, there was no gender job differentiation for the four youngest and particularly for the last two of us. That was Dean and me. Woman's work would probably have meant that washing clothes was something Dean and I didn't have to do, well you're wrong. We generally had to either do the wash, or help with it. Hell that was almost as hard as slinging shit from the wagon but it did smell better. The washing was done at the old well. We had a wash place where we lined up three number three washtubs, and filled them with water. In the first tub, we put the whites, which included pillowcases and sheets, in the water and washed them on the scrubbing board, and I do mean one of those little monsters called a "wash board". No, we didn't make music on those damned things, they were just an instrument of torture for shirt buttons and us. For the white things, we "renched" [rinsed] them through the second and third tubs. At the end, we would wring all the water we could get from them, and then hang them on the clothesline. Dark Clothes were shirts, and overalls and anything else that could stand up to the work we were doing. We would do an initial wetting and scrubbing on the washboard, and then put them in a big cast iron "washpot" which already had been fired up to heat the water. Some soap was thrown in, and the fire stoked and the water was boiled for about half an hour. Then the clothes were taken from the washpot and scrubbed again to get the last dirt out, renched twice, and 'wrung out' and hung on the line to dry. Be careful around me when you call that woman's work.

Ironing, as woman's work, didn't fly any better than washing did in my sand bed. The clothes dried in the sun, which left an aroma of "clean" that was and is impossible to match. Then it was time to iron everything, and I do mean everything. For years I have wondered if we didn't have some Chinese laundryman's blood somewhere, given the amount of time I spent washing and ironing. Ironing meant getting the stove going, in the summer as well as the winter, and putting about six flat irons on it to heat. The way to know if they were hot enough was to put as much spit as would stay on your right or left index finger, pick the iron up from the stove with the other hand, and slap that spit covered finger on the bottom of the iron. If you did it correctly, the spit sizzled, and the finger didn't even get warm. If you didn't do it right, you had a blister to show for it. The sound of the sizzle would tell you the iron was just right. Now that was a real sissy job, yeah.... want to break your damned back, it was as bad as picking cotton. You never can tell how "bad things" can turn into "good things" though. When I went into the Air Force, and we couldn't get laundry service, I made some good money dealing with idiots who just "didn't know how to iron". By that time, I had it made, I had figured out the complex issue of plugging in, and actually using an electric iron.

* * *

This is about some more "sissy stuff", if you had the gonads to say it to my face. There was a time somewhere in my growing up where I was big enough to want to go out, and girls were looking mighty fine, somewhere about eleven to fourteen, but I just was not allowed to really get loose. So, for about two or three winters, aside from reading, I had some time on my hands. I don't know if Mama wanted to help me or if I asked her to show me how to embroider, and I tell you now, I got better than walking around good at it. I could put some pretty fancy designs on pillowcases, and bureau scarfs. Next she later taught me how to crochet and "tatting" [the precursor to macrame] and what I referred to as creative knotting.

Grandma did something I always wanted to try but never did get around to, she was one of the most unbelievable seamstresses I had ever heard of. What she could do with a pedal powered Singer Sewing Machine was a talent to behold. I watched her take measurements from women after they had selected the dress they liked from the Sears and Roebuck Catalog, she was ready to sew. Fortunately, in those days the catalogs gave a front and back view of the dresses. If she thought the dress chosen was going to give a bit of difficulty, she would pull out some old newspapers and cut a pattern for it. If it was a simple one for her to make, she just threw the cloth on the floor and started cutting. I wanted to try that, but she had more gumption than I did. She wouldn't let me.

Sure as hell, just as anybody with good sense would know, word got out about my handiness with needles, threads and hooks or as some might have thought, my "sissy stuff". They might have thought it, but I didn't have to take any razzing because of all the fights Dean and I had over the years, and my boxing at school. I had a reputation as someone who could and would put a "major hurt" on you. I knocked a number of people out cold while boxing, and at one time thought I wanted to do more of it. While I never really got tagged hard enough to even make me dizzy, I finally decided boxing would be one stupid way to make a living.

Boxing taught me a valuable lesson about taking care of myself, and rather than getting me into fights, it really saved me from many more, not only at school, but later one in life as well. I learned a lot of people really got into pre fight yelling or, verbal exchanges, trying to convince themselves they wanted to fight and maybe also to try to figure a way out of a fight their mouth had fooled them into. That is probably where the old saying came from, "Don't let your mouth overload your ass." Boxing gave me more assurance than I had ever had and most likely I started from a higher level of it than was appropriate. Other kids in school knew it was hard to hit me, that I could take a punch, but even worse, I could and would put them down in a flash. When somebody who didn't know that started "bowing up", and telling me all the bad things they were going to do to me, I would look them in the eyes, and never raise my voice while telling them something they didn't really want to hear. "You may be just as bad as you think you are, but I'll bet you I have knocked people out in fights more times than you have ever even been in fights in your whole life." That quiet approach seemed to calm all sorts of problems, and I can't count but about five or six fights that ever started after that bit of information exchanged.

Sissy or not, I still cook. Every year, I think at my family's insistence, I make at least one huge fruitcake, usually two. Currently there seems to be some sort of "anti culture think" that says as long as you are under forty, "thou shalt not like fruitcakes". All of which seems stupid to me, cause made right, they are just flat good eating. How in the hell can you eat sushi [raw fish], or fish eggs [caviar], crayfish [eyes and all] and rave all the while about, "just how magnificent", and have the nerve to complain about dried fruit baked into a cake? I have come across folks like that, but that's mainly because they have never had Mama's, and now, my fruitcake.

I think I have demonstrated that the fact of the matter is we were ahead of our time. My family didn't haved to get involved in heavy sensitivity training, we had no gender-determined jobs in our sand bed. Except when it came to Daddy, he was the bull, and bulls just do bullish things. Mama worked in the fields alongside us all day long, but when Grandma got too sick to cook, she would leave us picking cotton, or whatever, to go get dinner ready. Sometimes she would send one of us to do it. She always said time and again, she wouldn't send us to the fields to work alone as long as she was able to stand.

Pure pride and respect for mama demanded that we respond in the same way and we did. Some people need to remember that gender is a condition, and sex is an activity. Doing the work we were doing had absolutely, for damned sure, had nothing to do with sex, and gender was considered totally inconsequential.

* * *

CHAPTER IX

EDUCATION IN THE SAND BEDS

Education in PO country didn't just happen at the schoolhouse. At the outset, let me admit to a level of arrogance that may not be at all becoming. For that, I will not apologize one smidgen. It was necessary, required and appropriate while I was in the process of becoming pretty self confident that I also become arrogant. That was preferable to, and better than, becoming "cowed" by some dumbass. There was a time, when I had just discovered that one of my prime goals in life was to get away from the farm, woods and sand beds. Imposing the goal of correct grammar on myself in the fourth grade was probably the first move I made toward getting away from the Sandbed hell of a dirt farm. I guess I was about in the fifth or sixth grade, when I noticed some folks seemed a little smug about competing with me in various activities. Especially smug, when they didn't know anything about me, that is, except that I was from a little country school. Poor damned fools, I had probably read several dozen more books than they had ever checked out, and at least a hundred times more comic books.

Daddy may not have had anything except a fourth grade formal education, but a day wasn't right if he didn't have either his *"Augusta Chronicle"*, or '*Savannah Morning News"* and the same was true for the weekly *"The True Citizen"*. He read every page, and passed each section on to me. I do not have a photographic memory, but damned close. I could effectively memorize those newspapers. Nasty, nasty was me.... I would look for opportunities to get in conversations with adults about stories in the newspapers and when I could find they were in error, it gave me a rush to know not only as much, but more about the subject than they did. You must understand, it took a real skill to maneuver it around so they knew they were wrong, but that they hadn't really been confronted. Because in Girard, Georgia, any kid who had more information and got into a confrontation with an adult could get in deep shit faster than castor oil runs through a new baby.

Girard did have a post office, and Miz. Grail was the postmistress. She was pretty well educated, and also seemed to be a genuinely nice person, so on many occasions we would talk about a wide variety of topics. Daddy came home one day and asked me if I knew her, and what we talked about so much. It seems she was trying to get a better bead on me and why I had so much information on just about everything. She wasn't being mean or nasty, I think just surprised. But that was an object lesson for me - in shovels - [never spades], don't talk to the same person too often, because there was a good chance you wouldn't be dealing with someone who had reasonable sense like her and you could catch hell for being a smartass!!

* * *

The dumb and the smart of education. I started the first grade in the September of 1939, after I had turned six in January. It would seem all school systems must have some rigid rules that don't necessarily make sense, just to satisfy their innate power drive, so I was six years and nine months in first grade. I could have started September of 1938 and been about five years and nine months old but that just didn't work, Being a little older worked out better for me since Girard school had only eleven grades. So I graduated in June 1950, the last year before all schools in Georgia were required to have twelve grades. When I graduated I was still only seventeen and a half years old. Why in the hell would I have needed to get out of high school a year earlier? I surely didn't have any money to go to college and at sixteen and a half, I couldn't have gone into the military even with parental consent for at least six months.

Maybe my first grade experience in a cap and gown was to portend my life. Sadie, my sister, was a senior in 1939, and the graduating classes all had mascots. Seems to me they had both boy and girl mascots and I was the male mascot that year. I was decked out in a cap and gown and I still have pictures from that event. Mama was a grade mother every year. Everybody knew she was a good cook and would be willing to cook about any time. She and various other women, over the course of my school years were always there for Easter egg hunts, May Day celebrations, Christmas parties, Halloween, and end of the year picnics. We also were likely to have other special purpose celebrations, which meant we celebrated something almost every month and Mama was always there.

During my first several years a number of good things occurred, and I guess the not so good things weren't too important. To this day I have no idea how many of my teachers had a degree from anywhere, and how many didn't. I suspect most of my grade school teachers had no more than two years of college, and some didn't have that much. I think I know who among my high school teachers had a college degree in something, even if they were doing what we now call "teaching out of field". Funny thing about it is, in retrospect, I know all the grade school teachers were good and dedicated individuals. They worked hard to give us the fundamentals. We wore out flash cards for the alphabet, addition, subtraction, multiplication and division.

We were pushed and shoved into printing and writing in script, and learning all the verb conjugations, inside out, backwards, forward, and every whichway. We had to do maps of the United States and be able to identify each state, know its capital city, and other details. To show you how sick I was, and I'm sure it was a serious indictment of me, I thoroughly enjoyed it. About the second grade I got hooked on books and reading. I read every book in the little elementary school library from cover to cover before I went up to high school. It didn't matter what the topic was, whether it was for males or females, I read it. That same appetite for books stayed with me through high school as well. I enjoyed having teachers do serial reading in my grade school classes. There was so much to learn about voice, voice control, inflection, pronunciation and articulation. By the third grade about three of us were reading stories to the rest of the class, which was probably not the best thing since the rest of the class may have been better served to do more reading them selves.

* * *

I can't recall doing anything really bad, or getting caught at it anyway, while in grade school. A few things would have been frowned on right much, I'm sure if they had been known. In the fifth grade, when the grass had turned brown, it seemed to me to be a good opportunity to excite a few kids, and some teachers too. I could flick a stove match with my fingernail and start it almost every time. That skill meant that when I walked past the open unscreened classroom window, about one of every three matches I flicked outside would start a grass fire. Since it started slowly, nobody ever connected the fire to my passing the window. It was just a little diversion to get us out of class to put the fire out, and it only took about thirty minutes out of our day. Anyway, grass was the sworn enemy of any kid who lived on a row crop Sandbed farm in the PO part of Georgia.

Another 'for instance' of a not "really bad" thing involved a pear tree. There was an old pear tree on the edge of the school property, right across the fence from the house of my oldest aunt. During the season, there were pears all over the ground, in various stages of rotting, and it tolled in yellow jackets from what must have been miles and miles. Yes Sir, there were thousands of yellow jackets, and that presented a serious temptation for me. I enlisted the aid of a couple of other boys in the sixth grade and we got to work during recess.

I used a small, clean mustard jar and we began catching yellow jackets. This was done by pressing them down where they sat on a rotting pear with a small stick, then taking hold of them between the thumb and forefinger of one hand, putting them up to the calloused skin on our other thumb, just close enough for the stinger to stick in the skin. By moving the finger away at just the right moment, the stinger would pull out of the bee, and we would drop that sucker in the jar. The final scenario may be too evident, but I'll spell it out anyway. When recess was over, and we went back into class, I gently slipped the lid off the mustard jar, and urged the little jackets to fly. You must have one hell of an imagination to come close to the confusion about ten yellow jackets can cause in a classroom. I guess we did that about four or five times during the pear season, and I have no doubt all of us would have had "stinging butts" from paddles, if we had ever been caught.

One other "derring-do" was totally on me. I was in the sixth grade and somebody had told me that white-headed bumblebees had no stingers. They even demonstrated it to me. I had catalogued that away, you never know when information like that is going to be important. Sure enough, one day the biggest bumblebee I had ever seen came flying through the unscreened classroom window. Everybody went crazy, but in the most mature manner I could muster, I assured everybody not to worry, that I would catch the bumblebee, and put it outside. I had already checked out Mr. Bee, and was sure his head was white, so I knew I was safe.

I got up in one of the windows where he was buzzing against the pane, and caught him, with full intentions of letting him go back outside, but that was not to be. That damned bumblebee twisted his tail around and slammed a stinger into my thumb at the joint nearest my palm. All I could do was just squeeze that sucker into a grease spot between my thumb and forefinger. I got down from the window ledge, and basically threw out the grease spot, went back to my desk and put the most seriously throbbing thumb God had ever permitted on a twelve year old, in my overall pocket. Fortunately that took place about an hour before school was out for the day. I sneaked a look at it once or twice being "most careful" not to let anybody see me. I would have preferred being shot to having anybody know I had been stung. Fortunately, I was not allergic to bumble bee stings, and if ever proof was needed, that was it.

* * *

In the seventh grade, we were in the high school building, even though we were not considered high school until the eighth grade. I still have trouble figuring out just why so much confusion goes on with new names for school grades every few years, pre kindergarten,

kindergarten, pre school, primary grades, lower grades, low middle school, middle school, upper middle school, charter school, magnet schools, and God knows what else.

Teacher's aides were unknown in Girard. It would have been considered ludicrous to even think that a teacher couldn't control a class and do her job. However, when a teacher was sick, there was little chance a substitute teacher could be found, let alone afforded. So the answer was, if you were an "A" student in the seventh grade you would be asked, or ordered, to take over a fifth, or lower grade class for the absent teacher. As the "A" students went up to the next grade, they were assigned one grade higher, up to the seventh grade level. The teacher closest to the room where the "A" student was filling in would check in to see if any help was needed, and give whoever was taking the class over, the assignments for each subject. In the main, however, we "student teachers" were on our own. Frankly, I think that system had fantastic benefits for both the classes and the student teachers. Thinking back, I don't ever recall any discipline problems when we took over the classes.

My graduating class was very small, I doubt if we had more than twenty kids in the first grade, and along the way, we lost some because they moved away. I don't recall any in my class who were left behind, however there were some "social" promotions. The strange thing about it was that we gained some kids in the second and third grades who were not advanced with their classes. When my class graduated, I thought we had fourteen in it, even though I knew in my own mind some of them couldn't, or didn't. do the work. I learned recently, at our first, and probably only, class "reunion" that only ten of us had actually gotten diplomas. The important thing to remember though, is that to the best of my knowledge, all members of the class have been successful in life and that seems to be the real measure of a school doing their job as well as the abilities of the Youngens would permit.

Whatever might be said about that little school in Girard, which has long since been closed, I learned, and I got a solid foundation, most of it by some darned good teaching. In high school, some of what I got was on my own. There were three of us who went past what the teachers knew in the math and science areas, and we had to teach ourselves. Surprisingly, some of the poorest teaching was from teachers with four-year degrees. But not surprisingly, I later learned they had never been prepared for teaching high school algebra, physics, or chemistry. The complex of variables as to why some of us were able to get such a good foundation must be specific to the individual, however, in my case I basically felt I had no choice, remember my whole focus was on getting away from PO.

Mama was very supportive of education and my going to school. She was never far from her dictionary. She absolutely shredded one Webster's Dictionary and was well on the way to doing bodily harm to the second one when she died. In addition to that, my sister, Sadie had graduated from Warren A. Candler School of Nursing in Savannah, Georgia, and somehow she had gotten her hands on a spare medical dictionary, which Mama proudly claimed. She probably spent more time reading that dictionary just for the joy of learning, than Sadie ever did out of necessity. I spent a good bit of time reading it also, however, for other reasons. Even though I knew a lot about animal sex, there never was any "big discussion" between Daddy and any of us boys. Nobody ever mentioned that at puberty, the phenomenon of "wet dreams" or as it was described in the medical dictionary, nocturnal emissions, was to be expected. I damned sure didn't know to expect it, and I was sure death was the next step. I can tell you that I started reading that dictionary with real purpose, and the other nursing medical textbooks I found in the bottom of a dresser. I finally pieced it all together before I imploded from fear. I then started holding classes during recess at school, cause nobody else really knew anything for sure either.

Mama finished the tenth grade at "Molly Pond" school. There was an eleventh grade in Girard, but that was about ten miles away, and there were no such things as school buses back then, so the "trek" was out of the question. I have wondered many times just what she could have done with the opportunity for higher education. I do know that when she challenged you on word usage, or spelling, your best choice was to give up gracefully. On the very few occasions she was wrong, it never flustered her, but, you can bet she'd never make the same mistake twice.

Jumping way ahead, to an example of how Mama operated, one day Mama and my wife, Deborah were talking and "Impetigo" came up in the conversation. Deborah decided that maybe they weren't talking about the same thing since she was almost sure Mama was saying "Infantigo". Deborah started trying to reconcile what she thought might be a mistake on her part, or Mama's. Mama immediately went to the medical dictionary, and discovered she had been wrong all those years, and so had everybody else around Girard. It was so logical since mostly infants were bothered by it, that she never even thought to challenge it. Mama really strutted with pride that she, with Deborah's help, had discovered an error of long standing. Within ten minutes, she accosted her sister in law with the new information. Now this particularly woman was about as hard headed as one of the mules I had plowed. Her reaction was swift and sure...."I don't care what Deborah says, and I don't care what that medical dictionary of yours says, it has been Infantigo all my life and it is going to stay Infantigo."

Another reason that education was so important to me was that Daddy had quit school after the fourth grade and he realized what he had missed. He surely did not dwell on it, but he had educated himself by reading newspapers. Believe it or not, his ability to write in longhand was probably better than mine ever was. No, he didn't always have the verb conjugations perfectly under control, but at the same time, he didn't have the utter disregard for the spoken word that so many of the uneducated people in rural Georgia did. Also, I think social and economic changes had changed Mama and, most particularly, Daddy by the time there was just my nearest brother, Dean and I who were left on the scene and the changes in their attitudes favored our chances of getting away from our PO situation. Education was recognized as another way, in addition to the military, as a ticket out.

For all intents and purposes, I never had to study any of the courses in high school, I did have to pay a little bit more attention to Algebra, Geometry and Physics, however. The reason for that was that the principal of the school was the teacher for algebra and geometry, and he didn't have a clue, notta cubed, or exponentially, as to what it was all about. He couldn't even work the problems following the teacher's guide and get the right answers. By reading the book, and working the examples, I could handle the subject pretty well. I think the hardest part of the course was to work the problems, and somehow or another let him think it was because of him that we were able to do the work. Only a few of us in the entire class ever had a clue as to what we were supposed to get out of the courses.

By the time my junior year arrived we had a new principal. I knew he was a college graduate, in just what, I never had an inkling. I did notice he had some sort of honor society pin that he wore, but it was wasted on us, because who in the world would have told us about academic honor societies at colleges. We had a Beta Club for awhile, but there were very few who met the standards, most were girls, and it went down the tubes. While I liked girls, I was not interested in an all girl organization, thank you.

Anyway, Mr. Floyd Boyner was the new principal, and I knew I wanted a physics course for my senior year, so I put pressure on him for it. He knew he would have to teach it, and tried to avoid offering it. I managed to get the other students to support me even though most of them had no idea what the course was about, and I surely didn't tell them. Anyway Mr. Boyner caved and we got the physics course. Whatever college or university he had been to and the honor society he had been in, the curriculum hadn't demanded much math, and definitely nothing on physics. Again, it fell my lot to try to interpret the book for myself. I don't think that guy ever really understood how a rocket could be propelled in outer space. He had no understanding of Goddard's research, and I think he believed that the German V-1 and V-2 rockets were just a new type airplane. Maybe he thought Goddard had done something like the "Smith Brothers" and their cough drops.

Chemistry and Biology were courses we had under a young woman who had completed college, and she was a good teacher in both subjects. However, she was handicapped by the absence of a laboratory for biology, and the virtual absence of a chemistry lab. Funny thing though, there had been a pretty good chemistry lab in the little farm community school a few years before. It was evident from all the beakers, test tubes and Bunsen burners strewn around in the room that had been a lab, but it was too far gone to try to resurrect it. What we really had were courses in descriptive chemistry and biology.

We did have good training in social studies, history, and literature. I would be willing to bet I read every book in that high school library, and yes, there were more than two books. I would also bet I was the only person in the school who read them all. I learned later that I had been very well trained in poetry, and literature from the fifth grade through high school. When I got to the University of Georgia, much of the memorization required was of the same passages I had studied in my little country school. Fancy that, I was ahead, or at least up to par, on some topics at the University of Georgia.

One of the best courses a few of us pushed for in high school was a course in typing. There was a typing room with about fifteen old Underwood manual typewriters sitting on typing tables. They were the training machines with no letters on the keys. The only way to know what you were going to get was to either hit the key, or go by the huge diagram on the wall. I can't recall if we were in the tenth or the eleventh grade, but we turned the screws on the principal again, and won again.

We promised that if we could use the typing room, we would not expect any teacher to supervise us, that we would follow the old Gregg typing book, lesson by lesson, and at the end of each six weeks, we would administer the timed typing test to each other, and give the papers to a teacher to assign the grades. We taught ourselves typing for a half year, and frankly that course in manual dexterity very possibly changed the course of my life in that it kept me from getting some really horrible jobs later.

It almost changed my life another way as well. There was a little storage room off the typing room, and while it wasn't my first encounter, an attractive classmate and I were involved in a little groping ceremony after class, when we heard the outside door open. We had just enough time to make it look like we were busy counting supplies. If the teacher knew any better, she didn't say anything. Bad timing on the part of everybody!

* * *

The reason I was so interested in getting some of the difficult courses taught was that I knew first hand what the situation was going to be without them. I had watched my two brothers who had fought in Europe come home to a tough situation trying to get jobs. Both had quit school, and even then it was tough to get much without a high school diploma. There was a real problem finding anybody to help us understand what opportunities might exist to get us out of the sand beds. Counselors didn't exist, or if they did somewhere in the county school system, they damned sure didn't pass information along to the likes of us PO Youngens.

I thought it might be possible to get into West Point, or Annapolis, fat chance. I wrote to my Congressman and Senator, and was promptly advised that all appointments for the next two years had already either been made, or promised. However, they may still be able to put me on the alternate list. To me that meant, maybe your Mama and Daddy will be dumb enough to vote for me next time. Basically, my interpretation of their letter was, "Go to hell, you hick!!" I was the one who had to scrounge up the information and write letters to the Congressman and Senators, and I probably didn't kiss their asses properly with a lot of "Honorables" in their addresses. I surely didn't have any help from school, and I just as surely, had no political connections of any consequence.

During the process of collecting data about West Point and Annapolis, near the end of the tenth grade, I did learn about the Merchant Marine Academy and that admission was based on competitive examinations and I applied, without the school's help, or knowledge. In fact it is doubtful they ever knew about my application. I went to Savannah to take the test, and got creamed in physics. Why not, I had never had the course. In chemistry the results were just about the same, but again, I had never had anything but one descriptive course in chemistry. Naturally, I didn't get selected. However, I did get several letters from the academy encouraging me to go to Marion Institute, an excellent prep school I later learned, in Alabama, for my senior year and retake the test. What that really meant was to take the eleventh and twelfth grades there, since we only had eleven grades in Sandbed Hell. From what I understood, I had not missed acceptance by much, and the Academy had Marion Institute send me brochures and enrollment forms. Can you imagine how much it must have cost, even back then, to go to a boarding school for two years? Selling the farm, selling Mama and Daddy into servitude, and everything else, wouldn't have been enough.

Another thing I learned years later was that the State of Georgia had a program for high school graduates with high grade point averages that would allow them to go to the University of Georgia, and on to The Medical College of Georgia with full scholarships. In exchange, the State of Georgia required an agreement to practice medicine in rural Georgia for some specified number of years. A boy who went to Sardis High School, about seven miles away from my little school, and whose family had heard of the program, helped him take advantage of it. I knew everybody in the entire county had more money that we did, so I assumed they had the money to pay for him to go to the University of Georgia. What I didn't know was that he was a premed student, or that the program he was going under even existed. I have often wondered about it, and still to this day believe that I was discriminated against because of being PO!! Some people think discrimination only goes on in racial or gender situations, think again. You can forget that crap. That program was still in effect when I returned from the Air Force in 1954, and I still never knew anything about it. That's okay, by God I made it through, and graduated from engineering school in spite of all the damned odds and any sneaky bastards who may have privately snickered at this PO youngen. The G.I. Bill, which I considered back pay for Korea, and part time jobs, paid for every damned thing I got.

* * *

Girard was indeed a different and unusual place for education to take place. One principal who came before the two I have already mentioned was basically a basketball coach. He had a fiery temper, and he carried that with him both on and off the court. He really considered himself to be "badder" than he was. I don't think he had ever been a school principal in "Mule Country" before.

Anyway one of the taller and more hardheaded boys in the school, worked after school at a garage and filling station in down town Girard. Claiford was skinny, and well over six feet tall, and just a hard working kid. Mr. Principal had already caused him to quit the basketball team for some unknown reason, so Claiford didn't feel too friendly toward the man. To top that off, Mr. Principal had said, or done, something to one of Claiford's sisters, so that made Claiford somewhat more aggravated with him.

When the hot tempered Mr. Principal stopped at the garage to get gas, Claiford, who was the designated gas pumper was involved in changing a tire, which for no apparent reason, immensely irritated Mr. Hot T. Principal, and that was too bad for him. He forgot he was not on school property where he was King. Bad, very Bad, he shot off his mouth, ordering Claiford to get over there and pump his gas, and NOW! Claiford looked over at him and told him to wait a minute until he got to a place to stop. Now old Mr. H. T. Principal made an even more serious mistake by charging over to where Claiford was working, apparently with the intent of kicking his ass. Claiford, with a tire iron in his hand, came around on him with perfect timing. One stroke was enough.

Mr. H.T. Principal went down like a ton of bricks. He wasn't knocked out completely, but he sure as hell didn't want anymore of that tire iron. After he got his senses unscrambled, he was so mad he was almost frothing at the mouth. Unfortunately for him, several people had seen the entire episode and they held a little court session right there. A self appointed panel of judges told Mr. Principal that he had committed a serious error in judgment in not knowing where school property ended, and even worse, not knowing he wasn't on it. Mr. Principal was also told that since he was known to be such a big badass, that Claiford had every reason to think he was being attacked, and every right to defend himself. All the time that was going on, Claiford was standing off to one side of the "court session", Just staring at that badass, with the tire iron still in his hand.

That episode pretty much put a lid on Mr. Principal's bad temper, and I think it made him a better coach too. I never see the hot-tempered Mr. Knight, basketball coach at Indiana, acting like a damned fool on the sidelines, that I don't wonder if a tire iron up side his head wouldn't work for him. However, on him it might take several strokes.

Mr. Principal had one child, a boy named Clyman who seemed to be fairly intelligent, but he didn't have a grain of country sense. His mama was raising him to be upper class, and it was apparent to all of us. Every time we did anything, he thought he was supposed to be in charge. I think he arrived in September, in time for the fifth grade at Girard, and by March he had made himself into a pain in the ass. Several of us were looking for a way to bust his bubble, or his ass. Now most of us knew what oranges were, we just didn't get to have them much, except as a part of Christmas, but Clyman seemed to always have oranges. We were envious, and hell, just downright jealous. However, those oranges seemed to be the perfect vehicle to use to mess with his mind, and maybe something more as well.

There was a family who lived down near the Savannah River who looked almost yellow, no, they weren't Chinese, but they had a really an unhealthy looking, sallow skin color. Daddy said it was because of some root they were using for medical purposes. He said he didn't know how or why, but all he knew was that anybody he had ever known, except that family would get ill from using it. He called it "hip po root". I have described that plant to a number of botanist, but I could never give them enough information to identify it. To this day I know I could still recognize it in the spring of the year. Anyway, all it takes is about one drop of the milky juice in the root to get unbelievable results in less than an hour.

Young Clyman always had his orange at recess, but if you asked him just a slightly difficult question, he would immediately get so importantly involved that he needed both hands to answer it. Fine, one day, just after he had rolled his orange, cut a hole in the end of it and was ready to suck the juice, we asked him a question. True to form, he put his orange down to explain the answer to us PO country Youngens. Bad choice, that was my cue to put one tiny drop of the hip po root juice in the hole of the orange. When he finished his answer to the question, he picked up his orange and started sucking the juice from it. Back in the classroom, and less than an hour later, that boy had covered his pants, his desk and the floor, and not a bit of that mess was vomit. Talk about one smelly situation. Fortunately, he only had to make it to the edge of the school property since his house was there. That was a "bad" on my part, and in retrospect, I never should have done it. Most of the ones who knew what had happened didn't feel sorry for him. I think we had all been pushed too far by "upper class" or elitism, and country PO was pushing back!

* * *

Public schools in Georgia could cure a lot of problems if they would just go back to what we had when I was growing up. Oh yes, we had the county school board, and the county superintendent, but most importantly, each school had what was called the "Local School Board". Now I don't know for sure whether or not the teacher's contracts were signed by the county superintendent, or the local school board, but I do know that nobody, and I do mean nobody, including the principal, was ever hired without the local board's approval. At the same time, each contract renewal absolutely had to have the local board's approval. They call that involvement at the local level. Now we have so many brilliant school educational managers that ordinary mortals are basically never allowed to question the judgments of any of them. Make that, without going to court. That is stupid! There were three buildings, not counting outdoor restrooms at Girard school, one building was the grammar school, which had the basketball gymnasium, and another was the old school house, which housed the home economics classes and the cafeteria, and the high school building. I seriously doubt there were ever more than two hundred students from the first through the eleventh grade. Mr. Floyd Boyner was the principal during my junior year, and since I was sixteen for most of the year, and had my driver's license, he used me to run errands in his Pontiac for various supplies needed for the school. I thought he was a pretty nice guy. Until I got a really loud wake up call early in my senior year.

Almost all of the boys in the senior class smoked, and some of the girls did too. No smoking was permitted anywhere at school, except at the smoking tree. However, one day five of us senior boys were in one of the dressing rooms just off the gymnasium in the grammar school with the doors closed, smoking. A little dipshit in about the fourth grade yanked the door open, and saw us smoking. He took off on the run to report his great discovery. We knew what he was going to do, so we put out the cigarettes, left the room open to get the smoke out, and went back up to the high school building.

Within half an hour, Mr. Boyner had rounded us all up and we were in his office. We had agreed none of us were going to admit to smoking. We all stood in front of his desk while he harangued, and harangued, and demanded that we admit we had been smoking. Not a living soul said anything, we just stood and looked at him. Finally he went down the line, one by one demanding that we admit that we had been smoking. None of us said anything. What the hell, he didn't smoke, all he had to do was walk up close to us and he would have been able to smell the tobacco smoke on us. Damned if we ever figured out what his purpose was.

Finally, he seemed to be running out of verbal abuse for us and that was when he made what I considered a colossal mistake. He said, "Well, since none of you are going to admit it, I'm going to let you go.... But I just want to know if any of you are man enough to admit that you smoked." I was man enough to beat the hell out of anybody in the school at that time including Mr. Boyner, with or without boxing gloves on, and I had never allowed a pair of damned old mules to get the better of me so I asked him what he had just said. He repeated, "I'm not going to do anything to you, I just want to know if any one of you is man enough to admit smoking". I looked at him and said, "since you said you are not going to do anything about it, I'm man enough to tell you I smoked and if that kid hadn't yanked the door open there would have been no problem."

With that, that son of a bitch told the other four they could go, but for me to stay in his office. After the other were gone he began to tell me what he was going to do to me, I asked him why he had lied to me. He allowed as how he thought it was funny that I would have believed him. To this day, I remember the vase of flowers sitting on his desk. I made a swinging motion with my left hand and they went flying up against the wall, shattering the vase. Then I started cussing him for everything I could think of, screaming every word at the top of my lungs. I told him I dared him to get out of his chair. I fully planned to throw his ass out the window. He was about the color of chalk, and he stayed in his chair. That was fortunate for both of us as I was totally out of control.

One of the women teachers, who always had presented herself as one tough woman, came flying across the hall and into Boyner's office. She ordered me to get out of the office, and I turned and moved to within about two feet of her, and told her that she had put her ass in something that she wasn't bad enough to control and that if she was smart, she would get back to her classroom. She left.

By the time I finished swearing at Boyner, the school busses had gone for the day. In the meantime, I was still in such a rage that I had walked the hall for I guess about ten minutes. Somewhere along the way I had picked up a three-foot section of beaded pine ceiling board, and was splintering it with my bare hands. Then I went back into his office. I have never figured out why he hadn't gotten the hell out of there, but he was still sitting there. He told me to go home. I told him, the busses had already run, and I was not walking home. I then demanded that he take me home and he agreed that he would. On the way I told him that he wasn't going to just drop me off, he was going to tell to Mama everything that had happened. God I hoped Daddy wasn't there, not for my sake, but I didn't want somebody else to kill the bastard. If anybody did, it was going to be me. Mr. Boyner wasn't too happy at the prospect of talking to Mama.

When we got to the house, I told him to get out of the car and get on the porch, I'd get Mama. I found Mama and quickly told her exactly what had happened. She came out on the front porch and Mr. Boyner started his story, and to his credit, he did tell it pretty much correctly. Including the vase, and the fact that I had been cussing him something fierce. He admitted he had lied to me, but he thought it was acceptable since all five of us had lied about smoking by refusing to admit it. Miranda was not in vogue at that time.

With that, Mama asked him, "Are you supposed to be setting an example for a bunch of Youngens or are you supposed to be showing them how it pays to try to lie and deceive them." She made the point that he couldn't have had any doubt that we had been smoking, so why didn't he just go ahead and punish us. While she didn't say it in so many words... "just cut the crap". She laid into him just the way I thought she would, she really worked him over. Finally he saw a way to get loose, and he wanted to know if there was anything he could do. Her reply was "You have already done too much, just leave." Mama and I both knew that was not the end of the situation. I expected I was going to be expelled, but I remembered Mr. Lonnie who was on the local school board.

Mr. Lonnie, as one member of the local school board, was PO just like most of us down there, however, somehow or another he had been taught to read aerial photographs. Farms all over the country had been mapped that way to be sure acreage controls on subsidized crops could me policed. One of the ways he was able to keep hide and hair together was to be a supervisor of that measuring process. I worked for him between my junior and senior year in high school. He was a prince of a fellow and we became good friends during that summer.

I went to see Mr. Lonnie that same Friday night and I told him the absolute truth about everything that had happened. He told me that he would probably be in worse trouble than I was, if it had been him in the same situation. However, he never told me in so many words that he would support me, so I was worried. I told Mr. Lonnie "You are sure going to be hearing about this, I expect Mr. Boyner is going to insist on a called meeting to get me expelled." Sure enough, he rounded up everybody for a local school board meeting the next day, Saturday afternoon. According to Mr. Lonnie, Boyner came in expecting a slam-dunk expulsion.

The problem for Boyner was he didn't know how well I knew Mr. Lonnie, and that I had told him the entire story. When Boyner told his story, he made a serious mistake. He left out all about his promise of no punishment, if anyone admitted to it. By the time he finished, it sounded like I had just lost it for no reason, and that I had been the organizer of the entire smoking event. Apparently after Boyner's encounter with Mama he had decided the only way to get out of the hole he had dug for himself was to lie by omission. Bad, bad, serious mistake. Mr. Lonnie asked him to repeat the part about what had caused him to let the others go and what happened just before I lost it. He also asked him to tell the board some of the things I had been shouting at him, aside from cussing him. Some of the other board members were in a hurry to vote, run me off, and go home but Mr. Lonnie started losing his temper and getting hot with them and with Mr. Boyner.

Finally, he told Boyner, "You have been lying through your damned teeth," and proceeded to tell the board what really happened. He made them all sit there and listen while he corrected Boyner's story. Then he told them that I had worked for him all the previous summer, and from what he knew of me, the only thing that would have set me off like that was just what I had told him. According to what another board member told me, he had never seen Mr. Lonnie so damned mad in his life. I can believe he was mad because the only time I saw him really mad [angry] he pulled his pocket knife out, opened it and started cleaning his nails, very deliberately.

I don't know everything that went on in the board meeting, but I was told Mr. Lonnie did clean his fingernails in the meeting. It apparently was one heated meeting. Boyner didn't get what he wanted. They refused to expel me, and they must have given him something to think about for his future. He never mentioned that episode in his office to me again. To this day, I believe it is scumbag behavior by people in authority that causes one hell of a lot of the problems we have with children today. Hell, in today's world, I would have been in a Youth Development Center [YDC] until I was 21, and Boyner would have been given a medal for being brilliant enough to lie. Anyway, Mr. Lonnie saved my ass and because of it, I always made it a point to see him whenever I went back down to Girard. I wonder if Mr. Lonnie ever thought that his act of kindness and backbone, made it possible, so far as I know, for the only graduate of Girard High School to finish Engineering School and later, to get his Ph.D.

* * *

If Mr. Ralph Lewis were still alive, he probably would be surprised to find his name in a section dealing with education in PO country, and in particular, my education. This really is about education, and work, as well as the positive things that a person can do when they don't really have to. I don't know if the office even exists in Burke County any longer, however, it was called the Agricultural Stabilization Committee. That is as close as I can recall, and it seems to me its abbreviation was ASC.

Anyway, I had heard that the ASC office in Waynesboro needed to hire what they called "Performance Reporters" to measure land and plot it on aerial photographs so I decided to get one of those jobs. I was just past sixteen years old, and just through the tenth grade. I got dressed in the best clothes I had, borrowed Daddy's truck, and went to Waynesboro to see Mr. Lewis. I got in to see him, but he was clearly not at all pleased that I had gotten past his secretary and through to him.

Our interview was about to be quick, very definite, and very definitely a NO. He was in the process of telling me I was too young, and that I should try to get on as a chain puller for a field reporter. Just for your information, a chain was what was used to measure distances. Somebody had to pull the suckers and put little sticks in the ground. Like I said, arrogance was a well-ingrained part of me, so I interrupted him and told him that I didn't much like the idea of being dismissed purely because I was young. Since I was on a roll, I told him he hadn't considered that I was in a tie for the top of my class, and that I guessed my being fool enough to take the hardest courses like algebra and geometry didn't really mean anything. After saying that, I just shut up and looked at him, fully expecting him to order me from his office.

Surprise of all surprises, he just stared at me for what seemed like hours, but most likely it was about two minutes, and then he said, "You know what boy, I'm going to hire you just so I can have the opportunity to fire you." I thanked him very much, and at the same time told him there was no way he was going to get a reason to fire me. I went through the training, and was assigned to Mr. Lonnie's group. That year, I was number one in accuracy on the basis of spot checks and rechecks. The next year, they came looking for me. Mr. Ralph Lewis, or if any of your family should read this, I salute you for having been open minded enough to listen, and take a calculated risk on a young punk like me.

What I really wanted to tell was about Mr. Lewis, however, there were some aspects of measuring land seem to qualify it as a strange job worth mentioning. It was seasonal work, and demanding, but the hours were somewhat flexible. Mr. Lonnie, who was the field supervisor, didn't care when we started, or stopped as long as he knew the hours we were in the field, so I hired a chain puller, rather than being one, as Mr. Lewis has suggested at first. We would work from 6:00 a.m. to 2:00 p.m., Monday through Friday, Working straight through, eating a biscuit along the way, if we had brought any. Mr. Lonnie would show up at strange times as if he was trying to catch me screwing off, but he never did, because I was really doing the job. Not all the performance reporters were keeping honest hours, however I believe Mr. Lonnie caught them every time. He seemed to have an innate ability to know when somebody might not be on the job.

After 2:00, I dropped off my chain puller, and went home to eat and start plowing those damned mules until nearly night. I would take over from Daddy. I can tell you one thing, he got the best part of my working my ass off, since I had to rent the pickup from him for forty dollars per month, not including gasoline and oil, and on top of that I had to pay my chain puller fifteen dollars per week. My total pay, before expenses were $165.00 per month, so you figure it out.

* * *

Comic books may not be "proper" literature, and I know there are many people today who believe comic, or funny books are a horrible thing for children to read. I also know there were many in 1945 who believed that also, and some of them were involved in the school system. It was a major criminal offense to be caught with a comic book on school property since the "all knowing authorities" had divine communication with some person of superior logic, from somewhere, who said they were destructive to young minds. Bull feathers!!!

Reading books, comic or otherwise, was actually a means of my finding out what had happened, or what people had thought years before. Comic books seemed to really be a window to the future especially if you consider miniature circuits and other science fiction concepts that are now commonly accepted things. When I said books was a means of finding out that had happened, we are really talking history, as most of the books in our sand bed library were at least twenty years old, and many were older. The general logic of keeping us away from the evils of comics may have been to some extent accurate, if reading them had impaired my reading of books in the library. However, that logic was just plain wrong for me, since I had read all the books in the library. I was looking for every source of information I could get because I knew there had to be a way out of Sandbed hell, and maybe it was in print somewhere.

Anyway, a kid in my class lived with his grandmother, and worked for his uncle. His mother and the rest of his family lived in Savannah. I barely knew the others in his family and didn't need to, except I did know one thing about them. Without a doubt, they must have read the most comic books of anybody in Georgia. After the Savannah family members had read their comic books, they sent them on to their brother in Girard. He read them, and when the next shipment arrived, he would tell me to come get the stack he had finished. When I say stack, that is exactly what it was, a stack was from twenty four to thirty inches high. I must have read every Superman comic up until 1949; I don't believe many escaped me. Other comic heroes were Dick Tracy, Flash

Gordon, Wonder Woman, the Green Hornet, Batman and Robin, Aqua man, Red Ryder, Roy Rogers, Gene Autry, Road Runner, The Lone Ranger, and a litany of other titles there would be no way to recall.

When the new stack was picked up, I would return any that had been marked that my friend wanted back, and start on the new batch. Surprisingly enough, they did use some words I had never heard before and if the context didn't give me the meaning, Mama's favorite dictionary was at hand to see what they were trying to run past me. Much of the time, the context gave me the meaning. Reading those comic books was an interesting challenge because Mama and Daddy absolutely did not consider comic books as anything but pleasure reading, with no direct relationship to my school performance.

I read mostly after supper because I was never denied afternoon study time, if my homework had not been completed in study hall. Study Hall was mandatory for everybody at the school since most parents wouldn't permit homework to be done at home. This says pretty quickly that most parents weren't heavy into the education of their Youngens. If I had time to read comics in the afternoon, then my schoolwork was done, and it was off to the fields to work. Like I said, most of my book reading of all kinds was done after supper. Reading became a deeply ingrained habit, which virtually became obsessive compulsive.

In relation to the comics, I could expect a call about 9:30 p.m. to "blow out the lamp" and go to sleep. So I would move the kerosene lamp from by my bed over to a table or mantle piece and blow it out. If you have ever had to rely on kerosene lamps and lanterns for your only source of light, you know that lamp was handled carefully. You didn't knock over a lamp holding a pint of kerosene, with a paper-thin glass "chimney" on it, first because of the chance of starting a fire, which would have spread like wildfire in that old heart pine house.

Second, there was the expense of replacement of the lamp chimney or the entire lamp, and third, the kerosene would leak out even if the lamp base didn't break and the odor of kerosene was with you forever.

After "lights out", if the weather was warm enough where we only needed a sheet, I would slide down in the bed, pull the sheet up over my knees, and head and turn on a flashlight and read until I got sleepy. Mama and Daddy had to know what was going on, not that they ever caught me, because it was about impossible to sneak up on anybody in that old house, every board in the floor had its own particular squeak or groan The reason I think they had to know was that flashlight batteries needed replacing faster than they would have with regular usage. I was very diligent about switching flashlights every chance I got, I never wanted any one flashlight identified as mine, cause I would have been caught for sure. Maybe that worked well enough to keep them from really understanding just how long flashlight batteries could last, if used reasonably.

Anyway, if anyone in that comic book reading family from Savannah reads this, they will in all likelihood recognize themselves. Being able to read all those comic books meant a lot to me and I want you to know it.

I mentioned that I became obsessive compulsive about reading, however, I didn't know others around Girard were really aware, anyway many years later I learned about it. One of my older brothers, Clifford was talking to a classmate of mine who had dropped out of school about the ninth grade. Rusty Willard asked him when he had last seen me and Clifford dryly told him "O' Hell, he is in Milledgeville, been there for years". He didn't elaborate at all, to which Rusty replied, "You know, I sure am sorry to hear about that, but he always did have his head in a book. I guess it just got to him" What you need to know is that Milledgeville was known all over Georgia as 'Sylum City'. It was the site of the state mental institution and Rusty immediately knew too much reading and becoming a patient were closely connected. Clifford didn't bother to tell him there were other things people could do in Milledgeville besides be mental patients. Rusty died about two years later, and when Clifford got around to relating the tale to me, he had already died so he never knew he had jumped to a wrong conclusion! When I first moved there, many people would make what they considered jokes such as "I didn't know they let people out on furlough" or other "touching" comments. I discovered a good line, which usually worked. I assured them I was on the other side of town, away from the mental hospital, however, I did have many close professional friends who worked there, and my recommendations would be taken very seriously. Somehow or another they got the idea I just might remember their names when I got back home.

* * *

Elitism and Radio can be twisted together. Reading wasn't the only way to pipe information into the Georgia sandbeds. We had a radio from the time I could remember. The first one I remember, and I think it was the first one the family had, was in a big cabinet. It had to be a big cabinet to hold the radio and the batteries. I do mean batteries in the plural sense, it took three of them, one was called an "A" battery, which weighed about a pound and a half and was smaller than the "B" and "C" batteries. Both of the larger batteries were really big and heavy and weighed about seven to ten pounds each. Listening time was rigidly controlled, and for a long time, I thought everybody on radio sounded like Walter Winchell. Anybody who was listening was expected to double check and be absolutely positive the set was switched off. Leaving the radio on overnight was about the same as being sure you wouldn't have any radio until the money could be scraped together to buy all the batteries again.

I was sure technology would never get beyond a later little tan portable Philco radio Daddy got from somewhere. It used one small battery, but it could have been used on electricity, that is if Georgia Power or REA had been there. After late 1948, we got electricity, so he could use it without the battery. After we got electricity, from one place or another, I got my hands on several old non-working radios. I started taking them apart, one by one, trying to decide which part would work, and which wouldn't. It was pretty much like holding somebody's hand and assuring them they had some dreaded disease. What I did would have caused an electrical engineer's hair to stand straight up, and it is a wonder I didn't get the same results.

Finally, I had a bunch of parts jammed together, crowned by a speaker facing down on the tubes, crazy looking, but it worked. There was surely no way to ever get that mess back in the case again, I didn't care, I had a radio. The volume control came out the wrong side, the variable condenser for changing stations was in a new location, but "by damn" it worked! I hooked the antenna wire to the window screen in my room, and I had volume. After I ran it out about fifty feet and hooked it to a tree, at night I could get WCKY Cincinnati, Ohio and Del Rio Texas. I never left that monster on when I was going to be away since nobody else could have figured out how to turn it off. I was so unsure about it that I even unplugged it so it couldn't cause a fire.

I listened to "Lum and Abner at the JottemDown Store", and "Amos and Andy and the Kingfish" and "The Shadow". I used the comment "Only the shadow knows for sure" with a fiendish laugh so much that my daughter found all the tapes and gave them to me for Christmas one year. Along with those shows, I remember listening to country music from WCKY, "The

Louisiana Hayride", the Grand Old Opry, and some western music out of Del Rio, Texas. Progress was a wonderful thing.

However, what caused me to equate the radio with learning was what I later discovered was the "elitism" of some of the educated. Shortly after I got my radio going, I found music on Sunday afternoon "Brought straight to you from the ballroom of the Roosevelt Hotel in....." and "The Metropolitan Opera brought to you by Texaco... you can trust your car to the man who wears the star...." I listened to a lot of strange music for a country hick. This is not to say I understood it. They didn't do much explaining of anything concerning the operas. If you knew the title, it was presumed you knew the rest. Second, there seemed to be something plebeian about doing a song in English, so I heard a lot of Italian and German opera. My reason for listening was to be able to say I had heard opera, and classical music of Bach, Beethoven, Mozart or whomsoever. Later I joked I had listened to opera, classical and big band music, anything to be different and know about something someone else didn't. Actually I enjoyed the music, and still do.

What was amusing was that one day my soon to be wife, who came from very distinctly different circumstances, was talking about listening to the opera with her grandfather, and how much she had loved it. In the conversation, she told me it was sponsored by Texaco. She was more than slightly surprised to learn that the person she was to later marry, had been listening to the same performances albeit under very different circumstances. I was stretched out across my bed in that old corncrib of a house, with the windows open, and a cobbled up radio, and she sitting in the loggia of a huge, servant filled home, listening to a fancy Grundig radio. God, it must be difficult for the wealthy to know that some of "their" music got out to heathens in the country sand beds of the backwoods, in the middle of nowhere.

* * *

The smartest man I ever met was when I was measuring land. I know to call him the smartest man I have ever met could be called a broad and sweeping statement. However, he was intelligent beyond about anything I had ever seen at the ripe old age of sixteen and a half years. It took me some years, reflecting back on my encounter, to fully appreciate what I had been privileged to observe. I went to see one of the big farmers in the area and told him I was ready to start measuring his cotton and peanuts. He told me to check with his "Overseer", and that he would have him meet me at the first field to measure.

When my chain puller and I arrived, he was sitting at the corner of the road. We started talking. I knew who he was, but had never had any reason to talk with him. He was gray headed, and looked to be about forty or fifty years old, which at that time in my life, was older than God. Anyway, I told him I needed to check all fields on the maps of the farm to verify what was planted, and measure the cotton and peanuts. He listened and quietly pulled a little spiral notebook from his pocket and started telling me where each field was, and how many acres, according to them, were in the field. They had about twenty-five different fields, so it was going to be a week's work. I moved a little closer to him as we talked, and caught a glance at his book. The pages had nothing but a bunch of crazy marks on them, so I asked him how he could tell me all the information he was giving me from that book. His reply was pretty direct, "There was no school for black boys to go to when I was a youngen so I didn't learn to read and write like white folks, so I just made up my own things," and he proceeded to show me what each character meant. Now that language was good only for him, but it worked. He had created a written language that allowed him to keep records as accurate as anyone who could read and write in the standard form. He could function in the world of farming as well as any man. It took me a number of years to fully comprehend what he had accomplished. Would you have felt comfortable in a discussion of symbolism with him? He was an extraordinary man and surely much smarter than anybody he was working for, and most likely smarter than anybody else I've ever met.

* * *

Want to be called a crazy? Just try something out of the ordinary for where you live and see what happens. The "Sandbed telegraph" said a farmer, old man Luncan Blisson, who lived about five miles from us, was doing some strange things and we should go and look at one of his cotton fields. He had a tractor, which meant I couldn't like him too much, no matter what. I wanted his tractor. Anyway, from the tone of voice we knew it was something strange, so Daddy, Dean and I went to see what it was all about. Sure enough, what we saw was more than strange. He had planted what appeared to be about twenty acres of cotton and it was growing quite well, or as we would have said, "That shore is pretty cotton".

We weren't the only people there that day, leaning up on the fence outside the field, gawking at what was out there. You have to understand we were heavily into what was called "Row crop" farming where the rows were expected to go from one side of the field to the other in perfectly straight lines. Yes, Luncan sure enough had rows of cotton, but his rows were in a huge circle. Each row was adjusted to the previous circle, and he kept planting in an ever smaller circles. When he got to where his tractor wouldn't cultivate correctly, he put in the minimum number of straight rows in the center of the field. He pulled his wagon or truck in toward the straight rows in the center of the field, mashing down what he had to, so he could refill the seed, or fertilizer as necessary.

Yes sir!! That was the talk of the community for quite awhile. It was obvious to everybody that old Luncan Blisson had lost it, and everybody worked overtime making every contact they had with him over the previous fifteen years into something that proved he was just a little looney and had been crazy for years. It was years later, but after studying something about invention and innovation I realized that we were the fools, not him. Not a soul, except Luncan, had ever stopped to think about what he had saved. When you cultivate rows, at both ends, you must turn the mules, or tractor around, and lose the time to get everything lined up, just in time to do it again, perhaps three hundred yards away. There was some pretty high speed plowing going on back then, and for all I know it still is today. It all revolved around setting a hand throttle for a particular gear and the cultivator. The "Indy 500" drivers would go down the rows as fast as the plows would allow.

Another funny thing that I noticed about tractor drivers, particularly after high-speed hydraulic lifts were put on the tractors, was that the driver would use every bit of speed he could while plowing on the row. At the end of the row, on both ends, there was usually a fence that was supposed to be standing after the tractor turned and started back. If the fence posts weren't still standing it was because the drivers seemed to have a motto that any post that didn't have John Deere green, or Ford Ferguson gray, or Allis Chalmers orange, or Farmall red on it meant the field was either being plowed by mules, or an inept tractor driver who couldn't handle the "challenge of the fence posts", which loosely translated meant, "nick'em but don't knock'em down."

At the end of the row, the driver hit the hydraulic pedal with the heel of his left foot, jammed and locked the left or right wheel brake, depending on the direction they were turning, and locked the steering wheel in the direction of the turn. In an instant, the front end of the tractor was airborne and the driver slammed the steering wheel back to straight forward while still in the air, and again jammed the hydraulic pedal to lower the cultivator back into the ground. The engine throttle was never touched, and the front end of the tractor - hopefully - had missed the fence, or the fence post, by no more than two inches. Could you even imagine the speed of that front end flying through the air? A miss of more than two inches plainly told anybody watching that you were a "wuiss". Yes, there were some tractors that couldn't survive that maneuver, but there were many that could. Today's tractors are so big and heavy, and so costly that I suspect a driver would never get but one chance to try a stunt that.

Anyway, later reflections indicated to me that old Luncan Blisson had at least looked for an efficient solution, and apparently it worked for him. However, I don't think anybody adopted it anywhere else, but I do know the diffusion of that innovation did not happen in the Girard farming community.

* * *

Fonzie and his experience with the graveyard on the way to his house was one of those things that were part of the Sandbed folklore around Girard. It isn't directly connected to education, but at least the Willis' lived on the corner on the way to the schoolhouse, which qualifies this story being here, one way or another. Fonzie Kohen wasn't a tenant on Willis' farm, but he did work for them most of the time. The Willis brothers were prone to pulling pranks on anybody, black or white. However, in this instance, Fonze was a black man, and no, I don't have a clue as to how he got to have what sounded like a Jewish name. It was general knowledge that Fonzie had an unnatural fear of dead people, and he didn't like to be anywhere around a graveyard during the day, and absolutely, not at night. He lived on Fire Tower Road, about a half mile beyond the graveyard, a distance which Fonzie considered entirely too close to his house.

An old man named Hulmy had died about a month before, and had been buried on the corner where Fire Tower road dead-ended into the Rockville road. Bethany Methodist Church was on one side of Fire Tower road and the cemetery was across the road. Mr. Hulmy had been a big old man, deep voiced, and just as mean and vicious as hell. Whites didn't particularly like him, and while Blacks didn't let it be known much, they hated and feared him. The Willis' men decided they were going to have some fun and take advantage of Fonzie's dislike for old man Hulmy and his fears of the unnatural.

They set everything up and made sure they kept Fonzie working until it was black night, nearly 9:00 p.m. Fonzie was told that he couldn't take the truck home as he usually did since they were going to use it the next morning. However, H. I. Willis said he would take Fonzie home. The front seat was loaded on purpose, so Fonzie had to ride in the back of the truck. It was about a mile from H.I.'s place to Fire Tower road and the cemetery. Both the roads were unpaved, dirt roads, and just as Mr. H. I. slowed the truck to jump the ruts to turn on fire tower road, he shut the engine down. Back then, the ignition and the starter were separate so you could leave the switch off, and grind the starter until forever, and the engine would never start.

Old Hulmy's grave wasn't more than twenty feet away from the old truck. Fonzie started to begging "Mr. Willis...Mr. Willis. please git the truck started, and let's git out of here". Of course it was never going to happen. Brother W. C. and a friend were ready and waiting. They had gotten white sheets and put them on and started to moving around old man Hulmy's grave and among the tombstones close by, making moaning sounds. They asked, "Are you there Fonzie?" It didn't take but just one time, and in two seconds flat, he really wasn't there, he was gone. Fonzie became airborne from the truck bed and he must have set a record for the half-mile getting to his house. They never got a chance to tell him they had come to get him. His wife Maude told the rest of the story. According to her, he was hollering at the top of his lungs from the time he hit the road to the house "Open the door, open the door by the time I git there". Maude must have been a little slow in moving, or maybe he was just much moving a mite faster than even he thought he was. Anyway when he saw the door wasn't open, he started running around the house, screaming, "Open the door by the time I git back".

Maude was thoroughly confused because she could hear him repeating the same thing over and over, but from what sounded like everywhere, from the woods around the house. She stayed at the front door and as she thought he was getting closer, she opened the door, and he came flying in at a full run. She said she thought he was going to die on the spot. He survived, but I think, had I been Fonzie, I would have been willing to see if those two clowns could have explained directly to old man Hulmy about what had transpired at his grave site. The strange thing about what happened was, none of the people involved thought there was anything racial about the prank. I have serious doubts there was myself, but I'll never be sure one-way or the other.

* * *

CHAPTER X

CHURCHES, RELIGION, REVIVAL MEETINGS AND DINNER ON THE GROUND

Churches, religion, revival meetings, and dinner on the ground were things that were very important to the PO in Sandbed Hell. It was pretty hard to avoid some aspects of zealotry no matter what. Blacks and whites had their own separate churches from the time I could remember, though at the little Baptist church we went to, there was a black cemetery adjoining the white cemetery and it was still actively used for burial in the late thirties and early forties. Since a grave with a mound of dirt on top looked pretty much the same to me, the only difference I knew was something I have never been able to get an answer for, from old blacks, or whites. When a black was buried, particularly the very old, I noticed they had the top of the grave, starting at the head, and then as far down as it took, covered with medicine bottles of all shapes, sizes, and colors put in the soft dirt. Some of them had caps on them and some didn't. If you have an answer as to why that was done, and what it signified, you've got one on me. I have yet to hear anything except rank speculation. I have done enough speculating and gotten no provable reasons for my trouble.

Close in to Girard we had Bethlehem Baptist, Botsford Baptist, Girard Methodist, Molly Pond Methodist and Bethany Methodist churches. The Christian Church and the Wesleyan Methodists were also in there taking care of the souls for the community. In Sardis, just seven miles away, they had even more. Can you believe we still never felt totally safe from bad things with all that religion over, under and around us? There were plenty of black churches scattered around too, whether they did any good for us heathen folks or not.

Mama was a member of the Christian church, a bit farther away than Bethlehem Baptist, where I think Daddy was a member, but I never remember him saying he was. He would go occasionally, every now and then, but he never was involved too much in what happened there. Church services, unless it was right in town, were held, every other Sunday at the very most. The collections never were enough for any more than that. Some of the time, church started at 1:00 p.m. which gave the preacher enough time to get to us from the church where he made his living. The rest of the time, church started about 11:00 a.m. There were sporadic attempts to have Sunday School, but it would ebb and flow for reasons I never understood...maybe I didn't care enough to ask too many questions.

There wasn't much chance of anybody really going to sleep in old Bethlehem Baptist Church. First off, there were no screens in the windows, and in the summer any bug that wanted to join in prayer could just boogie on down. Man, some of the mosquitoes were huge, and some of their size may have been that Bethlehem Church was less than a quarter mile from Briar Creek where mosquitoes flourished. Aside from that, another reason nobody could get a good nap was the benches were made of unpadded long leaf pine. The back piece was about twenty-four inches wide, and more than two inches thick, and at least twenty feet long. Both the back and the seat was a single board, with no knots to bleed "pine tar" and get on your clothes or to stick your ass to them. The seat was slightly angled to lean you back so you wouldn't roll forward, but, man, was that seat hard! Some of the most ample ladies had no problem, but if you had any tendency toward being skinny, your butt bone was ready to leave an indentation by the time services were over. I was always more than ready to get up and sing "mouth" the last song to get out of there.

Most of the preachers, up until the last one I remember, would get in the church, and really start building up a head of steam. I guess some of my irreverent behavior was getting a foundation because I kept wondering if he thought everybody in the church had a hearing problem, and then on other occasions, I wondered if he was preaching to God, and he thought God had a hearing problem. The last preacher I recall before leaving home kept his sermons on a more even "speaking" level, both when it seemed he was talking to God or to us. What's more, he had two daughters. One whom I dated a few times, the other was too young for me, but both were 'fine'.

PO people always had to have revivals. You see PO people had all this bad stuff just start "bunching up" on'em and the only way to take care of it was to sorta give us religious shock treatment to get the demons out. Just like they did at the "sylum" at Milledgeville, except Georgia Power wasn't involved. I never could quite understand how we could afford to pay for a revival, when we couldn't pay for regular preaching. Since I was a youngen, to have asked that question would have gotten my revival immediately through my backside. Only thing

I could ever figure out was that the visiting preacher and the regular preacher got together, and decided on how they were going to divide the pot [collection plate] and be satisfied with what they could scare up.

I'm not going to say too much about revivals, because of my getting religion at about thirteen, which really meant I got to go swimming in April rather than June. Baptizing in the Baptist Church meant total immersion. We didn't have a pool or fount or whatever you call it at the church because there was no electricity to pump water, we used Briar Creek at Ellison's Bridge. Now that may not seem exciting to you, but since total immersion was the name of the game, and the deep spots in the creek usually shifted over the winter, it could get really exciting. You could lose a converted sinner before you knew what was happening and get no chance to say Amen! We nearly had that happen one time when unbeknownst to anyone, the preacher couldn't swim, and most of the converts couldn't either. One of the larger sized, more fully formed ladies who had gotten the "calling", was more than the preacher could handle. He had about five or six converts in the water with him. He got her dunked backwards, under the water in fine form, but in the process of trying to stand her back up, he stepped backwards and into a hole over his head. All were rescued, but his sermons and the quality of his religion took on new fervor for the rest of the revival!!

* * *

Dinner on the ground was a requirement for a revival. Ever been to a dinner on the ground at the kick off of a revival meeting? Back then a bunch of the men would get together and put up about sixty feet of wooden tables out under the oak trees on Saturday before the services started on Sunday. People from all over everywhere would be invited, and some would invite themselves. A few free loaders would invite about twenty people, and bring enough food for ten, but that didn't really matter, because most of us brought enough food for thirty more than the crowd we came with.

There may be a lot wrong with living in the sand beds, but one thing that was right was the cooking. About 9:30 a.m. Sunday morning people started arriving and putting their food out on the tables, meats on the first table, on the next table there would be vegetables and non meat dishes, and on the next table there would be pies, cakes and puddings. The end table was for iced tea and lemonade. You might recall my description of the table at home, loaded with everything and I was accustomed to that every day. The table at home was enough to cause a belly ache from eating too much, but it would have been just an appetizer for this spread.

As soon as everybody got all the food out, they covered it with cloths to keep the insects away. By that time it was getting close to eleven o'clock, and time for the morning service, so all except a few who watched to make sure stray dogs didn't start eating without us, went into the church. I think most of us had our minds on that food, but finally the hellfire and brimstone preaching would end, and we would go outside, and from about noon until two o'clock it was like what a medieval feast must have been. If there was any debauchery, it sure had to be minimal, I just don't think people who have overeaten that much can do a whole lot of "bauching" or debauching!! Then it was time for church again, so from two until about three o'clock, we were reminded once again, of what sinners we were. Fortunately for us, the preachers, like us, had eaten as much as they could too, and that may have accounted for the reason that most of the afternoon session was singing. Another reason, irrespective of those bone killing pine seats, everybody would have fallen asleep after that big meal if they had been just listening. I have never seen a person fall asleep in the middle of a song they were singing. The singing part was one I thoroughly enjoyed even if I couldn't carry a tune in a bucket with a lid on it back then, and according to some, I still can't.

* * *

Cutting oats on Sunday really got tongues into overdrive in the Georgia sandbeds. Girard was in the Bible belt, in fact it could have been said it was the headwaters of some very religious folks who twisted everything you did or didn't do into something that was distinctly heavenly or distinctly hellish. I lived there too long to be fooled into that heavenly crap, but we did have our camps of the 'good' and the 'bad'. Then too, there was the even larger group who pretended membership in either the "good" or the "bad" other, you just couldn't be sure when they were in which one. Does the word hypocrite mean anything to you? We were eaten up with them, and there could have been some inbreeding between the heavenly and the hellish, which I suppose made some of them hermaphrodites.

One thing Daddy never did was work on Sunday. It sure wasn't because he was that religious, but I think he figured his mules deserved a rest. I don't know if we, the Youngens, figured in that equation or not. Anyway oats were ready to combine, and the weather had been rainy and just not suitable for harvesting until this particular Sunday. For anyone who doesn't know, once the oat straw started to break and let the heads fall, you were in deep dookey. Well, Gene McNugger and Herbert Sasser, who owned an oat combine together, were afraid they were going to lose their entire crop. However, on Friday, the sun came out and on Saturday the fields dried, but the weather forecast said there would be rain again before the end of the next week. You know the story; Gene and Herbert started cutting just as early as possible on Sunday, and ran just as hard and fast as they could until the next rain.

The word got out about their working on Sunday, and those two guys caught unmitigated hell for a very long time. I didn't see Gene that much, but I did see Herbert Sasser quite often, and he kept defending himself for the choice. I thought he was crazy as hell to even talk about it with people who were basically religious hypocrites anyway, and aside from that they just wished more than anything else that they owned a combine themselves.

* * *

Death in po country, I swear, is different from most other places. For most of my life, few of the bodies were ever embalmed for the PO, and that made undertakers very unhappy. However, not as unhappy as they would have been if they had embalmed a body and not gotten any money for it. If it was warm weather, the funeral was held quickly. In the wintertime, a little more time could pass before the funeral, however in those instances where the family was scattered everywhere, it was more likely embalming would be done. When the word got out that someone had died, unless they were really hated by just about everybody, something akin to dinner on the ground was sure to follow. The family surely may have problems because of their loss, but food was not one of them, and it still isn't unless I have lost touch with Girard and Sardis entirely.

One of the things I remember vividly about the sandbeds were the wakes. Just in case you don't know, they were all night affairs. Now, everybody goes to the funeral home, and for a limited time, say two hours, where you can view the newly departed and express your sympathy to the family. Not so, if you were from the real south, and were involved in the send off of a friend. What happened at the wake varied with the time of the night, and who might be there at that time. I went to many of them. Sometimes the entire wake was held with everybody in the room with the body. Usually the earlier hours were when the older folks came, and things were very somber and solemn. It took until about two in the morning for things to lighten up, and the story telling would begin with telling lies and funny stories about the newly departed. The stories would get "out of hand" when the group got down to the "totally irreverent" people, and the stories went from "off color" to downright dirty. Sometimes the body was kept in the hallway, which was generally a wide connector to the entire house. That was particularly important when embalming was not done, and the room where all the living people were going to be was warmed by a roaring fireplace. You don't want much heat, in the same room with an unembalmed body, or bad odors were sure to follow. Only one person at a time stayed in the hall with the body for those occasions. The reason for that was, at least so I was told, that cats seemed to have an uncanny ability to figure out how to get in the room with the body, and eat the nose off the corpse. I can't be sure about the truth of that story, it never happened at any of the wakes I went to but I sure didn't want to be at a wake where it happened. In the meantime, the rest of the group was off in another room eating, drinking coffee, and sometimes a bit of "shine" and other times a whole bunch of "shine" was taken to ease the pain. One thing was for sure, telling lies, funny stories, and all the other things happened no matter whether the body was in the hallway, or the same room.

I went to funerals in every church within a ten-mile radius while I was growing up, and I never enjoyed a damned one. For the people I hated, I figured we both felt the same way about each other, so I didn't go to their sendoffs. For everything I am, there are a lot of things I am not. When I went to a funeral, I had to be very distant from the person who had died not to feel emotional. I have never totally understood why. Was it for the person who was dead, or for the people left behind, or was it the dislike at being put in a situation that forced me to realize that sooner or later, it would be me in that box? One thing I learned from going to funerals was to compartmentalize and how to concentrate on something other than what was being said in the eulogy. Many, many times I counted the beaded boards in the ceilings of those country churches to focus on something other than the message of sadness. It seemed to me the preacher's main goal was to break down the family and friends of the dead person, as though he was going to be paid more for causing even more grief than they already felt. I know if too many folks get my attitude about funerals, it will distress the funeral industry, but I honestly feel the way funerals are done today is nothing but a pagan ritual. I don't plan to be put in the ground, I will be cremated.

I'm neither an atheist, nor an agnostic, but my beliefs tell me that if I live my life every day being fair, and reasonable and pretty much following the golden rule, if there is a hereafter, I will be just as qualified as anybody else. If my survivors think they can get enough people together who can think of funny or outlandish stories about what I did or didn't do, I want them to spend up to a thousand dollars hosting a damned big party. If anybody cries, call them a cab and send them home - they're too drunk to appreciate the purpose of the party!!!

* * *

The preacher, the well and me was an unlikely combination of things, but they surely came together with a bang. You have heard about the old well at the house, you know, out by the mule lot. I think I also told you about how any horseplay around the well was not tolerated at any time. Everybody recognized that to fall in the well probably meant death, either from the fall, or drowning. From my earliest memories that message had been ingrained in my brain.

Water wells and religion seem disconnected, but in this case they were closely joined. When a revival meeting was going on they usually lasted for two weeks. Somehow, some divine intervention had told all the religious and pious folks that it would take just exactly two weeks to "jerk a knot" in all the sinners and put them on the straight and narrow. All the members were expected to invite the preacher, and his wife to have dinner, which in the sandbeds was in the middle of the day. As I grew older, I felt we had more than our share of the feeding. However, I don't think what happened to me, when I was about five years old had anything to do with that opinion.

Reverend Chatwell was the preacher, and again, it was our turn to feed him. I can tell you he didn't eat much during that visit, his ass had been reamed by a real professional, named Mama. She had this tendency to react viscerally when somebody scared one of her Youngens, especially when they were very young. Anyhow, in retrospect I know the guy was just playing, but at the time he scared the living hell out of me. Maybe it was appropriate, I don't know. Anyway, the family and the preacher were outside the sleeping porch, about fifteen feet from the well, Dean and I were just playing around in the sand yard.

All of a sudden, the preacher grabbed me, picked me up off the ground and told me "I'm going to throw you in the well" That of course, was the single most scary threat anybody could make as far as I was concerned. Preacher, or not, I was sure that adult was about to kill me. I started screaming and crying at the top of my lungs. That instantly paralyzed the Preacher man and then he was surrounded by my older brothers and Mama. Mama grabbed me and wanted to know what in the world was wrong with me. Between sobs I told her, "He said he was going to throw me in the well". It didn't take but about three seconds for the shit to hit the fan by the huge buckets full.

The preacher honestly thought he was playing and joking with me, but there were no jokes about an open well. PO folks don't have any money, but they don't want to lose their Youngens by having them fall or be thrown into a well. Mama was more than slightly plain spoken, and a thoroughly chastised preacher delivered a solemn blessing at the dinner table that day. I don't know if that preacher ever preached at the Christian church again, but I do know he never came back to our house. Frankly, I still wonder how he was able to get through dinner, it probably all tasted like sawdust, after all, Mama must have scalded his taste buds.

* * *

Playing around the well can be dangerous to the anatomy and I really learned it the hard way. This doesn't have much to do with religion, but it just sort of follows the other well story. Dean was nearly five years older than me. As a matter of fact, he still is. That means as a kid, he could "clean my plow" most of the time, with one hand tied behind his back. Aside from being older, he was strong as an ox. He was into doing "one handed" pushups long before it was in vogue. One time he did five, and on the last one picked up a straight pin in his teeth that was sticking straight up on the floor. Not for this boy, I could do pushups, but one handed wasn't something I aspired to. Quite often, as we got older, we would go to the fields by ourselves to work at one thing or another. He always had the ability to start an argument, even with a fence post, and then he wanted to knock the hell out of it because it wouldn't answer him. I argued with him on a regular basis and he would beat my butt on a regular basis. No matter how hard I fought, I knew I was going to lose. My only hope was to get a sandwich while he got a meal.

One day, we were at the house and Dean was drawing a bucket of water. Now, let me tell you, nobody was about to drop a bucket full of water from halfway up since it would likely "bust" the bottom out of the bucket, and at least both of us knew that. I was convinced I had the "old man" spotted down the hill toward the head of the branch, and I knew Mama wasn't home, so I felt pretty secure. Man did I have a chance to get a few good punches in since I knew Dean wouldn't dare drop that bucket full of water. I started flailing him with both fists, with real gusto and he was trying to lock the chain over the nail to keep the bucket from falling. He never really needed to work very hard to get that chain to hang on the nail because, all of a sudden, it felt like somebody had lifted me three feet off the ground. To this day, I still don't know how in the hell Daddy had gotten behind me, or what he was doing coming from the direction he did. I do know he had taken off his leather belt and he proceeded to make a believer out of me. He really tanned my backside and I deserved it. I didn't get but a few of those whippings, since most any youngen with any ability to learn, will put their brain into overdrive with just a little help from a leather belt.

I watched carefully as Dean worked himself into trouble with Mama and Daddy, and saw the price he paid for it. I may not have been the smartest youngen in the world, but even if I had been, he was drawing me pictures of what not to do, in minute detail. I didn't have to experience everything to learn that, at certain times and for certain things, just don't go there!! I saw Mama send him out the back door numerous times to get a switch off the peach trees. When you were sent for a switch, you had better not come back with one so small she had to go get one of the proper size, but damned if you wanted to come back with something too big. Now good buddy, if you want to understand the worst and most agonizing part of a switching, it was having to choose the "right sized" one! Care to tell me I didn't understand what it meant when somebody said something about "Being on the horns of a dilemma?"

Dean got a bunch more "attitude adjustments" than I did, but he really worked at it much more diligently than was necessary. Actually, I was whipped with a belt almost never, and maybe just a little bit more with a peach tree switch. One thing I can tell you though, was that I never had any doubts that if I got too far out on a limb, or got to be too much of a smartass, that the smart would drop away, and my ass belonged to Mama and Daddy. You bet your sweet ass I feared my Daddy. I didn't have that cowering fear abused kids have, but to this day, I tell anybody who will listen that the best thing a father can do is to instill a little bit of fear of him in the minds of his kids.

* * *

CHAPTER XI

MORE THINGS THAT HELPED GETTING OUT OF PO

There were things that helped me in getting out of PO. When PO Youngens got a chance to do things to expand their horizons and they took the opportunity it was a lead pipe cinch, that they, at that moment, didn't have a clue how the pieces fit into the mosaic. Only by looking back, with good ole twenty twenty hindsight, can some appreciation of the impact of those beginnings start to make sense. Earlier I mentioned about the 4 - H Club program, which provided a pig, to selected members, in exchange for an agreement to give back a female pig from the first litter. I have already told about the dividends that earned for me and the family. The proven method of introducing change and behavior modification to adults, through the actions and acceptance of the children had worked again.

It went much farther than that, however. In the club there were offices to fill with kids who were willing to risk just a little. I can't recall how often the offices changed hands however, I am sure it was frequently. I held every office at least once, and I think several times over about a three or four year span. It probably wasn't that I was that good, more to the point, we were such a small group that we all were encouraged to hold all the various offices. That was a strong building block for me, I can't even begin to count all the organizations I have held offices in during my later years.

Another building block for the future was camp. The first time I ever went to camp was in North Georgia and we went by a school bus, driven by a lady, Mz. Molton from Waynesboro. All the campers from Burke County were on that bus, along with Mr. Pogue, the assistant county agent. I don't know how the real costs were met, but I think Mama and Daddy, or me had to come up with about 15 dollars for the entire week and that included meals as well. At the time, it didn't cross my mind, or Mama and Daddy's that there was some type of subsidy from somewhere. For that I am thankful, as there was no way in hell that Mama or Daddy would have even thought of letting me go if they had suspected we weren't paying all of my fare. Not only that, I knew I was PO, but I also know I was entirely too proud to take charity. Since I didn't know, I got to go. In later years my suspicions developed and grew and I now realize everybody on that bus got the same price break, and I haven't spent any time regretting it.

There were two things I remember about the trip to get to the camp. First, riding a school bus from Waynesboro, Georgia to Camp Wahsega at Dahlonega, Georgia was one very long trip. Even for a young and resilient butt, it was a real bruiser. We had about thirty kids on that almost new yellow monster, and I was sitting in the very back of the bus, on the driver's side. The second thing I remember about that trip was that Mz. Molton was a good flatlands bus driver, but she sure had flunked both mountain roads and steep grades. It didn't take long to figure it out, either. Those mountain roads gradually got steep and curving, but when we got to a really steep hill, she missed the shift from fourth gear to third gear, that was bad. The she immediately tried to put it in second gear, called "low gear" on those old Chevrolet buses and that didn't work either. I learned later that to get into low gear while moving required double clutching, and quickly, I think she missed that also. There we were on a steep mountain incline, on a narrow dirt road, with thirty kids with that damned bus in a dead stall.

She was just about in a panic, or maybe it was me, or both of us. You see, she kept rolling back and my end of the bus seemed to hanging off the edge of the road, and I could see the deepest ravine I had ever seen in my life. At that moment, I had a serious concern that I may never get to see another one. Anyway, Mr. Pogue quickly got up to the door, and he grabbed the emergency brake, which was always on the right of the gear shift, and yanked it back and held it. It was one of the minor miracles in my life, up to that point, anyway. That was the first time I had never seen anybody who had an emergency brake that worked. Maybe it was because the bus was so nearly new.... Nobody ever repaired emergency brakes that I knew about, where in the hell was anything going to roll off to in flat sandbeds?

Mz. Molton finally got the engine started, and, all the time she had her left foot on the brake, she switched feet and got her right foot on the brake, and left foot on the clutch, and put it in first gear, called the "granny gear", and as she let the clutch out, she let the brake go, and jammed the pedal to the metal. At the same time, Mr. Pogue let the emergency brake off and we lurched forward. I don't really know how many more of the Youngens had my view of that mountain gorge but I had been closer to it than I wanted to be.

I could tell just how scared the two adults were because Mz. Molton was nearly wringing wet with sweat, and Mr. Pogue who was pretty much red headed with a fair complexion, was sweaty, and flushed for the next ten miles. That was a part of my education and a learning experience I would have happily missed.

I know that most of the buses now have automatic transmissions, but later, after I saw how a 'hill lock' worked on Studebakers I wondered why in the world all the smart people in charge of buses that hauled people in hilly areas didn't pass a law that required a hill lock. I guess that would be pretty much the same as never putting a railroad barricade up until ten people have been killed at that crossing. Go Figure.

Camp Wahsega was something to behold. I must have been all of maybe twelve years old, and to eat three meals a day in a cafeteria was something I didn't know people could do. The food was good, as far as I could tell. We were assigned to cabins, and the beds were metal folding cots with a mattress for us to put our own sheets and a blanket on. The shower rooms and commodes were things I didn't know much about, so I watched what others were doing. I think it was a case of the blind leading the blind.

I already knew how to swim, and so, after passing the swimming test, everybody swam two or three times a day, using the buddy system. They really knew what they were doing on that score. At unexpected moments the lifeguard would give a blast on the whistle, and you had better be able to grab your buddies hand and lift it high in the air. Just a little bit of tardiness, and both of you were out of the water for at least thirty minutes.

We had classes in everything from rocks to native flowers, and went hiking for what seemed like several miles up and down the mountains. The distance didn't bother me, but what did bother me was that I never could get oriented to where things were in those mountains. For all I knew, they could have had us walking in circles most of the time, even the sun didn't seem to ever be in the right place. I do know that it was a memorable week, and the experience was something to cherish.

The next year, I got to go again and I seem to recall it was even more fun than the first year, since I was a returning camper. More fun yes, but not the rush of discovery I had the first year. Those were the first chances to be somewhere, that by my standards, PO was not an operative word!!

During the years I was in the 4 - H Club other things happened that were "builders" for me. Members were expected to do at least one project per year. Mr. Pogue, the assistant county agent, encouraged me to develop a grain-treating model for Blue Lupine as a demonstration. If I had known exactly what he had in mind, I may have looked for something else. Anyway, I got the model finished, and a script for the demonstration. Then he had me present it to the local Farmer's Club at the schoolhouse, which went very well, since I knew all the people there. I thought the whole thing was finished. Ho, Ho....the next thing I knew, he let me hold a real surprise. He told me on Monday he was picking me up on Thursday night to give the same demonstration to some men's club in Waynesboro, the county seat. I don't know if it was Rotary or Kiwanis, or who, but I do know that it seemed like everybody who was somebody in the county was there. I was the only one there who qualified as "PO". The only one I knew well enough to talk to, aside from Mr. Pogue, was Mr. Gnann, the county school superintendent.

You have heard of rubber chicken dinners, I guess that could have been rubber chicken, damn if I knew for sure. I pretty well had myself under control I thought, until I heard the president introduce me. I got up, and put my demonstration on the table in front and started going through the steps.

The only problem was that while I was talking, I forgot to breathe. All I could do was talk with the air I had in my lungs. I just knew I was going to fall dead from lack of air. Finally, it was time to either “fess up or fall down”, so I took a step back, took a breath and told them, “I don’t think I have to tell you I’m scared to death, and my knees won’t stop knocking”. With that I got a genuine sympathetic laugh from the group. Thank God! I felt better and I stepped back up and finished the presentation.

Now that was a learning experience of the first order. I will never forget Mr. Gnann coming up and talking to me, after the formal meeting part of the program was over. He had a very deep voice and he stretched every word out the farthest I have ever heard by anybody. He smiled and said,

“Weeeellllllll Goooooorrrdddon, I saaaaaw yoooou geeeettttiiiinnnnnggggg in thaaaaattttt meeeeess buuuuuttttt I diiiiiiiddddnnnnnn’tttttt knnnnnoooooowwwww hoooooowwwww to heeeellllpppp yoooouuuuu, Buuuuuttttt whhhhaaaaattttt yoooooouuuuuuu diiiiidddd wooorrrrrkkkkkeeeedddd juuuuuussssstttttt fiiiiinnnnnneeeee.”

Translated that meant, “Well Gordon, I saw you getting in that mess, but I didn’t know how to help you, but what you did worked just fine.”

Happy hooray horseshit, there I was dying and he let me do it. Fortunately, public speaking does get much easier with practice. You just have to start somewhere, and that was a memorable beginning for me!! All the operettas and school plays I was in may have helped to some extent, but good buddy, I was a shriveled puppy from that experience!!

Other things that helped me were opportunities to enter poultry judging and livestock judging contests at various places. I generally scored extremely well, and each opportunity was another notch in my experiences.

* * *

Maybe there really are no fires to put out in camp cabins late at night, but we pretended we didn't know that. I went to Camp Laura S. Walker forestry camp down near Waycross, Georgia. It was another low budget operation I'm sure. That didn't bother me, even a low budget for most people was more than I felt we had. We were supposed to ride the Trailways bus to Waycross and be picked up at the bus station. Mama and Daddy bought me a ticket, and put me on the bus in Sardis. I rode that bus to Waynesboro, got off, cashed in the ticket, got a map and started hitch hiking. Since there was a layover for the bus in Augusta, or Macon or somewhere of several hours, I hoped to be able to beat the arrival time by going direct. It worked; I got into Waycross several hours ahead of the schedule and walked the last little way to the bus station to wait for counselors from the camp to pick us up. When the others arrived, I just melted into the crowd and nobody caught on.

We had good food, and what I thought were good cabins. I had never seen what I learned later were things called Bahamian shutters. So we are all on the same page, that meant the windows had screens in them, but there was a sloping roof over each window to keep the rain out. We had all sorts of demonstrations about tree planting, and controlled burning and ways of back firing, fire safety, and whatever.

I had no idea, nor did anyone else that we were going to be given a test at the end of the camp, but we were. There were prizes for the top three places, and since I had scored the highest, I got to choose first. The choices were somewhat directed toward what I suppose suppliers were willing to donate. I had a choice of a five gallon back pumper for knocking down a fire line, a chopping rake made from a short mowing machine blade, and a double bitted axe. I chose the five-gallon back pumper. The award was given the last night before camp was over early the next morning.

The temptation was just too much for me. There were fifteen cabins, with eight boys per cabin, all of which had those Bahamian shutters. None of the cabins had any electricity to them, and the only light in the cabins after dark was from flashlights. If we had to go to the bathroom, we used a flashlight to get to it since it was central to about half of the cabins. Late that night, my cabin organized a little expedition with my prize as the star attraction. We filled the back pumper with water, put the single stream nozzle rather than the sprinkler nozzle in place, and went to the farthest cabin. I had the pumper strapped on my back. I hit about four of the screens on the cabin with several good pump strokes of water. The distance the water would travel was about twenty-five feet. It didn't take but about a minute before the place was alive with screaming and swearing. We took off at high speed, but very quietly, and went to the next cabin, and the next, until we got about ten of the cabins. We emptied all of them and the woods were full of screaming kids looking for somebody, but they didn't know who was friend or foe. We got back to our cabin, and sprayed two of our own windows to throw off the counselors, and after draining the pumper, joined the "search".

Of course we were as innocent as angels, and fooled all but one of the counselors. He came looking for me, checked my pumper, and even though it was empty, he knew. He took me aside and told me, "You have caused enough hell and confusion for one night. It was a pretty damned good plan, just don't mess with my sleep again." He never said anything about it to anybody else as far as I knew.

The next morning, they took us in to Waycross to catch the buses back home. I just sneaked out a side door, and 'thumbed' my way back home. Hitch hiking with a five-gallon back pump must have looked pretty strange, but nobody who gave me rides asked about it.

Years later when I was in the Air Force, I found myself in downtown San Francisco with a parachute, and I did get some strange stares and questions about having a parachute slung over my shoulder riding a city bus. Mama and Daddy never knew about my hitch hiking experience until long after I returned from the Air Force, which was a long time from being fourteen years old.

* * *

Visiting Abraham Baldwin Agricultural College [ABAC] was an experience that was valuable for a PO youngen. About 1947 Dean was discharged from the Air Force, and with the GI Bill, he returned to ABAC in Tifton, Georgia. Before he had enlisted, he had completed two quarters. Working as much as he could to pay expenses, and after getting so far in debt that he didn't know of any way he could ever pay off the fifty dollars he owed, he enlisted. About two quarters after he returned, he asked me if I wanted to come down and stay with him for a few days. I was just about fifteen then, and Mama and Daddy agreed for me to go, and again bought me a ticket. I did the old "sell the ticket and thumb" routine, but buddy some of the roads to Tifton Georgia from Waynesboro were lonesome ole roads. I learned "the shortest distance between two places" was one thing, but if nobody was on those "short distance" roads, and the few who were wouldn't stop to let you ride, it could quickly become the "longest distance."

I have never asked Dean if he had to pay anything for me to stay with him but I don't think so. It seems to me that I slept in whatever bed in the dorm was vacant. I ate in the dining hall, but again, I didn't pay, and whether or not he did, I just don't know. My bet is he had some friends who just looked the other way.

Man, was that trip and visit an experience. I met a gal who was a student, naturally much older than my fifteen years, she was probably eighteen, with more equipment than I had ever seen on one person before. It was summer and everyone just naturally gravitated toward the swimming pool and that's where I met her. Her bathing suit showed about as much of her as any suit in that era could, and still cover something.. She seemed very willing to engage in some horseplay in the pool, and I know she wasn't fool enough not to know that every "feel" I got caused the water to boil around me. No, I couldn't do anything about it, but it felt so goooood, it hurt.

I really think that trip took the mystery out of college for me, and I could see that just regular people were there. Not that it made much difference; I didn't have, and saw no way, to get any money for college. But still, It was an important thing for me to experience and I honestly think some of the best recruiting of PO students, who have the intellect to do college work, could be done by somehow arranging a week's experience of shadowing a student at a college like that one. That will work as long as they have really knowledgeable financial aid advisors to let them know college is not financially out of the question for them. Something that hasn't been done well enough to let the PO and forgotten students have a real shot at college.

On the way back home, I followed the advice of Dean, the master hitchhiker, and thumbed on more traveled highways. It was much faster, and involved a lot less hiking!!! Didn't tell Mama and Daddy about that thumbing excursion either. Had they heard about one of my rides they probably would have "done a sideways brick." I don't know exactly where I was on the way home, but an old Pontiac pulled up by me and stopped. The four men in it looked about like I usually did when I was working. Dirty overalls, chewing tobacco, which I didn't use, and just generally disreputable. But...they were riding and I wasn't! It was a four-door car, and one of the men in the back seat slid over and I sat next to the passenger side rear door. Man, those were some "happy" people, in fact they kept getting even happier, and faster than I wanted them to. The way I knew what was happening was they started passing a half-gallon jug of "White Lightning" around. On the guess that it had been full when they started, I figured they were about "Three sheets in the wind, or half gassed" since about half the jug was gone. This was long before anybody really said anything about the driver not drinking with his buddies, so on the next passing, he got his turn at the jug, which was the second snort since I got in the car. When it came to the back seat I was fortunate they didn't push for me to have a drink. That stuff was usually about hundred to a hundred fifty proof, and that was strong enough to blow the top of your head off. I had been working on good reasons for not joining in, if they had insisted. They were going to go through one little town, and on to another, which was directly on my route home. However, I started thinking I needed a good reason for getting out as quickly as possible, particularly after the second passing of the jug. I noticed the driver was having more and more trouble staying on his side of the road. What's more, I was hearing more rowdy whooping and hollering than I thought was good for me. It was one thing if it was somebody you knew, but I didn't know that redneck crew and I wanted out. I made up a fairly slick lie and got out in the next town, thanking them "mightly" for the ride.

* * *

CHAPTER XII

SANDBED TRANSPORTATION

PO transportation covers a lot of topics, but none of the means of travel actually costed much either in terms of 1935 dollars, or even in today's dollars. You have already heard enough about mules to know that the country PO had a very close relationship with them. About the only thing I can even slightly remember other than gasoline vehicles, and that damned old two-mule wagon, was that we did have an old open one-mule buggy. What I don't remember was whether or not we also had an old car at the same time.

Though I can't remember what year it was, I do remember an old car, probably a model T Ford, with canvas side curtains. It seems to me we made one trip of about forty miles in it to Thomson, Georgia to see an Aunt who had been living there for a thousand years. After that, the first closed sedan automobile I can recall was a black, 1932 Chevrolet with little louvers on each side of the hood. Again, it was so early in my life, I don't know exactly but it must have been about 1938 or 1939. When we got it driving around in a gas vehicle was pretty much a luxury. Even when gas was anywhere from 16.9 cents to 21.9 cents per gallon, we didn't just go in and fill the tank. In fact, I don't think we ever got a whole tank full of gas. The usual was a half dollar's worth, and at most, we would get five gallons. After that '32 Chevy came an old four door 1936 Chevrolet which we had through World War II.

Somewhere in there one of my brothers, Clifford, the one who is about eight years older than I am, bought an old 1928, one ton Chevrolet truck. He had bought it from an old man who seemed to have some real problems of a nature we always called strange but I never heard anybody put a real name to. Anyway, in the interest of not getting sued, let's say Clifford named the old truck "Finch", after the man he bought it from. That was in late 1941 or early 1942, and not long before he went into the Army. He had dropped out of school, and was working, so he had to have some way to get to work. Deferments from World War II service were out of the question for people like us, and when the U.S. got into the war, we knew he would be drafted just as soon as he was old enough and it was legal. He was drafted the day that he turned eighteen and was old enough, gone in a heartbeat, but he did leave his old truck "Finch" on the farm.

That truck was five years older than I was, but it was a piece of work. From the best we could tell it had been a jail truck. It had a factory built wooden bed, with benches where the prisoners sat when they were picked up in Augusta, Ga. That thing had a four-speed transmission, which meant it was almost like a tractor when it was in the "granny" gear. Something else that was unusual to me was a "spark advance" on the steering column, and a hand set throttle on the opposite side, just like a tractor. It was quite a powerful truck, even if it had only four cylinders.

At a pretty young age Clifford had already learned to do more drinking than he needed to, and ole "Finch" seemed to protect him from himself. Meaning it had big truck tires, which helped to get out of various predicaments that might just come from nowhere and "attack that PO child." I swear to this day I believe Clifford loved that old truck better than any woman he ever chased, and that's saying a lot since I have yet, to this day, seen a man have so many women so interested in doing anything they could imagine he wanted done. He didn't even have to ask, they just offered, and remember, we are talking about the "pre - loose" generation here.

Anyway, Clifford went into the army, and after a brief training period, he was assigned to the 10th Mountain Infantry, the ski troopers, and according to him, also known as mountain goats. There must have been some great logic to that assignment, but we couldn't figure it out. He had probably never seen snow but once in his life, maybe. He was a Sandbed born and raised flatlander. I think the real reason was they were still using burros and donkeys and mules as pack animals when they were climbing mountains and Clifford knew enough about mules. Yep, he knew enough to be damned sure he wanted nothing to do with them, but war is hell, burros, donkeys and mules not withstanding.

Finch became the beast of burden for Dean and me during Clifford's absence, I don't ever remember Daddy getting in the cab even once. The reason he never wanted to even sit in that old truck was he didn't want anybody to start making comments that he was taking on traits of old Finch who was almost certifiable for the 'sylum' in Milledgeville. I started driving "Finch" when I was about nine or ten years old, not on the county roads, even though they were dirt, but on the field roads. One of my earliest recalls of working that old truck was hauling Citrons from the fields for the hogs and cows. If you don't know what a Citron is, it is not a strange looking little French car, rather it looks almost exactly like a watermelon. It just never ripens, but hogs in particular love them. And cows will eat them. Funny thing they always came up as volunteer plants, which mean they reseeded themselves by just coming up. We could haul five or six loads off every ten acres, usually after the first frost.

That business of loading old Finch with Citrons made work almost fun. I'd fire him up, and go down to the field to get started. I'd line the truck up where I thought it would go without me at the steering wheel. Then I'd put the transmission in neutral, and try to guess where the hand throttle on the steering wheel should be set be for "granny gear" to be about equal to my loading speed for citrons. That was mostly one major guessing game, sometimes you'd win, and sometimes you'd lose. When you lost it was damned hard to catch a one-ton truck if it had much of a head start. Anyhow, when things were adjusted just right, I'd get out and "scald it" to grab all the citrons on both sides of the truck, and sling them into the body just as fast as possible. Grabbing from both sides meant about a forty-foot path. Usually about two trips up and down the field was more than enough to load the body down to where Finch was moaning and groaning, so I would jump back in the cab, take over the throttle and head for the hog and cow lot. Man, driving Finch like that could've made a workaholic of dumb people like me, except I wasn't quite that dumb!!!

Clifford came home from Italy, and Austria, and on a thirty-day furlough before he was to leave for the invasion of Japan. He had been slightly wounded two times while in Italy, and another brother, Herbert, had also been slightly wounded twice as well, while he was in France and Germany. At that time Clifford was the major worry since he was about to be sent to the Far East. They both experienced the true terror and nightmares of war. They had made it through Europe without serious injury but Clifford still lives with those nightmares, and will for as long as he lives. What the hell would you expect, give an eighteen year old a Browning automatic rifle and put him on the front lines all through Italy, up to Austria? The life expectancy of an automatic rifleman was about thirty seconds.

I know that as a kid, during the years from 1941 to 1945, my life was hell also. I, and we, all were constantly worried about getting one of those damnable telegrams that said, “We regret to inform you....” As cruel as I can be about a lot of things, just writing about no more of it than this almost makes me emotionally lose it. Man were we glad when they got home. Without a doubt, many families in Japan and Germany suffered massive anguish, and I can honestly say, “I feel your pain”. I can, and must, also say honestly again, that if President Truman had withheld the use of the atomic bomb, and I had lost my brothers in that invasion, I would have never forgiven him. I think he knew the depth of emotions that would have confronted him if he had wavered.

Thinking back over the World War II situation, and how my family was affected almost frightens me to realize the intensity of my recall, and we were comparatively stoic. Just writing about a damned old truck dragged out some frazzled deep-seated emotions about my brothers and their safety. For that reason, it is worthwhile to remind people that, maybe we often have suppressed many feelings in our minds. In some cases maybe it is fine to recall some of them but maybe in some others, it isn’t helpful.

Back to PO folks transportation. After the war ended, Clifford took over his beloved Finch, but he didn’t stay home for more than a month or two after he was discharged.

That 1936 Chevrolet four-door sedan that we had during the war was the family transportation and work vehicle for Daddy. It was a pretty decent car. It was the same car I sat in while Daddy and his brother had the hell raising about stealing and selling the milk from our cow, that is until he made me get out and walk home from the pine thicket. It was the same car I watched and waited for Mr. Bonnie to get his ass kicked because of another old cow jumping a fence. Daddy used that car like a truck to haul firefighting equipment through the woods for several years. We worked hard to keep it in good running condition. I think that was the best car Daddy ever had. It had been a valiant warrior, and had won many battles, but no car should be expected to really survive the sand beds and woods it was forever required to work in.

Daddy replaced it with an old 1940 International truck. That thing was a flat head six and it had a gear ratio really good for hauling fertilizer and other stuff in the fields. The major problem was you could never keep the manifold tight on the engine, and there were fumes in the cab no matter what you did. Another problem was that it vibrated so badly that the rear fenders were always tearing and coming off. It looked like shit, and it rode the same way. In fact, I think the designer used a two-mule wagon as his guide. Every time something went wrong we had to take it to Waynesboro, which was twenty miles away to get it repaired. Most often they had to order the part, and every repair was twice as expensive as any ordinary pickup would have been. Daddy decided to unload that sucker, I know you can't tell how broken up I was about that.

It must have been about 1946 when we got a 1940 Chevrolet half-ton pickup. That was the one I rented from Daddy to use measuring land. That truck had been owned by H. I. Willis, and was the same one Fonzie had jumped from at the cemetery when, thanks to the Willis brothers, he got closer to the deceased Mr. Hulmy than he really wanted to. Before we had gotten it Willie, my brother in law, married to my oldest sister, Evangeline, had owned it. He had his eye on another truck, so Daddy bought it from him. Talk about a truck that was hard to steer, I can't imagine a ten-ton Mack truck being that hard to turn. Willie had told Daddy about the problem, and also told him neither he nor any of the mechanics in the shop knew what was wrong and even though they had tried everything, they had failed to correct the problem.

That truck was still hard to drive as long as Daddy owned it and except for that, mechanically it was in good condition. When we got it, the inside was showing rust all over and was just plainly disreputable. There was no such thing as air conditioning in vehicles then, and it was so far in the future that the front windshield of the truck cranked out with a handle in the center of the dash. With the windows down, and the windshield cranked out, it kept the air moving fast enough to feel cooler, but air conditioning would have been better. I could see the handwriting on the wall, and knew that old truck was all we were going to have for the next four years. The only way it was going to be something even PO me would be willing to be seen in, as I approached the magic age of sixteen, was for me to make it nicer. I got my hands on some sand paper, and scrounged up the money to buy the best tan colored interior hard enamel for metal I could find. I sanded that cab until it was skinned clean, and applied about four coats of paint, giving it plenty of time to dry between coats, The door panels, the metal head liner, and the dash looked like "new" to me. I carefully repainted all the pedals, the gearshift, and the steering column black, and the job was done. A wooden body was needed to haul hogs and cows, and I built it from oak boards. I used a hand-powered brace and bit to make the holes for the bolts to put it together, painted it gloss black. It looked pretty good and I kept it as clean as a whistle. I don't think Daddy ever said how much better it looked, maybe he suspected my efforts were not altogether altruistic and he knew I was doing some long range scheming.

Before I got my driving license, I made many trips to the cattle sales with Daddy in that old pickup. He would come to school at 1:00 p.m. to get me, and we would go home and load hogs or cows, and take off for the livestock auction in Sylvania, Georgia, another little town about twenty miles away. I still have a small knot in my head where I was chasing a damned hog who refused to go up the loading chute and onto the truck. I hit the edge of a board on the hog pen and I saw stars for a few minutes, then I got a hand full of blood for my trouble. As soon as the solar system stopped whirling around , we finished loading the hogs and got underway.

After I got my drivers license, I was glued to that steering wheel. I had to use that old truck for dating, just as I knew I would. It took a hell of a lot of character, or something, for girls to be willing to go out in that pickup, even though it showed the work that had been lavished on it. I was still eaten up with envy and jealousy. Of the seven boys in my class, five had at least one good family sedan to drive. Several had a choice of new pickups, and in addition, one or two had ton and a half trucks. Three of them had big Harley Davidson or Indian “hogs” to ride.

Dammit, I couldn’t get a tractor, and didn’t really have a decent way to travel. At that time, knowing that at least three of them would not be getting a diploma would not have resolved the anguish and disgust I felt. There was only one thing that was immutable in my mind and that was.... PO IS HELL. I don’t care what color you are, if you start trying to tell me I don’t know about discrimination, stand waaaaay back away from me, or be ready to defend yourself, even today. If PO built character, I ended up with a damned skyscraper.

* * *

CHAPTER XIII

THINGS THAT DON'T FIT ANYWHERE ELSE

This is a story about Handler Bickman's upscale grocery store in Girard that was immortalized by my brother, Dean, in a speech class at college many years ago. You may be sure the names are entirely fictitious, in the interest of self-protection. His speech had to be extremely descriptive, and clear to the audience. The professor wanted vividly clear pictures of what the student was telling them about. I read the speech as written, and it was pretty tough. Be advised at this point, you may want to just skip this little episode if you have a weak stomach. Believe me I have not plagiarized Dean, I was there.

Handler's store was about thirty feet wide, and maybe forty feet deep. It was a wooden frame building, covered with vertically applied pieces of tin, and with a tin roof, and no ceiling at all. The only light in the store came from four lights, hanging by electrical cord, or the front door being open, and occasionally the back door. I never saw more than two of the lights turned on at any one time. The counter and cash drawer were on the left as you entered, and about twenty-five feet from the front door was a single white enameled meat case, facing the door. Between the meat case and the counter there was a big butcher block sitting where you had to walk around it to get to the shelves to buy canned goods, beyond the counter. There was some sawdust on the floor, sometimes, most likely after a blood spill, certainly not before.

Let me tell you there was no routinely scheduled floor cleaning of cow blood, or hog blood, and to the best of my knowledge there was no human blood there to clean up. However, the smell of rancid, rotting blood can get strong enough to almost burn the nasal passages unless you were around it every day and couldn't tell incrementally how the pungency had increased. Couple that with almost no air circulation unless the doors were open and the air would fairly hang just from that odor alone.

This was middle Georgia, without insulation and it was usually either too hot, or too cold. There was only one little trash burner for heat in the winter, and not even one fan for the hundred plus degree summers. Most of the store customers were field workers who were carrying the newest dirt on them from that day's work. That new dirt was a nice new coating over the accumulations of dirt from the past week's work, and maybe some night play as well. In the summer particularly, you could almost see the odors reaching for the sky. In the winter, the odor would just get a musky, soured smell and it seemed to linger near the floor and ground.

Handler was about at least six feet three inches tall, slim for his frame, but not skinny. His hair was salt and pepper gray from the time I could remember, and it always looked like he had been in the woods for about two months, meaning it wasn't dragging long, but it sure wasn't a buzz cut. I never saw the man when he was clean-shaven. It looked like he had about two weeks growth, but I never could figure out how it stayed the same length all the time. He chewed tobacco continuously, and pretty often a bit of the brown juice would trickle down into the beard from the bottom lip. Most often it stayed there, for God only knows how long.

Once you had seen his clothes, there was no reason for further comment. He never changed them until they were "stand alone" filthy. I was told he stripped them off, put on new ones and threw the old ones in a fire and burned them. He wore Khaki pants and shirts with white socks, at least they were white when he put them on. He wore them and wore them and wore them until something made him decide to put on another pair. I'm pretty sure he didn't wear undershirts, and I don't even want to contemplate whether or not he wore under drawers. I suspect all the bugs and insects applauded the burning of his filthy clothes because I can't help but think even they had some standards.

His eyes seemed to be perpetually red and red rimmed. While they weren't squinty, they weren't what you would ever call wide-eyed. If he ever had clean fingernails, it must have been in an earlier life. I seriously wonder if anybody could have paid any manicurist enough money to tackle a cleaning job on those hands, particularly if any thought were given about where they had been between supposed "wash ups". How old he was, I didn't know, and I'm not going to go to the graveyard to check it out now. If he was twenty-two, he was in bad to worse than bad shape, if he was sixty-two, he still looked like he had been trashed for many years.

When somebody came in to buy a piece of meat, they told him what they wanted and he would go over to the meat case and grab the leg, or whatever, and throw it on the chopping block. Never was there any indication that he may want to sweep or scrape the block, he might expose something that was resting quietly somewhere in the filth about the second or third layer down. He would just grab a knife that probably had been cleaned only when he wanted to remove the grease to sharpen it, and start cutting away. The only clean thing in the whole operation was the brownish red butcher paper he tore off the roll and pitched the meat slices onto. He would wrap the meat up, put a piece of string around it, weigh it, and tell them what the price was.

God forbid if he had a cold and a congested nose while he was cutting, or at any other time for that matter. Handler had big nostrils, probably from the constant stretching by his fingers. He thought nothing of ramming one of his fingers right up there to grab a nose oyster with his finger nail, or what ever it would stick to and yank out about a half inch catch. It took a strong stomach to watch him use a practiced 'flick' to get the "booger" off his finger. In those instances where it didn't go flying off to land on the floor, he had an automatic wiping motion that started just below his back pocket, and down his right leg to get it off his finger. You could easily have told he was right handed because the right hand side of his pants leg had a slick look to the fabric much faster than the "scum" build up on the left side, from all the wipes down the leg.

Another skill he had was something you may have seen performed by some people out in the open, who forgot their handkerchiefs. Sometimes folks who should know better also do it in places where they really ought to know better. That skill was his expert aim, demonstrated as he used either the right or left index finger to seal off one nostril and with great lungpower, clean the other. Usually the missile was a mass of yellowish green "snot" that hurled toward the floor at mach speed. Then he would casually wipe his hands on his pants, if he felt they need wiping, and resume working.

That was about all it took to get me out of the place. I don't know about you, but even with my usually granite strong stomach, just writing about that causes a squeamish feeling, and starts my stomach to roll a bit.

How hungry would you have to be to buy a piece of barrel cheese there after what I have just described? I swear he had a whole wheel of cheese in its box, covered with the wooden top and then, when somebody wanted a pound or two, he would pop the top off, grab a butcher knife and take a swipe. With those same dirty hands, he would put it on the paper, and wrap it up. I couldn't have eaten anything from that place that had not arrived in a sealed tin can, or in sealed plastic. If Handler had ever been close to it, I didn't want it.

Why did I know so much about that place? Good question,...it wasn't like I was there very often, I already knew how dirty he was, but I went occasionally just to watch. Hey, what do you expect, I was just a youngen? It was worse than bad. I think Mama or Daddy would rather have eaten razor blades than eat anything from that place. For a study in contrasts however, he had two sons that I knew of, and they were fastidiously clean and well dressed. His daughter was also clean, well dressed, nice, and intelligent. Handler's wife was one of the nicest, quietists, church-going people you would ever want to see. Apparently the Youngens followed her example. They were PO, but still not as PO as we were, but let me tell you that was one situation where I was not jealous, or envious of a one of them.

* * *

The Georgia style of buying votes was really pretty simple. Given that I have harped on being PO, can you imagine just how big a nickel looked to me, or what could be bought with a nickel in 1939, or 1940? A nickel had to be as big as a number three washtub, and a quarter, for my own, was about the size of a large wagon wheel. I didn't have much trouble with the size of either since nickels were as scare as hen's teeth, and quarters as scarce as an eight-year leap year.

Anybody who walked around with a lot of change in their pants was likely to be followed in the hopes their pockets would spring a hole. There was a man I didn't have to follow, and I didn't have to wait for the money to fall out of his pocket either. It was the county sheriff. At the time I thought he was just a very nice person, now I'm not so sure, maybe it was election time. Mr. O. J. Cliett was not only the sheriff, he was the "law" for Superior Court, and he and his family lived at the jail. His wife was in charge of the cooking for the prisoners. He never looked or talked like the sheriffs I had read about, or the few I had seen in the shoot'em up Westerns I had seen in the traveling tent movies that came to Girard about two times each year. Sheriff Cliett was too heavy, but well dressed, very soft spoken, wore glasses, and looked almost like an accountant. He may have been mean as hell, but Daddy never let on if he was.

Every time I ever saw the man, he had a pocket full of nickels, and he would give me one, not two, but one. Hell, I probably would have peed in my pants if I had gotten two. I was not the only one who got the nickel, if there was one, or ten kids, he gave every kid a nickel. Later, I thought back and decided if presidential elections limited the candidates to just a nickel for a vote, we could eliminate election donations and vote buying scandals, and have much less money changing hands for elections. The parents of us totally PO kids were watching those nickels going into our hands. He didn't even have to ask the Mamas and Papas to vote for him. I don't think he ever had anybody run against him until after I left home.

One thing for sure, when I heard he had somebody running against him while I was in Korea, I sent an airmail request for an absentee ballot. Yes, I voted for him, and if he were to run today, my vote for him was bought and paid for, with just a few nickels!!!

* * *

This little story is all about being just too good to a youngen. The more I read the paper, listen to television, hear people give extremely enlightened talks about teaching children right from wrong, and also being made to feel all parents should have a doctorate in psychology to raise decent kids, the more I am convinced we have too many idiots running their mouths and even more idiots listening to them. So far, it seems to me that the current generation is doing one hell of a lot worse job of being parents than their parents and grand parents and great grand parents did. I am convinced we have entirely too much conversation and explanation going on rather than demonstration. My children were trained pretty much the same way my siblings and I were. When you were told to stop in mid stride, if your foot was twelve inches off the ground, you held that foot up until you were told it was okay to put it down.

That was something like hearing “incoming” in Korea, no explanation was necessary, that meant instantaneous reactions because mortar rounds don’t wait for explanations. Now, in today’s world a committee meeting would have to be called to decide if it was appropriate to jump in a foxhole or not. You and I both know everything was not perfect from 1800 to 1950 on child rearing, but I am going to tell you about a PO family who was way ahead of their time. They would have fit perfectly into the 1970 to 2000 child psychology, psychobabble crap.

This is a story about Dandy Nixon. Dandy was about eight years older than I was.. He had a very hard working Daddy and Mama, and he, like me, was the youngest in his family. I think he only had one brother and one sister though. Dandy was treated like he was a privileged twenty five year old when he was fifteen. He drank too much beer and white lightning, and was driving illegally day and night, all over everywhere, in the process he managed to wreck about three cars before he was seventeen. Mr. Nixon and Ms. Nixon couldn't help but smile when they talked about their Dandy. Their precious Dandy could read their idiot smiles quickly, and he did. What he read however, was not what I would have heard and understood long before the first wreck. I knew my first bad mistake had better be the last, because I don't think my ass could have carried two of what I would have gotten. Neither Mama or Daddy made any "allowances" for the thought that "boys will be boys."

Since Dandy was being allowed to believe he could part the Red Sea, he soon started getting mean and began fighting and it kept getting worse with his boozing. In the meantime, his parents who didn't have much anyway, had to borrow money to get him out of one scrape after the other, and "Dandy just had to have another car." They eventually lost their farm. One night Dandy was in one of his drunken binge rages, when he ran up on a guy, Teddy, who had been raised a little too 'sissy', by a bunch of women.

Teddy didn't have a Daddy that I had ever heard about, but he was just a nice person as far as I ever knew. Dandy started his usual abusive tirade, and when Teddy tried to side step it, Dandy would have none of that and, suddenly, for no known reason Dandy pulled a pistol from his pocket and shot Teddy in the stomach. Teddy nearly died, but after about two months, he was released from the hospital. Don't start wringing your hands until you break your wrists, neither Dandy nor his Daddy ever hunted anything, so far as I know. We did and none of us ever shot anybody, in this country anyway.

Dandy went to Reidsville State Prison for seven years minimum. When he came home, he was a lot different, seems he ran into some guards and wardens who didn't do any explaining why things were going to be done, or not done, it was do it or die. He was a much better person for years. After he got back home, he told me Reidsville had a policy that prisoners who had shot someone were put in cells in the same general area as death row inmates. When they planned to use the electric chair known sometimes as "old smokey" or "Sparky", that he and others like him had to clean the death chamber, and clean the prep room of the hair shaved from the head of the condemned. After the electrocution, they had to clean the death chamber again and since all control over bodily functions were gone, there was much more to clean up. It also was something you didn't forget. I think that must have been before they started using plugs in the body orifices, stoppers, and whatever to contain the mess. But he told me he would never forget as long as he lived the odor of burned human flesh. He had finally gotten the message.

I don't think he was completely cured though, as long after I left the area, he did a "back slide" or fell back, and died from acute alcoholism. No, I can't prove that he wouldn't have gone off the deep end no matter what, but I can tell you that even if my Mama and Daddy didn't engage in a lot of hugging and kissing between themselves and us Youngens that I ever saw, all of us Youngens knew they were doing their dead level best to give us good strong values.

* * *

Hallucinogenic substances were things I knew nothing about, but I did learn about green pecans and rabbit tobacco. Before we ever knew about the bad kinds of drugs out there, even in the backwoods of Georgia, it was considered a bad thing if people used morphine when it wasn't absolutely necessary. I knew of only one person who was supposed to be "taking something." Until recently, when I read about ""huffing" of all sorts of substances, did I realize just how close I could have come to something really bad happening to me. I enjoyed the smell of raw regular gasoline as it was being pumped into the gas tank. Not only was I smelling that odor, I later discovered that the four to six milliliters of tetraethyl lead [TEL] which is liquid lead, when combined with the gasoline fumes could have really done bad things to me. What is that old saying, "Too late we get smart?" Nobody had ever told us about the dangers of inhaling fumes, Hell, I didn't have a clue that Oleanders were deadly when burned, and there were about four big bushes around the yard. We regularly burned the dead leaves from them, guess I didn't get downwind and in the smoke.

Many Youngens who grew up in the country, and couldn't get their hands on Sir Walter Raleigh, or Prince Albert tobacco in a can, would settle for some Rabbit tobacco and rolling paper. When I first tried smoking, it was Rabbit tobacco rolled in brown paper from a grocery sack. One thing was for sure, that was not about to be addictive, at least for me. Looking back there may be a question about whether or not it was the burning brown paper, or the "tobacco" that had such a horrible taste. I think it was probably a combination of both. Rabbit Tobacco grows about eighteen to twenty four inches high on what looks like a stick slightly less than a quarter of an inch in diameter. The leaves are about one fourth inch wide and one and a half inches long, all attach directly to the main stem of the plant, and when they were dry and ready for smoking, they were brown on one side, and grayish white on the other. You had a choice of either crumbling them, or just rolling them into a cigarette. As far as I was concerned, a cigarette made from that crap would give you one hell of a sore throat, without inhaling, from just one cigarette. My smoking life would have been real short if Rabbit tobacco had been the only thing available.

I also tried to dip snuff, once and only once. I was about nine years old and to this day I still say the same thing, " God! How could anybody use that stuff?" My Grandma dipped Railroad brand snuff. Naturally I just had to sneak a "dip" of hers and try it out. The experience was just as bad as Rabbit Tobacco, except that I couldn't really get rid of that dark brown taste, even after "renching" my mouth with water. I think I would rather have chewed ground up mule shit.

When I started pitching baseball at school, I made one more try at using tobacco products. I was having some real problems with the game, first off I was a left handed pitcher without much speed, the ball speed was a hell of a lot closer to fifty miles per hour than it was to a hundred miles per hour. Second, if any of my pitches curved, it was because of a defect in the baseball. Third, left-handed pitchers are likely to be wild, and I was giving new definition to "out of control." Let me tell you though, I was committed to doing my dead level best to gain control. Somehow I had an idea that if I got me a plug of tobacco and got on the mound, then control would come. Well sir, not only did control not come, but dizzy, dizzy and dizzier did come. My heart rate went crazy, my eyes wouldn't focus, and my stomach was pitching, churning and raising hell. That was one long walk from the ball field back to the school buildings that day, what seemed like five miles was actually about two hundred yards!!! Hell, I was a total failure at three things, smoking rabbit tobacco, dipping snuff, and biting a plug off Brown Mule chewing tobacco. The only success I had was being able to smoke Prince Albert tobacco and roll my own. That was, when Daddy and Mama weren't in position to catch me.

About the weirdest thing I ever experienced came from green pecans. It is not my intent to start a trend of raiding pecan orchards while the nuts are still on the tree and just before the hulls fall off the pecans on the tree, but it might just start a trend anyway. We had about ten pecan trees near the house, and we used the nuts for everything, like in cakes, in a design on the chocolate icing on cakes, in candy, in cookies, and roasted. But one of the best uses was to fill a pocket, and while walking along take them out and crack them, one against the other. We could walk along, pick them out and eat'm along the way. The old crop from the year before had usually been used up long before the new ones fell, or were shaken from the tree. We would climb the big old trees, and get high enough up on small limbs and commence to stomping the limb as hard as we could to make the pecans fall. It was natural to want to rush the crop of pecans a little bit by looking for nuts with hulls that looked like they were nearest to opening and dropping the new crop of nuts. By using fingernails it was possible to shuck the nut from the hull, crack, and eat the not quite ready, green, nut. If you got them too early, the green meats had a slightly milky juice. Well, one-day temptation got the better of me, and I was eating on some juicy "green pecans". Mama saw what I was doing, and she told me I'd better quit, which I did. Oh, how I wished I hadn't messed with them, I felt a little funny, but it was nearly night, and supper was coming up shortly after she told me to quit eating them. Anyway, I didn't think anything more about it because eating a big meal was always a good cure for anything I had anyway. Now, while I know correlation doesn't prove causation, I also know I had a night of totally wild nightmares, that involved flashing lights, and things I had never thought of before or since. Rightly or wrongly, I made the connection with green pecans and in retrospect, felt they had acted as an hallucinogenic, even though I didn't know the word at that time. I don't want anymore green pecans.

I know one other thing for sure, about green nuts on trees, if you want to have a game warden on your case in a hurry, get some black walnuts while they are still in their green hulls, take a hammer and bruise the hulls some, then put them in a burlap bag, tie the top and put them in a fishing hole with little water current. That will knock fish out almost as fast as telephoning them. In case you don't know about telephoning fish, you probably don't need to, but the old hand crank telephones, with two wires in the water, and some rapid grinding would knock fish out long enough for you to scoop them up. That was not sport fishing, even in back woods Georgia.

Why in the world anybody intentionally uses LSD, or other mind-altering drugs has always been a mystery to me. I guess I have always been a control freak, especially when it comes to my mind and any alterations to my thinking processes.

Maybe there was another reason I have never done drugs, like having a vivid imagination. Yes, I did have one that was and is vivid! In the country, visiting neighbors was ordinary and expected. It wasn't unusual, especially in warm weather, for several families to just stop by and everybody would sit on the front porch and talk about nearly anything, however, sex was not included. It was always a little after dark that, as the youngest, I would be sent to bed. A lot of good that did, my bedroom window opened to the front porch and I could hear every word. That was when all the ghost stories started, and I mean some wild and strange stories would be flying around and the natural tendency was, as you would expect, that the next person had to tell a more implausible tale than the last person. There I was, about eight or nine years old, listening to all that trash. The hair on the back of my neck would stand straight up and I would begin shaking all over. Every nerve ending in my entire body must have been at attention.

Finally one night in particular, I drifted off to sleep, and immediately stepped into the stories that were being told. In my dream, I was in one hell of a mess, being chased by a ghost and all sorts of worse than bad demons. I started screaming and hollering and raising more hell than a peg legged man stuck in a row of postholes. That wasn't the only nightmare I had from some of those sessions. Who, in their right mind, would want to purposely take something to cause that kind of distress? But, if you were PO you didn't need anything more that some accomplished ghost taletellers!!!!

* * *

Few people under fifty have any concept of what it was like to live without electricity for lights, or heat, or just to operate appliances. Living in sand bed hell meant not being able to have so many of the things that would have made life so much easier. By not having electric power, we couldn't have "running" water unless we had a gasoline engine to drive the pump, or a windmill with a five hundred to one thousand gallon tank over twenty feet off the ground. No running water piped to the house meant we had to have a wash place with wash basins and it also meant having ten quart water pails and a long handled gourd for a dipper for drinking water, cooking water, and dish washing. To wash ourselves, we had to go to the well, and draw water to fill either foot tubs, or washtubs. That was one hell of a way to live in the mid twentieth century.

That same gourd dipper was used to fill the washbasins for hand washing and for drinking water from the ten-quart water bucket. We all used, and drank from the same dipper. Instead of having a sink in the kitchen, we again had to have buckets of water to use in the dishpans and rinsing pans. Those same kitchen buckets were used for water for cooking. At one time, we had a fifty gallon wooden barrel on the back porch, which we filled with water so it could be dipped into smaller buckets. I was about six years old when I ended that, or caused serious rethinking of that practice. There was always a wooden cover that fit tightly on the barrel to keep mice, or other small animals out. Nobody had reckoned with what I did. At the dinner table one day, someone noticed short dark brown hair floating in the water and iced tea glasses. Everybody was trying to decide just where that hair could be coming from. Very innocently, truly, truly, truly, I said "Maybe it came from "Rattler", our dog. There was a dead silence, while everyone seemed to be holding their breath, waiting to hear more. I continued, but nobody was drinking tea, "We were talking about dogs having to learn how to swim, and I didn't think Rattler could, so I put him in the barrel to see if he knew how, but he could swim." It was all in innocence, so I didn't get anything more than a scolding, and the job of cleaning out the barrel!

There were so many things we needed electricity for, so why didn't we have electricity? We were in the sand beds, plain and simple. Our house was nine tenths of one mile from the last pole Georgia Power had in Girard. Daddy tried every way he knew to get them to extend the line. The answer was always the same, it was too expensive to run the line for so few houses. Daddy joined a group, which must have numbered about forty houses over about ten miles, who didn't have electricity either. Georgia Power rejected the petition out of hand, simple economics we were told.

Enter the Rural Electrification Act [REA]. A cooperative was in the process of being formed, and just as things were looking good, guess who we saw, could it be Georgia Power? It was just plainly amazing how much more profitable that section of the sand beds had become. I know Daddy and Mama told them to go stuff it, and so did most of the others. Don't ever say anything bad about

REA to me. There wouldn't be electricity through that section of PO country now if that cooperative had not been formed. So in the late summer of 1948, we had the old house wired. It wasn't the most complete job every done, but it was purely luxurious beauty to me.

All we had was a sixty ampere service entrance fuse box, surface mounted on the wall, with one receptacle in each room, except for the dining room where we had one for the radio and one for the refrigerator. The lighting circuit supplied one bare electric bulb in the dead center of each room, hanging from the electric, romex cable. One extra line was run to the well for a pump, and a washing machine.

I was the happiest person you have ever seen digging a trench to put a cast iron pipe into the kitchen, to a sink at the washstand, and the cow and mule lot. Life was suddenly much better. It didn't happen until 1950, but a commode was put in, and I personally put a ton of screws through galvanized tin to build a homemade shower. I didn't get to see the rest of the changes until after I returned from Korea in 1952. We never took the bucket off the old well, it was a standby in case the pump failed, but we seldom had to use it. Life was changing - Thank God!!!

* * *

PO folks and their families had to scrape in every direction to make it. Daddy kept trying every way possible. One job was as a wagon driver delivering Coca Cola syrup. At that time Coca Cola was an upstart company, and it was having cash problems, so they couldn't meet payroll. They called Daddy at Buxton's store, almost the only phone in the area, and told him if he would keep on delivering they would pay him in stock. He had already been taken to the cleaners by the depression and bank closings, so he told them to send somebody for their wagon and team, because he was tying them up at a tree outside the store and going home. According to my brother, Dean, who researched it much later, just the stock he would have gotten would have been worth about a million dollars approximately sixty years later. Again, "Too late we get smart"!!!

If the stories are correct, Daddy most likely became a city marshal, a superior court bailiff, and a part time deputy sheriff because he was a failure at drinking. The story he told on himself was that he got roaring, puking drunk the first time he tried to drink, and really had the dry heaves "bad" before it was over. He made a solemn pact with the Massa, that's God in case you don't know, that if he would just let him live, he'd never drink again. He lived, and I never knew of his ever having another drink. Every one of his sons drank to varying degrees, and some had many more degrees than they should have.

Daddy's little try with liquor was also most likely, part of the reason he worked with the "revooners" tearing up stills in the woods. Given the hunting he did, he knew every road, path, and branch in the entire county, and he could find stills any time. I never knew when he was getting paid to be a marshal, or deputy and when he wasn't but he seemed to be going out at some strange hours most of my early life. If he was a zealot about anything, his crusade against booze was it. Maybe his support of old Gene Talmadge in all his elections was another. He never had any inkling that folksy "Ole Gene" with his signature red galluses and wool hat, was a law graduate from the University of Georgia, and most of his "down home" behavior was a damned act.

The job he had for nearly fourteen years was a seasonal forest fire warden in the southern section of the Burke County. At first, he was paid mileage for his old 1936 Chevrolet. Many times I rode to school with him, sitting with my feet wrapped around the five gallon back pack fire pumps and flaps, while he was on the way to the fire tower. Flaps were rectangular flat rubber pieces, which looked like small sections of a conveyor belt, attached to what looked like a hoe handle. It was used to slap out fire on a forest fire line.

Later they furnished him with a half-ton fire truck, it was painted fire engine red, with a flashing red light, and a siren that was about two feet long. The truck had six back pumps, about ten flaps and rakes, and an engine driven pump to provide pressure for pumping water from its hundred and ten gallon tank. After he got that truck, I enjoyed going with him to fight fires. The enjoyment was heightened even more when I got to be sixteen, and Daddy let me drive. The county forestry service had a small Piper Cub airplane as a spotter to back up the fire towers all over the county. At random hours of the day, the pilot would be flying to spot fires that were just starting. While I always jabbered with the pilot on the radio, I remember one particular time, he made radio contact with us and told us to really put the pedal to the metal and get to a place where he was watching a guy going through the woods setting a fire line. I was driving, and Daddy was riding shotgun. I flipped the switch on the red light, but that was mainly just showing off, there was no traffic anyway. I had "red lined" all four gears getting all that weight up to full speed, and we were moving about sixty miles per hour on deeply rutted sand bed roads.

We saw a car ahead, and with Daddy's approval, I flicked the switch on the siren a good four hundred yards behind the old car. There was a sudden almost right angle turn, and the old car hit the three foot deep sand ditch. By the time I got fairly close Daddy said, "That's old Sizemore". Sure enough, as we passed, he was shaking his fist and I know he was swearing and calling us every low life bastard name he could think of. We couldn't stop so I don't know how he got out of the ditch. That tickled the hell out of me and Daddy was laughing so hard he started coughing. We got there in time to catch the fool spreading the fire, and put it out before it burned more than ten acres. I guess idiot boy didn't think anybody in the plane could see him.

Daddy didn't let me drive because I was a better driver, he just wanted to give me some experience, and some enjoyment too. If he were still alive, and had the reflexes he had when I was twelve to sixteen years old, I could almost assure you of racing stripes in your drawers if you rode shotgun with him in the woods. How many times I saw him aim that old car, or the fire truck between two trees at about twenty five miles per hour and I just knew there was no way it was going to fit. If he ever put a scratch on either side, I never saw it or heard it, but I will tell you this, 20-25 miles per hours doesn't seem fast until you see a pine tree or oak tree zipping past the window about three inches away. More times than not, I had moved so far toward the center of whatever vehicle we were in that a really big man could have sat between me and the door by the time the ride was over. Damn, it scared me, and he would be smoking, and driving with one hand, and appeared to be looking off to the right or left, everywhere except at that damned cowpath road. Scarey? Hell yes, Fun? Hell yes!

We fought fires all over the southern part of the county, any time of the day, or night, but mostly for me, on nights and weekends. I knew about crown fires, that's when the fire is in the top of the trees and jumps from one tree to the other, but fortunately we never had one of them. I saw one in California one time, and it was scarey as hell. Several times, the winds were so high we had to work like hell to get us and the truck out and hightail it to another road to back fire. On the really bad fires, we would have to call in the crawler tractors to cut firebreaks and backfire, and then watch for hot spots for hours.

I was climbing fire towers from the time I was ten. They are of varying heights, but our county towers were one hundred two feet tall, with first set of steps going up about twenty feet to a landing about six feet long, and then another set of steps going up did the same, and that kept on until you got to the observation room at the top. In that flat country, you could see forever with just an elevation like that.

During the period of time that I was climbing the tower I really did a stupid thing, and Daddy let me do it. I can't recall my exact age, but we had climbed to the top, and the trap door to the observation room was "slammed shut and stuck". There was no way to get the thing open no matter what we did. I had the brilliant idea of climbing out underneath the observation room, grabbing the safety railing around the observation room platform, and climbing over it to get to the trap door from above. I did it, but after I got that trap door open, "Mr. Scared" walked in on me; I was weak as a kitten. Best thing I could think about that stupidity was that I didn't freeze and lock down about half way through it. Daddy never mentioned what I had done to anybody, and I damned sure didn't think I needed to brag about that level of stupidity. Sometimes PO folks who aren't ordinarily stupid can have a lapse!

I will never forget Mr. Will Quick who lived at the tower and worked with Daddy in later years. Mr. Will was a fairly large man, much too large to be as afraid of everything as he professed to be. His favorite expression for many of his funny stories about where he was scared because of something or another was, "Feets you better take care of my body". Another conversation he frequently had with his feet, according to him was "Feets, if you don't take care of my body, I ain't going to buy you no new shoes!" His wife, Miz Pearl, was a good, kind and well thought of woman, who climbed the fire tower anywhere from three to five times each day during fire season as a spotter, and tower telephone and radio operator.

Daddy's part time jobs, along with what we were able to do on the old farm made it possible for us to weather the official depression, and as I said earlier, our own private depression until 1950. PO folks who want a way to make a living will struggle at everything and every way to eke one.

* * *

CHAPTER XIV

GOODBYE TO THE SANDBEDS AND HELLO TO A FUTURE

It was time to say goodbye to the sandbeds. Staff Sergeant Bass, U. S. Army, drove an old silver and black Plymouth and as recruiter, he really didn't have to work very hard. It was about May 1950, and Korea was just beginning to get dangerously warm. In fact by the middle of June it was hot as hell, and the North Koreans and the Chinese were just about ready to push the U. S. forces into the bay at Pusan. The military draft was getting into full swing, and I was graduating from high school the next month, exactly six months before my eighteenth birthday. Since I couldn't afford to go to college, a deferment was out of the question. I didn't want to be in the Army infantry, so I was considering enlisting in the Marines. Fortunately for me, Dean jarred some sense in my head, and convinced me the Air Force was a much better "ride". I contacted Sergeant Bass and he came to give me the enlistment test. I wasn't totally sure the Marines were out of my mind, however, after the tests,

Sergeant Bass became seriously intent on my enlisting in the Air Force. He recruited Mama and Daddy more than me, since they had to sign because I wasn't eighteen. I was going to be in the United States Air Force leaving on July 5, 1950 from Millen, Georgia.

I was one eager youngen to get on The Nancy Hanks for my first train ride ever to Atlanta, and then to Lackland Air Force Base, San Antonio, Texas for basic training. Martin Luther King has been credited with "Free at Last, Free at Last, Great God Almighty, Free at Last," and he should be, but can I tell you that was about, word for word, what I felt like shouting every time we passed through the middle of some little town as I left Girard farther and farther behind. I didn't know it would be two years before I would get back home, and then only after spending seven months in Japan and eleven months in Korea. If I never did another thing in my life, I had escaped from the sand beds even if it might just be temporary! PO "me" had made it to some extent, I went so far west that I had been in the Far East!

* * *

Some concluding comments are in order, so what was all this crap about? First and foremost, it gives the highlights of just how hard life was for small dirt farmers and their Youngens in rural Georgia from the early to the mid 1900's. The best I could tell was that there wasn't much difference for the PO people from the early to late 1800's. It didn't matter what color your skin was, the work was back breaking, never ending, and for basically no pay. What struck me so vividly was that not everybody was PO, but it was a damned clear fact to me that there were more of us who were PO than weren't in my Sandbed hell. The discrimination I experienced was not from the color of my skin, but rather it was economic discrimination. I have long had the opinion that there was, and is a major difference between being poor and being PO, and never should one ever use the word PO except in caps to really put the emphasis on just how much more economically deprived PO meant, then and now.

So many of the things that appear to be just plain funny, when examined, even in the context of the technology and development of that time, in some respects have a poignancy all their own. No matter how hard you may laugh about Lucius digging stumps, there is a story within that story that is sad as well. Try to understand the complex relationships that existed between the Youngens, and the adults, and the way the farm animals were used to try and make sense of what it took to keep the family together and still have some humanness in the process. Will you get the true story about the school principal who lied, or will you only see the smart-ass juvenile delinquent who got away with something? Was there a complex, and highly developed value system designed to develop pride, determination and a willingness to risk everything for an ethical construct that could not have been articulated at the time? These remembrances are intended to be funny, and in some instances, to shock your sensibilities. Some of the language could have been cleaned up but the flavor of the sometimes senselessly hard work would have been lost. When you finish reading this please don't just put it down and forget it. Spend a few minutes reflecting on a glimpse about a tough way to live, but also on the fact that there are thousands of stories that are much sadder and more gripping. Irrespective of everything, I made it out of the sandbeds. Many others didn't have the abilities and luck of the dice rolling for them. I truly believe that "If you've got it, you'd damned sure better do your best to flaunt it!!"

ABOUT THE AUTHOR

J. Gordon LongPO, BSAE, MBA, Ph.D., Professor Emeritus, Georgia College & State University, University System of Georgia, Milledgeville, Georgia. The last of seven children, Gordon was born at home in Girard, Burke County, Georgia in the middle of the depression, that for his family would last long beyond what the rest of America endured. However, some strong teachings by his parents along with the Korean War provided the instant impetus and energized the motivation for this seventeen year old to get away from the sandbeds.

Fortunately PO doesn't have to be synonymous with stupid, and ignorance can be fixed, so beginning in about the fourth grade, Gordon's major goal was to figure out how to get away from the grinding poverty of his life. High School in a very small school, without all the frills of today's schools was unbelievably thorough, and proved to some extent that a person could get the background to compete and graduate from Agricultural Engineering at the University of Georgia. One year before his graduation, a young Atlanta woman decided she was willing to take a chance on a PO country fellow and after forty-four years, she still hasn't given up.

After graduation, Gordon worked as a Mechanical Engineer in Research and Development, and later moved into the mainstream of business. Business provided an opportunity for him to put on seminars and realize that he thoroughly enjoyed teaching. He knew if he wanted to teach at the University level he would need advanced degrees. Without looking back, and making a pact to never hindsight the decision, he jumped right in and picked up his Master's of Business Administration, while in the pipeline for his Doctorate in Business at the University of Georgia. Starting over at age thirty two, with a wife and two children was probably one of the biggest risks he had ever undertaken, particularly since scholarships were few and far between and part of the deal, which his wife met with great trepidation, was that she was to return and finish her degree.

Gordon moved his family to Milledgeville Georgia in June 1969 to teach at what was then known as Georgia College. While counseling students as a Professor he often used some of his personal experiences to make a point. It became clear to him that his escape from Sandbed Hell, with the good, bad and ugly that brought about his need to get away was not only instructive, but might be interesting enough to write about. He says the pathos, humor, grinding poverty, good livin; and the good and bad people who played a part in his growing up, hopefully combine to make this book worthwhile reading. Some who read it will be able to substitute their own circumstances, or maybe understand their parents or grandparents much better. This may well be a tome on motivation for some who think they are the only ones who ever had it tough!!